Good Reasons

Good Reasons

Lester Faigley
University of Texas at Austin

Jack Selzer
The Pennsylvania State University

Allyn and Bacon

Boston   London   Toronto   Sydney   Tokyo   Singapore

Vice President: Eben W. Ludlow
Editorial Assistant: Grace Trudo
Marketing Manager: Lisa Kimball
Editorial-Production Administrator: Annette Joseph
Editorial-Production Coordinator: Susan Freese
Editorial-Production Service: Omegatype Typography, Inc.
Text Design: Denise Hoffman
Electronic Composition: Omegatype Typography, Inc.
Photo Researcher: Linda Sykes Picture Research
Composition Buyer: Linda Cox
Manufacturing Buyer: Suzanne Lareau
Cover Administrator: Linda Knowles

Copyright © 2000 by Allyn & Bacon
A Pearson Education Company
160 Gould Street
Needham Heights, MA 02494
Internet: www.abacon.com

Between the time Web site information is gathered and published, it is not unusual for some sites to have closed. Also, the transcription of URLs can result in unintended typographical errors. The publisher would appreciate being notified of any problems with URLs so that they may be corrected in subsequent editions. Thank you.

Many of the designations used by manufacturers and sellers to distinguish their products are claimed as trademarks. Where those designations appear in this book, and Allyn and Bacon was aware of a trademark claim, the designations have been printed in initial or all caps.

Library of Congress Cataloging-in-Publication Data

Faigley, Lester
   Good reasons / Lester Faigley, Jack Selzer.
     p. cm.
   Includes index.
   ISBN 0-205-28586-4 (paper)
   1. Reasoning. 2. Rhetoric. I. Selzer, Jack. II. Title.
BC177.F35 2000
160—dc21   99-29376
                                     CIP

Text and photo credits appear on pages 331–334, which constitute a continuation of the copyright page.

Printed in the United States of America

10 9 8 7 6 5 4 3 2 1   04 03 02 01 00 99

In memory of our teacher and friend,
James L. Kinneavy (1920–1999)

 # Contents

Preface

Like many other college writing teachers, we have come to believe that a course focusing on argument is an essential part of a college writing curriculum. Most students come to college with very little experience in reading and writing extended arguments. Because so much writing in college involves arguments in the disciplines, a basic course in writing arguments is foundational for an undergraduate education. You will find that college courses frequently require you to analyze the structure of arguments, to identify competing claims, to weigh the evidence offered, to recognize assumptions, to locate contradictions, and to anticipate opposing views. The ability to write cogent arguments is also highly valued in most occupations that require college degrees. Just as important, you need to be able to read arguments critically and write arguments skillfully if you are to participate in public life. The long-term issues that will affect your life after your college years—education, the environment, social justice, and the quality of life, to name a few—have many diverse stakeholders and long, complex histories. They cannot be reduced to slogans and sound bites.

We find that other argument textbooks spend too much time on complicated schemes and terminology for analyzing arguments and too little time looking at why people take the time to write arguments in the first place. People write arguments because they want something to change. They want to change attitudes and beliefs about particular issues, and they want something done about problems they identify. We start out with why you might want to write an argument and how what you write can lead to extended discussion and long-term results. We then provide you with practical means to find good reasons for the positions you want to advocate. This book is also distinctive in its attention to the delivery and presentation of arguments and to arguments in electronic media. It encourages you to formulate arguments in different genres and different media.

Several textbooks on writing arguments have appeared in recent years that use Stephen Toulmin's method of analyzing arguments. We take a simpler approach. Toulmin's method provides useful analytic tools, but we do not find it a necessary one to teach the practical art of making arguments. In fact, our experience is that Toulmin's terminology is often more confusing than helpful.

The key to the Toulmin method is understanding how warrants work. *Warrants,* in the Toulmin scheme, are the assumptions, knowledge, and beliefs that allow an audience to connect evidence with a claim. We believe that you will understand this concept better if you focus on the rhetorical situation, examining what assumptions, knowledge, and beliefs a particular audience might have about a particular issue, rather than "Toulminizing" an argument. The only technical terms our book uses are the general classical concepts of *pathos, ethos,* and *logos.*

Likewise, you will not find explicit discussions of syllogisms, enthymemes, or fallacies in this book. We have avoided introducing these terms because, like the Toulmin terminology, they too often hinder rather than help. The crux of teaching argument, in our view, is to get you to appreciate its rhetorical nature. What makes a good reason good in public debate is not that it follows logically from a set of truth claims arranged in syllogisms but that the audience accepts the assumptions, knowledge, and beliefs on which the argument is based and thus accepts the reason as a good reason.

Another difference is that our book does not make a sharp distinction between what some people think of as rational and irrational arguments. Rationality is a socially constructed concept. Until the twentieth century, it was rational to believe that women should not participate in politics. To question the absolute nature of rationality is not to say that it doesn't exist. Driving on the right side of the road is rational in North, South, and Central America and most of Western Europe, just as driving on the left side is rational in Great Britain, Ireland, India, and Japan. But the insistence on a dichotomy between rational and irrational has some unfortunate consequences, including a sharp division between argument and persuasion. Advertisements are often held up as typifying persuasion that plays to the emotions rather than reason. Other pieces of writing, however, are not as easy to classify as either argument or persuasion. For example, multicultural readers are filled with narratives that include arguments. Personal narratives are critical in these essays to supply cultural knowledge of other perspectives and group experiences, which in turn enables the writer to employ good reasons. We treat narratives in this book as an important type of argument. We also pay attention to ads and other genres of persuasion that are usually not represented in textbooks on argument. You will find examples in the readings that illustrate the wide range of argument.

The dichotomy between rational and irrational also leads to almost total neglect of the visual nature of writing. Visual thinking remains excluded from the mainstream literacy curriculum in the schools; it is taught only in specialized courses in college in disciplines such as architecture and art history. This exclusion might have been justified (though we would argue otherwise) as long as writing courses were bound by the technology of the typewriter, but the great majority of college students today prepare their work on personal computers. Commonly used word-processing programs and Web page editors now allow users to include pictures, icons, charts, and graphs, making design an important part of argument. While we still believe the heart of an argument course should be the critical reading and critical writing of prose, we also believe that the basics of visual persuasion should be a part of that course. In chapter 11, you will find an extensive discussion of visual design and how good design can support good reasons.

If our goal is to help you become active citizens in a participatory democracy, then it seems counterproductive to ignore that most of the writing you will do in your future public and private life will be electronically mediated. Most students now have access to the most powerful publishing technology ever invented: the World Wide Web. Until very recently, students who published on the Web had to learn HTML and had to manipulate cumbersome file transfer programs. Current word-processing programs and WYSIWYG ("what you see is what you get") editors bypass the step of coding HTML, and the process of putting Web pages on servers has become almost as simple as opening a file on a PC. The Web has become a vast arena of argument, with nearly every interest group maintaining a Web presence. You will find in chapter 12 an introduction to arguments on the Web.

The popularity of argument courses is not an accident. Even though we hear frequently that people have become cynical about politics, they are producing self-sponsored writing in quantities that have never been seen before. It's almost as if people have rediscovered writing. Although the writing of personal letters may be becoming a lost art, the number of people who participate in online discussion groups, put up Web sites, and send email is expanding at an astounding rate. Citizen participation in local and national government forums, a multitude of issue-related online discussions, and other forms such as online magazines increase daily. You already have many opportunities to speak in the electronic polis. We want you to recognize and value the breadth of information that is available on the Internet and to evaluate, analyze, and synthesize that information. And we want to prepare you for the changing demands of the professions and public citizenship in your future.

Acknowledgments

We are much indebted to the work of many outstanding scholars of argument and to our colleagues who teach argument at the University of Texas and at Penn State. In particular, we thank the following reviewers for their comments and suggestions: William A. Covino, Florida Atlantic University; Richard Fulkerson, Texas A & M University–Commerce; David Harvey, Central Arkansas University; Jeffrey Walker, The Pennsylvania State University; and Stephen Wilhoit, University of Dayton.

We are especially grateful to our students, who have given us opportunities to test these materials in class and who have taught us a great deal about the nature of argument.

We appreciate the work of all those who contributed to this book, including Janet Zepernick, who offered her good ideas on effective research in chapter 13, and Eric Lupfer, who prepared the excellent Instructor's Manual for *Good Reasons*. Our publisher, Eben Ludlow, convinced us we should write this book and gave us wise guidance throughout. Grace Trudo, Lisa Kimball, Annette Joseph, Susan Freese, and the expert production staff at Omegatype all contributed their many talents to our book. Finally, we thank our families, who make it all possible.

Good Reasons

 # Part I

Persuading with Good Reasons

What Do We Mean by Argument?

For the past thirty years, the debate over legalized abortion has raged in the United States. The following scene is a familiar one: Outside an abortion clinic, a crowd of pro-life activists has gathered to try to stop women from entering the clinic. They carry signs that read "ABORTION = MURDER" and "A BABY'S LIFE IS A HUMAN LIFE." Pro-choice supporters are also present in a counterdemonstration. Their signs read "KEEP YOUR LAWS OFF MY BODY" and "WOMEN HAVE THE RIGHT TO CONTROL THEIR BODIES." Police keep the two sides apart, but they do not stop the shouts of "Murderer!" from the pro-life side and "If you're anti-abortion, don't have one!" from the pro-choice side.

When you imagine an argument, you might think of two people engaged in a heated exchange or two groups of people with different views, shouting back and forth at each other like the pro-choice and pro-life demonstrators. Or you might think of the arguing that occurs in the courthouse, where district attorneys and defense lawyers debate strenuously. Written arguments can resemble these oral arguments in being heated and one sided. For example, the signs that the pro-choice and pro-life demonstrators carry might be considered written arguments.

But in college courses, in public life, and in professional careers, written arguments are not thought of as slogans. Bumper stickers require

*Demonstration outside the Supreme Court in
Washington, D.C., December 1993*

no supporting evidence or reasons. Many other kinds of writing do not offer
reasons either. An instruction manual, for example, does not try very hard to
persuade you. It assumes that you want to do whatever the manual tells you
how to do; indeed, most people are willing to follow the advice, or else they
would not be consulting the manual. Likewise, an article written by someone
who is totally committed to a particular cause or belief often assumes that
everyone should think the same way. These writers can count on certain
phrases and words to produce predictable responses.

Effective arguments do not make the assumption that everyone should
think the same way or hold the same beliefs. They attempt to change people's
minds by convincing them of the validity of new ideas or that a particular
course of action is the best one to take. Written arguments not only offer evidence and reasons but also often examine the assumptions on which they are
based, think through opposing arguments, and anticipate objections. They explore positions thoroughly and take opposing views into account.

Extended written arguments make more demands on their readers than
most other kinds of writing. Like bumper stickers, they often appeal to our
emotions. But they typically do much more. They expand our knowledge with

the depth of their analysis and lead us through a complex set of claims by providing networks of logical relations and appropriate evidence. They explicitly build on what has been written before by offering trails of sources, which also demonstrates that they can be trusted because the writer has done his or her homework. They cause us to reflect on what we read, in a process that we will shortly describe as critical reading.

Our culture is a competitive culture, and often the goal is to win. If you are a professional athlete, a top trial lawyer, or a candidate for president of the United States, it really is win big or lose. But most of us live in a world in which the opponents don't go away when the game is over. Even professional athletes have to play the team they beat in the championship game the next year.

In real life, most of us have to deal with the people who disagree with us at times but with whom we have to continue to work and live in the same communities. The idea of winning in such situations can only be temporary. Other situations will come up soon enough in which we will need the support of those who were on the other side of the current issue. Probably you can think of times when friendly arguments ended up with everyone involved coming to a better understanding of the others' views. And probably you can think of other times when someone was so concerned with winning an argument that even though the person might have been technically right, hard feelings were created that lasted for years.

Usually, listeners and readers are more willing to consider your argument seriously if you cast yourself as a respectful partner rather than as a competitor and put forth your arguments in the spirit of mutual support and negotiation—in the interest of finding the *best* way, not "my way." How can you be the person that your reader will want to cooperate with rather than resist? Here are a few suggestions, both for your writing and for discussing controversial issues in class:

- **Try to think of yourself as engaged not so much in winning over your audience as in courting your audience's cooperation.** It is important to argue vigorously, but you don't want to argue so vigorously that opposing views are vanquished or silenced. Remember that your goal is to invite a response that creates a dialog.
- **Show that you understand and genuinely respect your listener's or reader's position even if you think the position is ultimately wrong.** Often, that amounts to remembering to argue against an opponent's position, not against the opponent himself or herself. It often means representing your opponent's position in terms that your opponent himself or herself would accept. Look hard for ground that you already share with your reader, and search for even more. See yourself as a mediator. Consider that neither you nor the other person has arrived at a best solution, and carry on in the hope that dialog will lead to an even better course of

action than the one you now recommend. Expect and assume the best of your listener or reader, and deliver your own best yourself.

- **Cultivate a sense of humor and a distinctive voice.** Many textbooks on argument emphasize using a reasonable voice. But a reasonable voice doesn't have to be a dull one. Humor is a legitimate tool of argument. Although playing an issue strictly for laughs risks not having the reader take it seriously, nothing creates a sense of goodwill quite so much as good humor. You will be seen as open to new possibilities and to cooperation if you occasionally show a sense of humor. And a sense of humor can sometimes be especially welcome when the stakes are high, the sides have been chosen, and tempers are flaring.

Consider that your argument might be just one move in a larger process that might end up helping *you*. Most times we argue because we think we have something to offer. But in the process of developing and presenting your views, realize also that argument might help you—that you might learn something in the course of your research or from an argument that answers your own. Holding onto that attitude will keep you from becoming too overbearing and dogmatic.

Chapter 1

What to Argue About

A Book That Changed the World

In 1958, Rachel Carson received a copy of a letter that her friend Olga Huckens had sent to the *Boston Herald*. The letter described what had happened during the previous summer when Duxbury, Massachusetts, a small town just north of Cape Cod where Huckens lived, was sprayed several times from an airplane with the chemical pesticide DDT to kill mosquitoes. The mosquitoes came back as hungry as ever, but the songbirds, bees, and other insects vanished except for a few dead birds that Huckens had to pick up out of her yard. Huckens asked Carson if she knew anyone in Washington who could help to stop the spraying.

Rachel Carson

The letter from Olga Huckens struck a nerve with Rachel Carson. Carson was a marine biologist had worked many years for the U.S. Fish and Wildlife Service and had written three highly acclaimed books about the sea and wetlands. In 1944, she had written an article on how bats use radarlike echoes to find insects, which was reprinted in *Reader's Digest* in 1945. The editors at *Reader's Digest* asked whether she could write something else for them, and Carson replied in a letter that she wanted to write about experiments using DDT. DDT was being hyped as the solution for controlling insect pests, but Carson knew in 1945 that fish, waterfowl, and other animals would also be poisoned by widespread spraying and that eventually people could die too. *Reader's Digest* was not interested in Carson's proposed article, so she dropped the idea and went on to write about other things.

Huckens's letter brought Carson back to the subject of chemical spraying. In the late 1940s and 1950s, pesticides—especially the chlorinated hydrocarbons DDT, aldrin, and dieldrin—were sprayed on a massive scale throughout the United States and were hailed as a panacea for world hunger and famine. In 1957, much of the greater New York City area, including Long Island, was sprayed with DDT to kill gypsy moths. But there were noticeable side effects. Many people complained about not only birds, fish, and useful insects being killed but also their plants, shrubs, and pets. Other scientists had written about the dangers of massive spraying of pesticides, but they had not convinced the public of the hazards of pesticides and of the urgency for change.

Rachel Carson decided that she needed to write a magazine article about the facts of DDT. When she contacted *Reader's Digest* and other magazines, she found that they still would not consider publishing on the subject. Carson then concluded that she should write a short book. She knew that her job was not going to be an easy one because people in the United States still trusted science to solve all problems. Science had brought the "green revolution" that greatly increased crop yields through the use of chemical fertilizers and chemical pesticides. Carson's subject matter was also technical and difficult to communicate to the general public. The public did not think much at that time about air and water pollution, and most people were unaware that pesticides could poison humans as well as insects. And she was sure to face opposition from the pesticide industry, which had become a multi-million-dollar business. Carson knew the pesticide industry would do everything it could to stop her from publishing and to discredit her if she did.

Rachel Carson nonetheless wrote her book, *Silent Spring*. It sounded the alarm about the dangers caused by the overuse of pesticides, and the controversy it raised has still not ended. No book has had a greater impact on our thinking about the environment. *Silent Spring* was first published in installments in *The New Yorker* in summer 1962, and it created an immediate furor. Chemical companies threatened to sue Carson, and the trade associations that they sponsored launched full-scale attacks against the book in pamphlets and magazine articles. The chemical companies treated *Silent Spring* as a public relations problem; they hired scientists whose only job was to ridicule the book and to dismiss Carson as a "hysterical woman." Some even accused *Silent Spring* of being part of a communist plot to ruin U.S. agriculture.

But the public controversy over *Silent Spring* had another effect. It helped to make the book a success shortly after it was published in September 1962. A half million hardcover copies of *Silent Spring* were sold, keeping it on the best-seller list for thirty-one weeks. President John F. Kennedy read *Silent Spring* and met with Carson and other scientists to discuss the pesticide problem. Kennedy requested that the President's Scientific Advisory Committee study the effects of pesticides and make a report. This report found evidence around the world of high levels of pesticides in the environment, including the tissues of humans. The report confirmed what Carson had described in *Silent Spring*.

In the words of a news commentator at the time, *Silent Spring* "lit a fire" under the government. There were many congressional hearings on the effects of pesticides and other pollutants on the environment. In 1967, the Environmental Defense Fund was formed; it developed the guidelines under which DDT was eventually banned. Three years later, President Richard Nixon became convinced that only an independent agency within the executive branch could operate with enough independence to enforce environmental regulations. Nixon created the Environmental Protection Agency (EPA) in December 1970, and he named William Ruckelshaus as its first head. One of the missions of the EPA, according to Ruckelshaus, was to develop an environmental ethic.

The United States was not the only country to respond to *Silent Spring*. The book was widely translated and inspired legislation on the environment in nearly all industrialized nations. Moreover, it changed the way we think about the environment. Carson pointed out that the nerve gases that were developed for use on our enemies in World War II were being used as pesticides after the war. She criticized the view of the environment as a battlefield where people make war on those natural forces that they believe impede their progress. Instead, she advocated living in coexistence with the environment because we are part of it. She was not totally opposed to pesticides, but she wanted to make people more aware of the environment as a whole and how changing one part would affect other parts. Her message was to try to live in balance with nature. The fact that we still talk so much about the environment is testimony to the lasting power of *Silent Spring*. In 1980, Rachel Carson was posthumously awarded the highest civilian decoration in the nation, the Presidential Medal of Freedom. The citation accompanying the award expresses the way she is remembered:

> *Never silent herself in the face of destructive trends, Rachel Carson fed a spring of awareness across America and beyond. A biologist with a gentle, clear voice, she welcomed her audiences to her love of the sea, while with an equally clear voice she warned Americans of the dangers human beings themselves pose for their own environment. Always concerned, always eloquent, she created a tide of environmental consciousness that has not ebbed.*

Why *Silent Spring* Became a Classic

A book that covered much of the same ground as *Silent Spring*, titled *Our Synthetic Environment*, had been published six months earlier. The author, Murray Bookchin, writing under the pen name Lewis Herber, also wrote about the pollution of the natural world and the effects on people. Bookchin was as committed to warning people about the hazards of pesticides as Carson, but *Our Synthetic Environment* was read only by a small community of scientists. Why, then, did Carson succeed in reaching a larger audience?

Rachel Carson had far more impact than Murray Bookchin not simply because she was a more talented writer or because she was a scientist while Bookchin was not. She also thought a great deal about who she was writing for—her **audience.** If she was going to stop the widespread spraying of dangerous pesticides, she knew she would have to connect with the values of a wide audience, an audience that included a large segment of the public as well as other scientists.

The opening chapter in *Silent Spring* begins not by announcing Carson's thesis or giving a list of facts. Instead, the book starts out with a short fable about a small town located in the middle of prosperous farmland, where wildflowers bloomed much of the year, trout swam in the streams, and wildlife was abundant. Suddenly, a strange blight came on the town, as if an evil spell had been cast upon it. The chickens, sheep, and cattle on the farms grew sick and died. The families of the townspeople and farmers alike developed mysterious illnesses. Most of the birds disappeared, and the few that remained could neither sing nor fly. The apple trees bloomed, but there were no bees to pollinate the trees, and so they bore no fruit. The wildflowers withered as if they had been burned. Fishermen quit going to the streams because the fish had all died.

But it wasn't witchcraft that caused everything to grow sick and die. Carson writes that "the people had done it to themselves." She continues, "I know of no community that has experienced all the misfortunes I describe. Yet every one of these disasters has actually happened somewhere, and many real communities have already suffered a substantial number of them. A grim specter has crept upon us almost unnoticed, and this imagined tragedy may easily become a stark reality." Carson's fable did happen several times after the book was published. In July 1976, a chemical reaction went out of control at a plant near Seveso, Italy, and a cloud of powdery white crystals of almost pure dioxin fell on the town. The children ran out to play in the powder because it looked like snow. Within four days, plants, birds, and animals began dying, and the next week, people started getting sick. Most of the people had to go to the hospital, and everyone had to move out of the town. An even worse disaster happened in December 1982, when a storage tank in a pesticide plant exploded near Bhopal, India, showering the town. Two thousand people died quickly, and another fifty thousand became sick for the rest of their lives.

Perhaps if Rachel Carson were alive today and writing a book about the dangers of pesticides, she might begin differently. But remember that at the time she was writing, people trusted pesticides and believed that DDT was a miracle solution for all sorts of insect pests. She first had to get people stirred up enough to accept the reality that DDT could be harmful to them. In the second chapter of *Silent Spring* (reprinted at the end of this chapter), Carson continued appealing to the emotions of her audience. People in 1962 knew about the dangers of radiation even if they were ignorant about pesticides. They knew that the atomic bombs that had been dropped on Hiroshima and Nagasaki at the end of World War II were still killing Japanese people through the effects of radiation many years later, and they feared the fallout from nuclear bombs that were still being tested and stockpiled in the United States and Soviet Union.

Tactics of *Silent Spring*

Chapter 1 of *Silent Spring* tells a parable of a rural town where the birds, fish, flowers, and plants die and people become sick after a white powder is sprayed on the town. At the beginning of chapter 2, Rachel Carson begins her argument against the mass aerial spraying of pesticides. Most of her readers were not aware of the dangers of pesticides, but they were well aware of the harmful effects of radiation. Let's look at her tactics:

> The history of life on earth has been a history of interaction between living things and their surroundings. To a large extent, the physical form and the habits of earth's vegetation and its animal life have been molded by the environment. Considering the whole span of earthly time, the opposite effect, in which life actually modifies its surroundings, has been relatively slight. Only within the moment of time represented by the present century has one species—man—acquired significant power to alter the nature of his world.

This simple truth about the environment was not as well understood in 1962 as it is today. The interrelationship of people and the environment provides the basis for Carson's argument.

Carson shifts her language to a metaphor of war against the environment rather than interaction with the natural world.

> During the past quarter century this power has not only increased to one of disturbing magnitude but it has changed in character. The most alarming of all man's assaults upon the environment is the contamination of air, earth, rivers, and sea with dangerous and even lethal materials. This pollution is for the most part irrecoverable; the chain of life it initiates not only in the world that must support life but in living tissues is for the most part irreversible. In this now universal contamination of the environment, chemicals are the sinister

People in 1962 had learned about the dangers of nuclear radiation, and in 1963 the first treaty was signed by the United States and the Soviet Union that banned the testing of nuclear weapons above ground, under water, and in space.

(continued)

and little-recognized partners of radiation in changing the very nature of the world—the very nature of its life. Strontium 90, released through nuclear explosions into the air, comes to earth in rain or drifts down as fallout, lodges in the soil, enters into the grass or corn or wheat grown there, and in time takes its abode in the bones of a human being, there to remain until his death. Similarly, chemicals sprayed on croplands or forests or gardens lie long in soil, entering into living organisms, passing from one to another in a chain of poisoning and death. Or they pass mysteriously by underground streams until they emerge and, through the alchemy of air and sunlight, combine into new forms that kill vegetation, sicken cattle, and work unknown harm on those who drink from once-pure wells. As Albert Schweitzer has said, "Man can hardly even recognize the devils of his own creation."

The key move: Carson associates the dangers of chemical pesticides with those of radiation.

Albert Schweitzer (1875–1965) was a concert musician, philosopher, and doctor who spent most of his life as a medical missionary in Africa.

Getting people's attention by exposing the threat of pesticides wasn't enough by itself. There are always people writing about various kinds of threats, and most aren't taken seriously except by those who already believe that the threats exist. Carson wanted to reach people who didn't think that pesticides were a threat but might be persuaded to take this view. To convince these people, she had to explain why pesticides are potentially dangerous, and she had to make readers believe that she could be trusted.

Rachel Carson was an expert marine biologist. To write *Silent Spring,* she had to read widely in sciences that she had not studied, including research about insects, toxic chemicals, cell physiology, biochemistry, plant and soil science, and public health. Then she had to explain complex scientific processes to people who had very little or no background in science. It was a very difficult and frustrating task. While writing *Silent Spring,* Carson confided in a letter to a friend the problems she was having: "How to reveal enough to give understanding of the most serious effects of the chemicals without being technical, how to simplify without error—these have been problems of rather monumental proportions."

To make people understand the bad effects of pesticides required explaining what is not common sense: why very tiny amounts of pesticides can be so harmful. The reason lies in how pesticides are absorbed by the body. DDT is fat-soluble and gets stored in organs such as the adrenals, thyroid, liver, and kidneys. Carson explains how pesticides build up in the body:

This storage of DDT begins with the smallest conceivable intake of the chemical (which is present as residues on most foodstuffs) and continues until quite high levels are reached. The fatty storage deposits act as biological magnifiers, so that an intake of as little as $\frac{1}{10}$ of 1 part per million in the diet results in storage of about 10 to 15 parts per million, an increase of one hundredfold or more. These terms of reference, so commonplace to the chemist or the pharmacologist, are unfamiliar to most of us. One part in a million sounds like a very small amount—and so it is. But such substances are so potent that a minute quantity can bring about vast changes in the body. In animal experiments, 3 parts per million has been found to inhibit an essential enzyme in the heart muscle; only 5 parts per million has brought about necrosis or disintegration of liver cells.

Throughout the book, Carson succeeds in translating scientific facts into language that, to use her words, "most of us" can understand. Of course Carson was a scientist and quite capable of reading scientific articles. She establishes her credibility as a scientist by using technical terms such as *necrosis*. But at the same time she identifies herself with people who are not scientists and gains our trust by taking our point of view.

To accompany these facts, Carson tells about places that have been affected by pesticides. One of the more memorable stories is about Clear Lake, California, in the mountainous country north of San Francisco. Clear Lake is popular for fishing, but it is also an ideal habitat for a species of gnat. In the late 1940s the state of California began spraying the lake with DDD, a close relative of DDT. Spraying had to be repeated because the gnats kept coming back. The western grebes that lived on the lake began to die, and when scientists examined their bodies, the grebes were loaded with extraordinary levels of DDD. Microscopic plants and animals filtered the lake water for nutrients and concentrated the pesticides at 20 times their level in the lake water. Small fish ate these tiny plants and animals and again concentrated the DDD at levels 10 to 100 times that of their microscopic food. The grebes that ate the fish suffered the effects of this huge magnification.

Although DDT is still used in parts of the developing world, the influence of *Silent Spring* led to the banning of it and most other similar pesticides in the United States and Canada. Rachel Carson's book eventually led people to stop relying only on pesticides and look instead to other methods of controlling pests, such as planting crops that are resistant to insects and disease. When pesticides are used today, they typically are applied much more selectively and in lower amounts than was common when Carson was writing.

Rachel Carson's more lasting legacy is our awareness of our environment. She urges us to be aware that we share this planet with other creatures and that "we are dealing with life—with living populations and all their pressures and counterpressures, their surges and recessions." She warns against dismissing the balance of nature. She writes:

> The balance of nature is not the same today as in Pleistocene times, but it is still there: a complex, precise, and highly integrated system of relationships between living things which cannot safely be ignored any more than the law of gravity can be defied with impunity by a man perched on the edge of a cliff. The balance of nature is not a *status quo;* it is fluid, ever shifting, in a constant state of adjustment.

Since the publication of *Silent Spring,* we have grown much more conscious of large-scale effects on ecosystems caused by global warming, acid rain, and the hole in the ozone in addition to the local effects of pesticides described in Carson's book. The cooperation of nations today in attempting to control air and water pollution, in encouraging more efficient use of energy and natural resources, and in promoting sustainable patterns of consumption is due in no small part to the long-term influence of *Silent Spring.*

Analyzing Arguments: Pathos, Ethos, and Logos

When the modern concept of democracy was developed in Greece in the fifth century B.C.E., the study of rhetoric also began. It's not a coincidence that the teaching of rhetoric was closely tied to the rise of democracy. In the Greek city-states, all citizens had the right to speak and vote at the popular assembly and in the committees of the assembly that functioned as the criminal courts. Citizens took turns serving as the officials of government. Because the citizens of Athens and other city-states took their responsibilities quite seriously, they highly valued the ability to speak effectively in public. Teachers of rhetoric were held in great esteem.

In the next century, the most important teacher of rhetoric in ancient Greece, Aristotle (384–323 B.C.E.), made the study of rhetoric systematic. He defined *rhetoric* as the art of finding the best available means of persuasion in any situation. Aristotle set out three primary tactics of argument: appeals to the emotions and deepest held values of the audience (*pathos*), appeals based on the trustworthiness of the speaker (*ethos*), and appeals to good reasons (*logos*).

Carson makes these appeals with great skill in *Silent Spring.* Very simply, her purpose is to stop pesticide pollution. She first appeals to *pathos,* engaging her readers in her subject. She gives many specific examples of how pesticides have accumulated in the bodies of animals and people. But she also engages her readers through her skill as a writer, making us care about nature as well as be concerned about our own safety. She uses the fate of robins to symbolize her crusade. Robins were the victims of spraying for Dutch elm disease. Robins feed on earthworms, which in turn process fallen elm leaves. The earthworms act as magnifiers of the pesticide, which either kills the robins outright or renders them sterile. Thus when no robins sang, it was indeed a silent spring.

Carson is also successful in creating a credible *ethos.* We believe her not just because she establishes her expertise. She convinces us also because she establishes her ethos as a person with her audience's best interests at heart. She anticipates possible objections, demonstrating that she has thought about opposing positions. She takes time to explain concepts that most people do not understand fully, and she discusses how everyone can benefit if we take a different attitude toward nature. She shows that she has done her homework on the topic. By creating a credible ethos, Carson makes an effective moral argument that humans as a species have a responsibility not to destroy the world they live in.

Finally, Carson supports her argument with good reasons, what Aristotle called *logos.* She offers "because clauses" to support her main claims. She describes webs of relationships among the earth, plants, animals, and humans, and she explains how changing one part will affect the others. Her point is not that we should never disturb these relationships but that we should be as aware as possible of the consequences.

Reading Arguments

If you have ever been coached in a sport or have been taught an art such as dancing or playing an musical instrument, you likely have viewed a game or a performance in two ways. You might enjoy the game or performance like everyone else, but at the same time, you might be especially aware of something that you know from your experience is difficult to do and therefore appreciated the skill and the practice necessary to develop it. A similar distinction can be made about two kinds of reading. For the sake of convenience, the first can be called *ordinary reading,* although we don't really think there is a single kind of ordinary reading. In ordinary reading, on the first time through, the reader forms a sense of content and gets an initial impression: whether it's interesting, whether the author has something important to say, whether you agree or disagree.

For most of what you read, one time through is enough. When you read for the second or third time, you start to use different strategies because you have some reason to do so. You are no longer reading to form a sense of the overall content. Often, you are looking for something in particular. If you reread a textbook chapter, you might want to make sure you understand how a key concept is being used. When you reread your apartment contract, you might want to know what is required to get your deposit back. This second kind of reading can be called *critical reading*. Critical reading does not mean criticizing what the writer has to say (although that's certainly possible). Critical reading means beginning with questions and specific goals.

Writers of arguments engage in critical reading even on the first time through. They know that they will have to acknowledge what else has been written about a particular issue. If the issue is new (and few are), then the writer will need to establish its significance by comparing it to other issues on which much has been written. Writers of argument, therefore begin reading with **questions.** They want to know *why* a particular argument was written. They want to know *what* the writer's basic assumptions are. They want to know *who* the writer had in mind when the argument was written. Critical readers most often read with pen or pencil in hand or with a window open on their computer in which they can write. They write their questions in the margins or in the file.

Critical readers do more than just question what they read. They **analyze** how the argument works. Critical readers look at how an argument is laid out. They identify key terms and examine how the writer is using them. They consider how the writer appeals to our emotions, represents himself or herself, and uses good reasons. They analyze the structure of an argument—the organization—and the way in which it is written—the style.

Finally, critical readers often **respond** as they read. They don't just take in what they read in a passive way. They jot down notes to themselves in the margins or on the blank pages at the front and back of a book. They use these notes later when they start writing. Reading is often the best way to get started writing.

Reading with a Pencil in Your Hand

The best way to read arguments is with a pencil—not a pen or highlighter. Pens don't erase, and highlighters are distracting. Much of the time, you don't know what is important the first time through an argument, and highlighters don't tell you why something is important. Use a pencil instead, and write in the margins.

If you are reading on a computer screen, open a new window in your word-processing program so that you can write while you read. Reading on a computer has the advantage of letting you copy parts of what you read to your file. You just have to be careful to distinguish what you copy from what you write. Always remember to include the information about where it came from. (Your Web browser allows you to copy text and paste it in a new file. Look in the Edit menu on Netscape or Internet Explorer.)

Before you start reading, find out when the argument was written, where it first appeared, and who wrote it. Arguments don't appear in vacuums. They most often occur in response to something else that has been written or some event that has happened. In this book, you'll find this information in the headnotes. You also have a title, which suggests what the argument might be about. This information will help you to form an initial impression about why the writer wrote this particular argument, who the writer imagined as the readers, and what purposes the writer might have had in mind. Then pick up your pencil and start reading.

Ask Questions

On the first time through, you need to understand what's in the argument. So circle the words and references that you don't know and look them up. If a statement part of the argument isn't clear, note that section in the margin. You might figure out what the writer is arguing later, or you might have to work through it slowly a second time through.

Analyze

On your second reading, you should start analyzing the structure of the argument. Here's how to do it:

- Identify the writer's main claim or claims. You should be able to paraphrase it if it doesn't appear explicitly.
- What are the good reasons that support the claim? List them by number in the margins. There might be only one reason, or there could be several (and some good reasons could be supported by others).
- Where is the evidence? Does it really support the good reasons? Can you think of contradictory evidence?
- Does the writer refer to expert opinion or research about this subject? Do other experts see this issue differently?
- Does the writer acknowledge opposing views? Does the writer deal fairly with opposing views?

Respond

You should write down your thoughts as you read. Often you will find that something you read reminds you of something else. Jot that down. It might be something to think about later, and it might give you ideas for writing. You might also think about what else you should read if you want to write about this topic. Or you might want to write down whether you are persuaded by the argument and why.

Finding Arguments

Rachel Carson did not so much find the subject for *Silent Spring* as the subject found her. She wrote about a subject that she had cared about for many years. Subjects that we argue about often find us. There are enough of them in daily life. We're late for work because the traffic is bad or the bus doesn't run on time. We can't find a place to park when we get to school or work. We have to negotiate through various bureaucracies for almost anything we do—making an appointment to see a doctor, getting a course added or dropped, or correcting a mistake on a bill. Most of the time, we grumble and let it go at that.

But sometimes, like Rachel Carson, we stick with a subject. Neighborhood groups in cities and towns have been especially effective in getting things done by writing about them—from stopping a new road from being built to getting better police and fire protection to having a vacant lot turned into a park. Most jobs that require college degrees sooner or later demand the ability to write extended arguments. Usually, it is sooner; the primary cause of new employees being fired during their first year at *Fortune* 500 companies is poor communications skills. If your writing skills are not up to speed, you may pay heavily down the road.

Position and Proposal Arguments

In *Silent Spring*, Rachel Carson made an effective argument against the massive use of synthetic pesticides. Arguing against the indiscriminate use of pesticides, however, did not solve the problem of what to do about harmful insects that destroy crops and spread disease. Carson also did the harder job of offering solutions. In her final chapter, "The Other Road," Carson gives alternatives to the massive use of pesticides. She describes how a pest organism's natural enemies can be used against it instead.

These two kinds of arguments can be characterized as **position** and **proposal** arguments.

Position Arguments

In a position argument, the writer makes a claim about a controversial issue.

- **The writer first has to define the issue.** Carson had to explain what synthetic pesticides are in chemical terms and how they work, and she had to give a history of their increasing use after World War II before she could begin arguing against pesticides.

- **The writer should take a clear position.** Carson wasted no time setting out her position by describing the threat that high levels of pesticides pose to people worldwide.
- **The writer should make a convincing argument and acknowledge opposing views.** Carson used a variety of strategies in support of her position, including research studies, quotes from authorities, and her own analyses and observations. She took into account opposing views by acknowledging that harmful insects needed to be controlled and conceded that selective spraying is necessary and desirable.

Proposal Arguments

In a proposal argument, the writer proposes a course of action in response to a recognizable problem situation. The proposal says what can be done to improve the situation or change it altogether.

- **The writer first has to define the problem.** The problem Carson had to define was complex. Not only was the overuse of pesticides killing helpful insects, plants, and animals and threatening people, but the harmful insects the pesticides were intended to eliminate were becoming increasingly resistant. More spraying and more frequent spraying produced pesticide-resistant "superbugs." Mass spraying resulted in actually helping bad bugs such as fire ants by killing off their competition.
- **The writer has to propose a solution or solutions.** Carson did not hold out for one particular approach to control insects, but she did advocate biological solutions. She proposed biological alternatives to pesticides, such as sterilizing and releasing large numbers of male insects and introducing predators of pest insects. Above all, she urged that we work with nature rather than being at war with it.
- **The solution or solutions must work, and they must be feasible.** The projected consequences should be set out, arguing that good things will happen, bad things will be avoided, or both. Carson discussed research studies that indicated her solutions would work, and she argued that they would be less expensive than massive spraying. Today, we can look at Carson's book with the benefit of hindsight. Not everything Carson proposed ended up working, but her primary solution—learn to live with nature—has been a powerful one. Mass spraying of pesticides has stopped in the United States, and species that were threatened by the excessive use of pesticides, including falcons, eagles, and brown pelicans, have made remarkable comebacks.

Being either inspired or required to write an argument is only the beginning. Once Rachel Carson decided that she wanted to write a book about the hazards of pesticides, she did her homework before she started writing. She used these questions as guides to her research:

- How do pesticides work?
- Why are pesticides used?
- Who and what benefits from the use of pesticides?
- Who or what is harmed by the use of pesticides?
- Who creates pesticides?
- Who supports the use of pesticides?
- When can pesticides be used beneficially? When is their use harmful?
- What alternatives to pesticides are feasible?

In much the same way, you can explore a topic by asking questions.

Carson also kept in mind what had been written before about the environment. She was trained as a scientist, and she could have written only for other scientists. But she wanted to reach a much wider audience, and she wanted people to think about more than just the hazards of pesticides. She wanted to create a revolution in the way we think about the environment. Carson's respect for the integrity and interconnectedness of life contributed a great deal to the power of her argument. Her goal was not so much to make chemical companies into the Evil Ones as it was to promote a different way of thinking that would reconnect people with the world around them. She alludes to Robert Frost's poem "The Road Not Taken" for her concluding chapter, "The Other Road." "We stand now where two roads diverge," she says, the one "a smooth superhighway on which we progress with great speed" but on which disaster lies at the end, the other the road "less-traveled" but on which is our chance to preserve the earth. The greatest legacy of *Silent Spring* is that we are still very concerned with and actively discussing the issues she raised.

 Rachel Carson

The Obligation to Endure

Rachel Carson (1907–1964) was born and grew up in Springdale, Pennsylvania, eighteen miles up the Allegheny River from Pittsburgh. When Carson was in elementary school, her mother was fearful of infectious diseases that were sweeping through the nation and often kept young Rachel out of school. In her wandering on the family farm, Rachel developed the love of nature that she maintained throughout her life. At twenty-two she began her career as a marine biologist at Woods Hole, Massachusetts, and she later went to graduate school at Johns Hopkins University in Baltimore. She began working for the U.S. government in 1936 in the agency that later became the Fish and Wildlife Service, and she was soon recognized as a talented writer as well as a meticulous scientist. She wrote three highly praised books about the sea and wetlands: *Under the Sea Wind* (1941), *The Sea around Us* (1951), and *The Edge of the Sea* (1954).

Carson's decision to write *Silent Spring* marked a great change in her life. For the first time, she became an environmental activist rather than an inspired and enthusiastic writer about nature. She had written about the interconnectedness of life in her previous three books, but with *Silent Spring* she had to convince people that hazards lie in what had seemed familiar and harmless. Although many people think of birds when they hear Rachel Carson's name, she was the first scientist to make a comprehensive argument that links cancer to environmental causes. Earlier in this chapter, you saw how Carson associated pesticides with the dangers of radiation from nuclear weapons. Notice how else she gets her readers to think differently about pesticides in this selection, which begins chapter 2 of *Silent Spring*.

The history of life on earth has been a history of interaction between living things and their surroundings. To a large extent, the physical form and the habits of the earth's vegetation and its animal life have been molded by the environment. Considering the whole span of earthly time, the opposite effect, in which life actually modifies its surroundings, has been relatively slight. Only within the moment of time represented by the present century has one species—man—acquired significant power to alter the nature of his world.

During the past quarter century this power has not only increased to one of disturbing magnitude but it has changed in character. The most alarming of all man's assaults upon the environment is the contamination of air, earth, rivers, and sea with dangerous and even lethal materials. This pollution is for the most part irrecoverable; the chain of evil it initiates not only in the world that must support life but in living tissues is for the most part irreversible. In this now universal contamination of the environment, chemicals are the sinister and little recognized partners of radiation in changing the very nature of the world—the very nature of its life. Strontium 90, released through nuclear explosions into the air, comes to earth in rain or drifts down as fallout, lodges in soil, enters into the grass or corn or wheat grown there, and in time takes up its abode in the bones of a human being, there to remain until his death. Similarly, chemicals sprayed on croplands or forests or gardens lie long in soil, entering into living organisms, passing from one to another in a chain of poisoning and death. Or they pass mysteriously by underground streams until they emerge and, through the alchemy of air and sunlight, combine into new forms that kill vegetation, sicken cattle, and work unknown harm on those who drink from once-pure wells. As Albert Schweitzer has said, "Man can hardly even recognize the devils of his own creation."

3   It took hundreds of millions of years to produce the life that now inhabits the earth—eons of time in which that developing and evolving and diversifying life reached a state of adjustment and balance with its surroundings. The environment, rigorously shaping and directing the life it supported, contained elements that were hostile as well as supporting. Certain rocks gave out dangerous radiation; even within the light of the sun, from which all life draws its energy, there were short-wave radiations with power to injure. Given time—time not in years but in millennia—life adjusts, and a balance has been reached. For time is the essential ingredient; but in the modern world there is no time.

4   The rapidity of change and the speed with which new situations are created follow the impetuous and heedless pace of man rather than the deliberate pace of nature. Radiation is no longer merely the background radiation of rocks, the bombardment of cosmic rays, the ultraviolet of the sun that have existed before there was any life on earth; radiation is now the unnatural creation of man's tampering with the atom. The chemicals to which life is asked to make its adjustment are no longer merely the calcium and silica and copper and all the rest of the minerals washed out of the rocks and carried in rivers to the sea; they are the synthetic creations of man's inventive mind, brewed in his laboratories, and having no counterparts in nature.

5   To adjust to these chemicals would require time on the scale that is nature's; it would require not merely the years of a man's life but the life of generations. And even this, were it by some miracle possible, would be futile, for the new chemicals come from our laboratories in an endless stream; almost five hundred annually find their way into actual use in the United States alone. The figure is staggering and its implications are not easily grasped—500 new chemicals to which the bodies of men and animals are required somehow to adapt each year, chemicals totally outside the limits of biologic experience.

6   Among them are many that are used in man's war against nature. Since the mid-1940's over 200 basic chemicals have been created for use in killing insects, weeds, rodents, and other organisms described in the modern vernacular as "pests"; and they are sold under several thousand different brand names.

7   These sprays, dusts, and aerosols are now applied almost universally to farms, gardens, forests, and homes—nonselective chemicals that have the power to kill every insect, the "good" and the "bad," to still the song of birds and the leaping of fish in the streams, to coat the leaves with a deadly film, and to linger on in soil—all this though the intended target may be only a few weeds or insects. Can anyone believe it is possible to lay down such a barrage of poisons on the surface

of the earth without making it unfit for all life? They should not be called "insecticides," but "biocides."

The whole process of spraying seems caught up in an endless spiral. Since   8
DDT was released for civilian use, a process of escalation has been going on in which ever more toxic materials must be found. This has happened because insects, in a triumphant vindication of Darwin's principle of the survival of the fittest, have evolved super races immune to the particular insecticide used, hence a deadlier one has always to be developed—and then a deadlier one than that. It has happened also because, for reasons to be described later, destructive insects often undergo a "flareback," or resurgence, after spraying, in numbers greater than before. Thus the chemical war is never won, and all life is caught in its violent crossfire.

Along with the possibility of the extinction of mankind by nuclear war, the   9
central problem of our age has therefore become the contamination of man's total environment with such substances of incredible potential for harm—substances that accumulate in the tissues of plants and animals and even penetrate the germ cells to shatter or alter the very material of heredity upon which the shape of the future depends.

Some would-be architects of our future look toward a time when it will be   10
possible to alter the human germ plasm by design. But we may easily be doing so now by inadvertence, for many chemicals, like radiation, bring about gene mutations. It is ironic to think that man might determine his own future by something so seemingly trivial as the choice of an insect spray.

All this has been risked—for what? Future historians may well be amazed by   11
our distorted sense of proportion. How could intelligent beings seek to control a few unwanted species by a method that contaminated the entire environment and brought the threat of disease and death even to their own kind? Yet this is precisely what we have done. We have done it, moreover, for reasons that collapse the moment we examine them. We are told that the enormous and expanding use of pesticides is necessary to maintain farm production. Yet is our real problem not one of *overproduction?* Our farms, despite measures to remove acreages from production and to pay farmers *not* to produce, have yielded such a staggering excess of crops that the American taxpayer in 1962 is paying out more than one billion dollars a year as the total carrying cost of the surplus-food storage program. And is the situation helped when one branch of the Agriculture Department tries to reduce production while another states, as it did in 1958, "It is believed generally that reduction of crop acreages under provisions of the Soil Bank will stimulate interest in use of chemicals to obtain maximum production on the land retained in crops."

All this is not to say there is no insect problem and no need of control. I am   12
saying, rather, that control must be geared to realities, not to mythical situations, and that the methods employed must be such that they do not destroy us along with the insects.

Theo Colborn, Dianne Dumanoski, and John Peterson Myers

Hand-Me-Down Poisons

A book published in 1996, *Our Stolen Future,* has had an impact similar to that of *Silent Spring,* catalyzing an interational debate over the threat of a new class of pollutants known as *endocrine-disrupting chemicals (EDCs).* These chemicals are referred to as "Gender Benders" in the press because one of their effects is to influence gender orientation in animals. *Our Stolen Future* was written by two zoologists, Theo Colborn and John Peterson Myers, and a journalist, Dianne Dumanoski. The book's main character is Colborn, a former Colorado sheep rancher who returned to college and was a fifty-eight-year-old grandmother when she received her PhD. She became well known among scientists for her work on environmental estrogens.

Like *Silent Spring* for Rachel Carson, *Our Stolen Future* marked a major shift in Colborn's writing. *Our Stolen Future* is written not as a scientific report but as a detective story. The first chapter, titled "Omen," relates reports of wildlife suffering from the inability to reproduce and disrupted sexual development. The second chapter describes how in 1989 Colborn joined a team assessing the health of the Great Lakes, which were then recovering from the severe pollution of the 1960s and 1970s. In spite of signs of improvement, there were still many unexplained effects in the Great Lakes and around the world: marine epidemics, same-sex birds nesting together, tumorous cancers in fish, declines in the reproduction of various species, and drastic increases in the rates of breast and testicular cancer among humans. Colborn's problem was trying to make sense out of all these trends. Many of the animals affected had 250 or more different chemical toxins stored in their body fat. Finally, she realized that the very expression *cancer-causing chemicals* might be concealing the obvious.

Something that could be traced to prenatal influences was upsetting the reproductive systems and gender identities of many species. The last section of chapter 2 describes how Colborn came to the conclusion that human-made chemical pollutants mimic natural estrogens and other hormones to produce devastating effects on the unborn. Why do you think Colborn, Dumanoski, and Myers chose to write *Our Stolen Future* as a scientific detective story?

Theo Colborn

1   As Colborn tackled the wildlife files for a second time, her mind kept returning to the female gulls nesting together. She pulled out the papers by Fox and Fry and carefully reread them. She sensed that the "gay gulls," as someone had

dubbed them, were an important piece of the puzzle, but she still didn't know how to put it all together. The feminization of the males was a consequence of disrupted hormones. That involved the endocrine system, which was composed of various glands that controlled critical functions such as basic metabolism and reproduction.

Well, that about summed up her knowledge of current endocrinology. She had taken courses in pharmacy school, but the intervening decades had revolutionized the field. And endocrinology was not standard fare in the training of ecologists. If she was going to pursue this line of inquiry, she would have to know more.

2

Several new endocrinology textbooks joined the stacks of wildlife files on the top of her desk. Her first efforts to master the basics of the endocrine system proved frustrating in the extreme. The texts were dense, unreadable, and full of acronyms that forced one to keep flipping back to earlier pages. Colborn only began making headway when she found a practical, accessible text, *Clinical Endocrine Physiology*, which she kept within reach through the months that followed.

3

As she focused on hormones, evidence that she had previously passed over gained new meaning. She recalled the keynote address by Bengtsson, the Swedish toxicologist who described how the size of fish testicles had diminished as contamination from synthetic organochlorine chemicals increased in the Baltic. Was this a sign of hormone disruption? She looked again at reports of abnormal mating behavior in bald eagles, which had preceded the appearance of eggshell thinning and the collapse of the eagle population. The birds had been disinterested in mating. Hormone disruption, Colborn now suspected.

4

Other things struck her, too, as she read through the wildlife files. A pattern began to emerge. Birds, mammals, and fish seemed to be experiencing similar reproductive problems. Although the adults living in and around the lakes were reproducing, their offspring often did not survive. Colborn began to focus on studies that compared Great Lakes populations to others living inland. In every case, the lake dwellers, who appeared otherwise healthy, were far less successful in producing surviving offspring. It seemed that the contamination in the parents was somehow affecting their young.

5

It dawned on Colborn that the human studies investigating the effects of exposure to synthetic chemicals had focused largely on cancer in exposed adults. Only a handful had looked for possible effects on the children of exposed individuals, but Colborn recalled reading one that had studied the children of women who had regularly eaten Great Lakes fish. She dug it out of her files and read it again. The study by Sandra and Joseph Jacobson, psychologists from Wayne State University in Detroit, had also found evidence the mother's level of chemical contamination affected her baby's development. The children of mothers who had eaten two to three meals a month of fish were born sooner, weighed less, and had smaller heads than those whose mother did not eat the fish. Moreover, the greater the amount of PCBs, a persistent industrial chemical that is a common pollutant in Great Lakes fish, in the umbilical cord blood, the more poorly the child scored

6

on tests assessing neurological development, lagging behind in various measures, such as short-term memory, that tend to predict later IQ.

7   The parallel between this human study and the offspring effects in wildlife was interesting as well as troubling.

8   Colborn moved on, following wherever the investigation led, but the Jacobson study hovered in the back of her mind, nagging at her like an unanswered question. Had scientists been looking in the right place in their search for effects? Perhaps the Jacobson studies were more important than anyone had realized.

9   As she dug deeper, more parallels became apparent. In the tissue analyses done on the wildlife, the same chemicals kept showing up in the troubled species, among them the pesticides DDT, dieldrin, chlordane, and lindane, as well as the family of industrial chemicals called PCBs, which had been used in electrical equipment and many other products. Of course, these results might be a coincidence, or they could well reflect technical limits and the small budgets for tracking contaminants. These were the chemicals toxicologists knew how to measure and the ones least expensive to analyze.

10   Whatever the reason for their repeated appearance, studies had found the very same chemicals in human blood and body fat. Colborn was particularly shocked by the high concentrations reported in the fat in human breast milk.

11   By the time the research deadline approached, Colborn had plowed through more than two thousand scientific papers and five hundred government documents. She felt like a beagle following its nose. She wasn't sure where she was headed, but propelled by her curiosity and intuition, she was hot on the trail. She had found so many tantalizing parallels, so many echoes among the studies. Somehow, she was certain, it all fit together, because she kept finding unexpected links. Her latest discovery had come while she reexplored the literature on the eerie wasting syndrome seen in young birds. The chicks could look normal and healthy for days, but then suddenly and unpredictably they would begin to languish, waste away, and finally die. The wasting problem, scientists were learning, was a symptom of disordered metabolism. The young birds could not produce sufficient energy to survive. Though one would not at first suspect that this problem had anything in common with the gay gull phenomenon, it also stemmed from the disruption of the endocrine system and hormones.

12   But the elation of discovery passed quickly. The deadline was looming. What did this all mean? She had pieces and patterns but no picture.

13   Maybe she could gain perspective if she laid it all out. Colborn began entering the findings from the studies on a huge ledger sheet, the kind used by accountants. When that became unwieldy, she turned to her computer and created an electronic spreadsheet, which scientists call a matrix. As she made entries

under columns headed "population decline," "reproductive effects," "tumors," "wasting," "immune suppression," and "behavioral changes," her attention came to focus increasingly on sixteen of the forty-three Great Lakes species that seemed to be having the greatest array of problems.

She sat back and looked at the list: the bald eagle, lake trout, herring gull, mink, otter, and the double-crested cormorant, the snapping turtle, the common tern, and coho salmon. What did they have in common?   14

Of course! Each and every one of these animals was a top predator that fed on Great Lakes fish. Although the concentrations of contaminants such as PCBs are so low in the water in the Great Lakes that they cannot be measured using standard water testing procedures, such persistent chemicals concentrate in the tissue and accumulate exponentially as they move from animal to animal up the food chain. Through this process of magnification, the concentrations of a persistent chemical that resists breakdown and accumulates in body fat can be 25 million times greater in a top predator such as a herring gull than in the surrounding water.   15

One other startling fact emerged from the spreadsheet. According to the scientific literature, the *adult* animals appeared to be doing fine. The health problems were found primarily in their offspring. Although she had been thinking about offspring effects, Colborn had not recognized this stark, across-the-board contrast between adults and young.   16

Now the pieces were beginning to fall together. If the chemicals found in the parents' bodies were to blame, they were acting as hand-me-down poisons, passed down from one generation to the next, that victimized the unborn and the very young. The conclusion was chilling.   17

But the host of disparate symptoms in everything from adult herring gulls to baby snapping turtles did not seem to add up. Some animals, like the gulls, exhibited strange behavior such as same-sex nests, while other species, including the double-crested cormorant, had visible gross birth defects such as club feet, missing eyes, crooked spines, and crossed bills. Again a pattern emerged from the confusing pieces of the puzzle as Colborn reflected on what she had learned by following her nose.   18

These were all cases of derailed development, a process guided to a significant extent by hormones. Most could be linked to disruption of the endocrine system.   19

This insight pointed Colborn's investigation in another direction. She began reading everything she could find about the chemicals that showed up again and again in the tissue analyses of animals having trouble producing viable young. She quickly learned that the testing and reviews done by manufacturers and government regulatory agencies had focused largely on whether a chemical might cause cancer, but she found enough in the peer-reviewed scientific literature to prove that her hunch had been correct.   20

21   The hand-me-down poisons found in the fat of the wildlife had one thing in common: one way or another, they all acted on the endocrine system, which regulates the body's vital internal processes and guides critical phases of prenatal development. The hand-me-down poisons disrupted hormones.

Getting Started:
Listing and Analyzing Issues

A good way to get started is to list possible issues to write about. Make a list of questions that can be answered "YES because . . . " or "NO because . . ." (Following is a list to get you started.) These questions all ask whether we should do something, and therefore they are all phrased as arguments of policy. You'll find out that often before you can make recommendations of policy, you first have to analyze exactly what is meant by a phrase like *censorship of the Internet.* Does it mean censorship of the World Wide Web or of everything that goes over the Internet, including private email? To be convincing, you'll have to argue that one thing causes another, for good or bad.

But it's hard to argue about something in which you have no interest. You have to identify what you are interested in first if you want to write an argument that expresses your own convictions.

Campus

- Should students be required to pay fees for access to computers on campus?

- Should smoking be banned on campus?

- Should varsity athletes get paid for playing sports that bring in revenue?

- Should admissions decisions be based exclusively on academic achievement?

- Should knowledge of a foreign language be required for all degree plans?

- Should your college or university have a computer literacy requirement?

- Should fraternities be banned from campuses if they are caught encouraging alcohol abuse?

Community

- Should people who ride bicycles and motorcycles be required to wear helmets?

- Should high schools be allowed to search students for drugs at any time?

- Should high schools distribute condoms?

- Should bilingual education programs be eliminated?

- Should the public schools be privatized?

- Should bike lanes be built throughout your community to encourage more people to ride bicycles?

- Should more tax dollars be shifted from building highways to public transportation?

Nation/World

- Should advertising be banned on television shows aimed at preschool children?

- Should capital punishment be abolished?

- Should the Internet be censored?

- Should marijuana be legalized?

- Should handguns be outlawed?

- Should beef and poultry be free of growth hormones?

- Should a law be passed requiring that the parents of teenagers who receive abortions be informed?

- Should people who are terminally ill be allowed to end their lives?

- Should it be made illegal to kill animals for their fur?

- Should the United States punish nations with poor human rights records?

- Should the United Nations recognize groups of people who are not defined by their national status, such as the Kurds?

After You Make a List

1. Put a check beside the issues that look most interesting to write about or the ones that mean the most to you.

2. Put a question mark beside the issues that you don't know very much about. If you choose one of these issues, you will probably have to do a lot of research—by talking to people, by using the Internet, or by going to the library.

3. Select the two or three issues that look most promising. For each issue, make another list:

   ■ Who is most interested in this issue?

   ■ Whom or what does this issue affect?

   ■ What are the pros and cons of this issue? Make two columns. At the top of the left one, write "YES because." At the top of the right one, write "NO because."

   ■ What has been written about this issue? How can you find out what has been written?

Getting Started:
Making an Idea Map

When you identify an issue that looks promising and interests you, the next step is to discover how much you know about it and how many different aspects of it you can think of. One way to take this inventory is to make an *idea map* that describes visually how the many aspects of a particular issue relate to each other. Idea maps are useful because you can see everything at once and make connections among the different aspects of an issue—definitions, causes, effects, proposed solutions, and your personal experience.

A good way to get started is to write down ideas on Post-it notes. Then you can move the Post-it notes around until you figure out which ideas fit together.

As an example, let's say you pick binge drinking among college students. Several stories have been in your campus newspaper this year about binge drinking. You read an article recently that reported the results of an annual study of student drinking behavior done by a Harvard professor. From this article you have a few statistics to go with your knowledge of binge drinking and what your school is doing to attempt to prevent alcohol abuse. Figure 1.1 shows what your idea map might look like after you assemble your notes.

Harvard survey released September 1998
- 43% of 14,500 students surveyed at 116 schools reported that they had binged at least once in the preceding 2 weeks
- Little change in drinking patterns since 1994
- Increase in drinking deliberately to get drunk, and in alcohol-related problems—including injuries, drunk driving, violence, and academic difficulties

Causes of binge drinking
- Binge drinking is a part of college culture
- Alumni and students binge at tailgate parties at sporting events
- Many bars and liquor stores close to campus
- Many alcohol promotions such as 2-for-1 happy hours and free nights for women
- Administrators condone drinking
- No exams on Friday allow students to binge Thursday through Sunday

Experience with binge drinking
- Three students on your dorm floor are regular binge drinkers and get rowdy
- Not enough alcohol-free alternatives at your school
- Legal drinking age of 21 leads to more drinking rather than less because it gives alcohol a mystique
- Students under much pressure and look for a release

Definition of binge drinking
- More than 5 drinks a night for men
- More than 4 drinks a night for women

Binge Drinking

Fraternities and sororities
- Harvard study reports 4 of 5 residents in fraternities and sororities binge
- Most recent alcohol-related deaths of college students involved fraternity parties
- High school seniors often go to fraternity parties
- Administrators hesitant to regulate fraternities for fear of angering alumni donors

Proposed solutions to binge drinking
- Education campaigns about risks of binge drinking
- Ban alcohol in residence halls and in fraternities and sororities
- Ban alcohol and alcohol ads at sporting events
- Punish disruptive behavior
- Provide alcohol-free alternatives

Effects of binge drinking
- Rise in alcohol-related deaths on campus
- Colleges are being sued by families of students injured by excessive drinking
- Rise in alcohol-related problems including drunk driving and academic difficulties
- Binge drinkers harm nonbingers, interrupting sleep, committing violent acts, driving drunk

Figure 1.1   Idea Map on Binge Drinking

 Chapter 2

Persuading with Good Reasons

The Basics of Arguments

Many people think of the term *argument* as a synonym for *debate*. College courses and professional careers, however, require a different kind of argument—one that, most of the time, is cooler in emotion and much more elaborate in detail than oral debate. At first glance an **argument** in writing doesn't seem have much in common with debate. But the basic elements and ways of reasoning used in written arguments are similar to those we use in everyday conversations. Let's look at an example of an informal debate:

Jeff: I think students should not have to pay tuition to go to state colleges and universities.

Maria: Cool idea, but why should students not have to pay?

Jeff: Because you don't have pay to go to high school.

Maria: Yeah, but that's different. The law says that everyone has to go to high school, at least to age 16. Everyone doesn't have to go to college.

Jeff: Well, in some other countries like the United Kingdom, students don't have to pay tuition.

Maria: The whole system of education is different in Britain from the United States. Plus you're wrong. Students started paying tuition at British universities in fall 1998.

Jeff: OK, maybe the United Kingdom isn't a good example. But students should have a right to go to college, just like they have the right to drive on the highway.

Maria: Jeff, you pay for driving through taxes. Everyone who buys gas and has a driver's license helps pay for the highways. Going to college isn't necessary, and not everyone does it. Only people who go to college should pay. Why should everyone have to pay taxes for some people to go to college?

Jeff: Because our nation would be better if everyone had the opportunity to college free of charge.

Maria: Why? What evidence do you have that things would be better if everyone went to college? It would put an enormous drain on the economy. People would have to pay a lot more in taxes.

Jeff: The way to help poor people is to provide them with a good education. That's what's wrong now; poor people don't get a good education and can't afford to go to college.

In this discussion, Jeff starts out by making a **claim** that students should not have to pay tuition. Maria immediately asks him why students should not have to pay tuition. She wants a **good reason** to accept his claim. A reason is typically offered in a **because clause,** a statement that begins with the word *because* and then provides a supporting reason for the claim. Jeff's first attempt is to argue that students shouldn't have to pay to go to college *because* they don't have to pay to go to high school.

The word *because* signals a **link** between the reason and the claim. When Jeff tells Maria that students don't have to pay to go to public high schools, Maria does not accept the link. Maria asks **"So what?"** every time Jeff presents a new reason. She will accept Jeff's evidence only if she accepts that his reason supports his claim.

In this small discussion, we find the basics of arguments. Jeff has a claim for which he offers a reason.

CLAIM ◄----- REASON

Every argument that is more than a shouting match or a simple assertion has to be supported by one or more reasons. That reason in turn has to be linked to the claim if it is to become a *good reason.*

CLAIM ◄----- *LINK (because)* ◄----- REASON

Jeff's problem in convincing Maria is that he can't convince her to link his reasons to his claim. Maria challenges Jeff's links and keeps asking "So what?" For her, Jeff's reasons are not good reasons.

CLAIM ◄----- LINK *(because)* ◄----- REASON

↑

CHALLENGES (So What?)

By the end of this short discussion, Jeff has begun to build an argument. He has had to come up with another claim to support his main claim, and if he is to convince Maria, he will probably have to provide a **series of claims** that she will accept as linked to his primary claim. He will also need to find evidence to support these claims.

CLAIM ◄----- LINK *(because)* ◄----- REASON ◄----- EVIDENCE

↑

CHALLENGES (So What?)

Benjamin Franklin observed that "so convenient a thing it is to be a rational creature, since it enables us to find or make a reason for every thing one has a mind to do." It is not hard to think of reasons. What is difficult is to convince your audience that your reasons are *good reasons.* In a conversation, you get immediate feedback that tells you whether your listener agrees or disagrees. When you are writing, you usually don't have someone reading who can question you immediately unless you are writing on a computer connected to other computers. Consequently, you have to be more specific about what you are claiming, you have to connect with the values you hold in common with your readers, and you have to anticipate what questions and objections your readers might have if you are going to convince someone who doesn't agree with you or know what you know already.

When you write an argument, imagine a reader like Maria who is going to listen carefully to what you have to say but is not going to agree with you automatically. When you present a reason, she will ask, "So what?" You will have to have evidence, and you will have to link it to your claim in ways she will accept if she is to agree that your reason is a good one.

To begin, there must be something that you want to claim. If that claim is very general, it is often very hard to argue. For example, Jeff's assertion that our nation would be better off if everyone went to college is almost like saying our nation would be better if everyone obeyed traffic laws. Jeff's claim seems unrealistic because it doesn't take into account what it would take to accomplish the goal or why things would be better as a result. He makes a more

National Archives building, Washington, D.C.

specific claim in response to Maria that education is the route out of poverty, but that claim too is very broad.

Your claim should be specific, and it should be contestable. If you claim that you like sour cream on a baked potato, your claim is specific but not contestable. Someone could tell you that a baked potato is less fattening without sour cream, but it still doesn't change the fact that you like sour cream. Besides, you might want to gain weight.

What Is Not Arguable

Just about everything is arguable, but much of the time certain kinds of argument are not advanced. Statements of **facts** are usually not considered arguable. Jeff's claim that students at universities in the United Kingdom do not pay tuition is a statement of fact that turned out not to be true. Most facts can be verified by doing research. But even simple facts can sometimes be argued. For example, Mount Everest is usually acknowledged to be the highest mountain in the world at 29,028 feet above sea level. But if the total height of a mountain from base to summit is the measure, then the volcano Mauna Loa in Hawaii is the highest mountain in the world. Although the top of Mauna Loa is 13,667 feet above sea level, the summit is 31,784 above the ocean floor. Thus the "fact" that Mount Everest is the highest mountain on the earth depends on a definition of *highest* being the point farthest above sea level.

Another category of claims that are not arguable are those of **personal taste.** Your favorite food and your favorite color are examples of personal taste. If you really hate fresh tomatoes, no one can convince you that you actually like them. But many claims of personal taste turn out to be value judgments using arguable criteria. For example, if you think that *Alien* is the best science fiction movie ever made, you can argue that claim if you set out evaluative criteria that other people can consider as good reasons. Indeed, you might not even like science fiction and still argue that *Alien* is the best science fiction movie ever.

Finally, many claims rest on **beliefs** that for some people are not arguable. If someone accepts a claim as a matter of religious belief, then for that person, the claim is true and cannot be refuted. Of course, people still make arguments about the existence of God and which religion reflects the will of God. Any time an audience will not consider an idea, it's possible but very difficult to construct an argument. Many people claim to have evidence that UFOs exist, but most people refuse to acknowledge that evidence as even being possibly factual.

The Basics of Reasoning

You decide to pick up a new pair of prescription sunglasses at the mall on your way to class. The company promises that it can make your glasses in an hour, but what you hadn't counted on was how long it would take you to park and how long you would have to wait in line at the counter. You jog into the mall, drop off your prescription, and go out of the store to wait. There's a booth nearby where volunteers are checking blood pressure. You don't have anything better to do, so you have your blood pressure checked.

After the volunteer takes the blood pressure cuff off your arm, he asks how old you are. You tell him you're twenty. He asks you whether you smoke, and you say no. He tells you that your reading is 150 over 100. He says that's high for a person your age and that you ought to have it checked again. "This is all I need," you think. "I have test coming up tomorrow, a term paper due Friday, and if I don't make it to class, I won't get my homework turned in on time. And now something bad is wrong with me."

When you get your blood pressure checked again at the student health center after your test the next day, it turns out to be 120/80, which the nurse says is normal. When you think about it, you realize that you probably had a high reading because of stress and jogging into the mall.

Your blood pressure is one of the most important indicators of your health. When the volunteer checking your blood pressure tells you that you might have a serious health problem because your blood pressure is too high, he is relying on his knowledge of how the human body works. If your blood pressure is too high, it eventually damages your arteries and puts a strain on your entire body. But he used the word *might* because your blood pressure is not the same all the time. It can go up when you are under stress or even when you eat too much salt. And blood pressure varies from person to person and even in different parts of your body. For example, your blood pressure is higher in your legs than in your arms.

Doctors use blood pressure and other information to make diagnoses. Diagnoses are claims based on evidence. But as the blood pressure example shows, often the link is not clear, at least from a single reading. A doctor will collect several blood pressure readings over many weeks or even years before concluding that a patient has a condition of high blood pressure called *hypertension.* These readings will be compared to readings from thousands of other patients in making a diagnosis. Doctors are trained to rely on **generalizations** from thousands of past observations in medical science and to make diagnoses based on **probability.** In everyday life, you learn to make similar generalizations from which you make decisions based on probability. If you are in a hurry in the grocery store, you likely will go to the line that looks the shortest. You pick the shortest line because you think it will probably be the fastest.

Sometimes we don't have past experience to rely on, and we have to reason in other ways. When we claim that one thing is like something else, we make a link by **analogy.** Jeff's attempt to argue that American colleges and universities should be tuition free because British universities are tuition free is an argument by analogy. Analogies work only if the resemblances are more convincing than the dissimilarities. Maria pointed out that Jeff simply didn't know the facts.

Another way we reason is by using **cultural assumptions,** which we often think of as common sense. For example, you walk down the street and see a 280Z speed around a car that is double-parked, cross the double line, and sideswipe a truck coming the other way. A police officer arrives shortly, and you tell her that the 280Z is at fault. Maybe you've seen many accidents before, but the reason you think the 280Z is at fault is because in the United States, drivers are supposed to stay on the right side of two-way roads. It is part of our culture that you take for granted—that is, until you try to drive in Japan, Great

Britain, or India, where people drive on the left. Driving on the left will seem very unnatural to you, but it's natural for the people in those countries.

Driving on the right or left side of a street is a cultural assumption. Many assumptions are formally written down as laws. Others are simply part of cultural knowledge. There is no law that people who are waiting should stand in a line or that people who are first in line should receive attention first, but we think someone is rude who cuts in front of us when we stand in a line. In some other cultures, people don't stand in line when they wait. Crowding up to the counter, which seems rude to us, is the norm for them. Other cultures sometimes find the informality of Americans rude. For example, in some cultures, calling people by their first name when you first meet them is considered rude instead of friendly.

Particular cultural assumptions can be hard to challenge because you often have to take on an entire system of belief. The metric system is much easier to use to calculate distances than the English system of miles, feet, and inches. Nonetheless, people in the United States have strongly resisted efforts to convert to metric measures. When cultural assumptions become common sense, people accept them as true even though they often can be questioned. It seems like common sense to say that salad is good for you, but in reality it depends on what's in the salad. A salad consisting of a lot of lettuce and a mayonnaise-based dressing has little nutritional value and much fat.

Finding Good Reasons

A good reason works because it includes a link to your claim that your readers will find valid. Your readers are almost like a jury that passes judgment on your good reasons. If they accept them and cannot think of other, more compelling good reasons that oppose your position, you will convince them.

Most good reasons derive from mulling things over "reasonably," or, to use the technical term, from logos. *Logos* refers to the logic of what you communicate; in fact, logos is the root of our modern word *logic*. Good reasons are thus commonly associated with logical appeals. Over the years, professional rhetoricians have devised a number of informal methods, known as *heuristics*, to help speakers and writers find good reasons to support their arguments. (The word *heuristics* comes from the same root as the Greek word *eureka*, which means "I have found it!") In the rest of this section, you will find a set of heuristics for developing good reasons for your arguments. Think of them as a series of questions that can help you to develop persuasive arguments.

These questions will equip you to communicate more effectively when you are speaking before a group as well as writing an argument. But do not expect every question to be productive in every case. Sometimes, a certain question won't get you very far; and often, the questions will develop so many good reasons and strategies that you will not be able to use them all. You will ultimately have to select from among the best of your good reasons to find the ones that are most likely to work in a given case.

If a certain question does not seem to work for you at first, do not give up on it the next time. Get in the habit of asking these questions in the course of developing your arguments. If you ask them systematically, you will probably have more good reasons than you need for your arguments.

Can You Argue by Definition—from "the Nature of the Thing"?

Probably the most powerful kind of good reason is an **argument from definition.** You can think of a definition as a simple statement: _____ *is a* _____. You use these statements all the time. When you need a course to fulfill your social science area requirement, you look at the list of courses that are defined as social science courses. You find out that the anthropology class you want to take is one of them. It's just as important when _____ *is not a* _____. You are taking College Algebra this semester, which is a math course taught by the math department, yet it doesn't count for the math requirement. The reason it doesn't count is because College Algebra is not defined as a college-level math class. So you have to enroll next semester in Calculus I.

Many definitions are not nearly as clear cut as the math requirement. If you want to argue that figure skaters are athletes, you will need a because clause that defines what an athlete is. So you start thinking about how to define an athlete. An athlete competes in an activity, but that definition alone is too broad, since many competitions do not require physical activity. Thus, an athlete must participate in a competitive physical activity and must train for it. But that definition is still not quite narrow enough, since soldiers train for competitive physical activity. You decide to add that the activity must be a sport and that it must require special competence and precision. Your because clause turns out to be as follows: *Figure skaters are athletes because true athletes train for and compete in physical sporting competitions that require special competence and precision.*

If you can get your audience to accept your definitions of things, you've gone a long way toward convincing them of the validity of your claim. That is why the most controversial issues in our culture—abortion, affirmative action, gay rights, pornography, women's rights, gun control, the death penalty— are argued from definition. Is abortion a crime or a medical technique? Is pornography protected by the First Amendment, or is it a violation of women's rights? Is the death penalty just or cruel and inhuman? You can see from these examples that definitions often rely on cultural assumptions for their links.

Because cultural assumptions on controversial definitional issues are so strongly held, people usually don't care about the practical consequences if they believe the definition. Arguing that it is much cheaper to execute prisoners who have been convicted of first-degree murder than to keep them in prison for life does not convince those who believe that it is morally wrong to kill anyone, no matter what they have done.

Can You Argue from Value?

A special kind of argument from definition, one that often implies consequences, is the **argument from value.** You can support your claim with a because clause (or several of them) that includes a sense of evaluation. Arguments from value follow from claims like _____ *is a good* _____ or _____ *is not a good* _____ .

You make arguments from value every day. Your old TV set breaks, so you go to your local discount store to buy a new one. When you get there, you find too many choices. You have to decide which one to buy. You have only $230 to spend, but there are still a lot of choices. Which is the best TV for $230 or less? The more you look, the more confusing it gets. There are several 19-inch TVs in your price range. All have remote control. Some have features such as front surround sound, multilingual on-screen display, and A/V inputs. But you realize that there is one test that will determine the best TV for you: the picture quality. You buy the one with the best picture.

Evaluative arguments usually proceed from the presentation of certain criteria. These criteria come from the definitions of good and bad, of poor and not so poor, that prevail in a given case. A really good 19-inch TV fulfills certain criteria; so does an outstanding movie, an excellent class, or, if you work in an office, an effective telephone system. Sometimes the criteria are straightforward, as in the TV example. The TV that you select has to be under a certain cost, equipped with a remote, and ready to hook up to your cable. After those criteria are met, the big ones are picture and sound quality. But if your boss asks you to recommend a new telephone system, then it's not quite so straightforward. You are presented with a lot of options, and you have to decide which of them are worth paying for. You have to decide how the phone system is going to be used, examine which features will be important for your office, and then rate the systems according to the criteria you have set out. The key to evaluation arguments is identifying and arguing for the right criteria. If you can convince your readers that you have the right criteria and that your assessments are correct, then you will be convincing.

Can You Compare or Contrast?

Evaluative arguments can generate comparisons often enough. But even if they don't generate comparisons, your argument might profit if you get in the habit of thinking in comparative terms—in terms of what things are like

or unlike the topic you are discussing. **Claims of comparisons** take the form
_____ *is like* _____ or _____ *is not like* _____. If you are having trouble coming up with good reasons, think of comparisons that help your readers
to agree with you. If you want to argue that figure skaters are athletes, you
might think about how their training and competitions resemble those of other
athletes. Making comparisons is an effective way of building common ground.

A particular kind of comparison is an analogy. An **analogy** is an extended
comparison—one that is developed over several sentences or paragraphs for
explanatory or persuasive purposes. Analogies take different forms. A **historical analogy** compares something that is going on now with a similar case in
the past. One of the most frequent historical analogies is to compare a current
situation in which one country attacks or threatens another with Germany's
seizing of Czechoslovakia in 1938 and then invading Poland in 1939, starting
World War II. The difficulty with this analogy is that circumstances today are
not the same as those in 1939, and it is easy to point out how the analogy fails.

Other analogies make literal comparisons. A **literal analogy** is a comparison between current situations, in which you argue what is true or works in
one situation should be true or work in another. Most advanced nations provide basic health care to all their citizens either free or at very minimal charges.
All citizens of Canada are covered by the same comprehensive health care
system, which is free for both rich and poor. Canadians go to the doctor more
frequently than citizens of the United States do, and they receive what is generally regarded as better care than their Southern neighbors, who pay the most
expensive health care bills on the planet.

The Canadian analogy has failed to convince members of the U.S. Congress to vote for a similar system in the United States. Opponents of adopting
the Canadian system argue that health care costs are also high in Canada, but
Canadians pay the costs in different ways. They pay high taxes, and the Canadian national debt has increased since the universal health system was approved. These opponents of adopting the Canadian system for the United
States believe that the best care can be obtained for the lowest cost if health
care is treated like any other service and consumers decide what they are willing to pay. Comparisons can always work both ways.

Analogies are especially valuable when you are trying to explain a concept
to a willing listener or reader, but analogies are far from foolproof if the reader
does not agree with you from the outset. Using an analogy can be risky if the
entire argument depends on the reader's accepting it.

Can You Argue from Consequence?

Another powerful source of good reasons comes from considering the possible
consequences of your position: Can you sketch out the good things that will fol-

low from your position? Can you establish that certain bad things will be avoided if your position is adopted? If so, you will have other good reasons to use.

Arguments from consequence take the basic form of _____ *causes* _____ (or _____ *does not cause* _____). Very often, arguments from consequence are more complicated, taking the form _____ *causes* _____ *which, in turn, causes* _____ and so on. In chapter 1 we saw that *Silent Spring* makes powerful arguments from consequence. Rachel Carson's primary claim is that *DDT should not be sprayed on a massive scale because it will poison animals and people.* The key to her argument is the causal chain that explains how animals and people are poisoned. Carson describes how nothing exists alone in nature. When a potato field is sprayed with chemical poison such as DDT, some of that poison is absorbed by the skin of the potatoes and some washes into the groundwater, where it contaminates drinking water. Other poisonous residue is absorbed into streams, where it is ingested by insect larvae, which in turn are eaten by fish. Fish are eaten by other fish, which are then eaten by waterfowl and people. At each stage, the poisons become more concentrated. Carson shows why people are in danger from drinking contaminated water and eating contaminated vegetables and fish. Even today, over thirty years after DDT stopped being used in the United States, dangerous levels exist in the sediment at the bottom of many lakes and bays.

All the big environmental debates revolve around arguments from consequence. Scientists generally agree that the average temperature on the earth has gone up one degree over the last hundred years and that the amount of carbon dioxide has increased by 25 percent. But the causes of those increases are much disputed. Some people believe that the rise in temperature is a naturally occurring climate variation and that the increase in carbon dioxide is only minimally the cause or not related at all. Others argue that the burning of fossil fuels and the cutting of tropical forests have led to the increase in carbon dioxide, which in turn traps heat, thus increasing the temperature of the earth. The major problem for all participants in the global warming debate is that the causation is neither simple nor direct. Therefore, powerful computer models have become an important part of this debate.

Proposal arguments are future-oriented arguments from consequence. In a proposal argument, you cannot stop with naming good reasons; you also have to show that these consequences would follow from the idea or course of action that you are arguing. As an example, let's say you want to argue that all high school graduates in your state should be computer literate. You want a computer requirement more substantial than the one computer literacy course you had in the eighth grade. You want all high school graduates to be familiar with basic computer concepts and terminology, to be able to use a word-processing application and at least two other applications, and to understand issues of ethics and privacy raised by new electronic technologies.

Your strongest good reason is that high school graduates should be competent in the use of computers, the tool that they will most certainly use for most writing tasks and many other activities during their lifetime. Even if your readers accept that good reason, you still have to prove that the requirement will actually give students the competency they require. Many students pass language requirements without being able to speak, read, or write the language they have studied.

Furthermore, you have to consider the feasibility of any proposal that you make. A good idea has to be a practical one. If you want to impose a computer literacy requirement, you have to argue for increased funding for expensive technology. High school students in poor communities cannot become computer literate unless they have access to computers. More teachers might also need to be hired. And you will need to figure out how to fit the computer requirement into an already crowded curriculum. Sometimes, feasibility is not a major issue (for example, if you're proposing that the starting time for basketball games be changed by thirty minutes); but if it is, you must address it.

Can You Counter Objections to Your Position?

Another good way to find convincing good reasons is to think about possible objections to your position. If you can imagine how your audience might counter or respond to your argument, you will probably include in your argument precisely the points that will address your readers' particular needs and objections. If you are successful, your readers will be convinced that you are right. You've no doubt had the experience yourself of mentally saying to a writer in the course of your reading, "Yeah, but what about this other idea?"— only to have the writer address precisely this objection.

You can impress your readers that you've thought about why anyone would oppose your position and exactly how that opposition would be expressed. If you are writing a proposal argument for a computer literacy requirement for all high school graduates, you might think about why anyone would object, since computers are becoming increasingly important to our jobs and lives. What will the practical objections be? What philosophical ones? Why hasn't such a requirement been put in place already? By asking such questions in your own arguments, you are likely to develop robust because clauses that may be the ones that most affect your readers.

Sometimes, writers actually create an objector by posing rhetorical questions such as "You might say, 'But won't that make my taxes go up to pay for computers for all students?'" Stating objections explicitly can be effective if you make the objections as those of a reasonable person with an alternative point of view. But if the objections you state are ridiculous ones, then you risk being accused of setting up a *straw man,* that is, making the position opposing your own so simplistic that no one would likely identify with it.

Questions for Finding Good Reasons

1. Can you argue by definition—from "the nature of the thing"?

- Can you argue that while many (most) people think X is a Y, X is better thought of as a Z?

  Example: Most people do not think of humans as an endangered species, but small farmers have been successful in comparing their way of life to an endangered species and thus extend the definition of an endangered species to include themselves.

- Can you argue that while X is a Y, X differs from other Ys and might be thought of as a Z?

  Example: Colleges and universities are similar to the public schools in having education as their primary mission, but unlike the public schools, colleges and universities receive only part of their operating costs from tax revenues and therefore, like a business, must generate much of their own revenue.

2. Can you argue from value?

- Can you grade a few examples of the kind of thing you are evaluating as good, better, and best (or bad and worse)?

  Example: There have been lots of great actors in detective films, but none compare to the best of Humphrey Bogart.

- Can you list the features you use to determine whether something is good or bad and then show why one is most important?

  Example: Coach X taught me a great deal about the skills and strategy of playing tennis, but most of all, she taught me that the game is fun.

3. Can you compare or contrast?

- Can you think of items, events, or situations that are similar or dissimilar to the one you are writing about?

  Example: We should require a foreign language for all students at our college because our main competitor does not have such a requirement.

- Can you distinguish why your subject is different than one usually thought of as similar?

  Example: While poor people are often lumped in with the unemployed and those on welfare, the majority of poor people do work in low-paying jobs.

(continued)

4. Can you argue from consequence?

■ Can you argue that good things will happen if a certain course of action is followed or that bad things will be avoided?

Example: Eliminating all income tax deductions would save every taxpayer many hours and would create a system of taxation that does not reward people for cheating.

■ Can you argue that while there were obvious causes of Y, Y would not have occurred had it not been for X?

Example: A seventeen-year-old driver is killed when her car skids across the grass median of an interstate highway and collides with a pickup truck going the other direction. Even though a slick road and excessive speed were the immediate causes, the driver would be alive today if the median had a concrete barrier.

■ Can you argue for an alternative cause rather than the one many people assume?

Example: Politicians take credit for reducing the violent crime rate because of "get-tough" police policies, but in fact, the rate of violent crime is decreasing because more people are working.

5. Can you counter objections to your position?

■ Can you think of the most likely objections to your claim and turn them into your own good reasons?

Example: High school administrators might object to requiring computer literacy because of cost, but schools can now lease computers and put them on a statewide system at a cost less than they now pay for textbooks.

■ Can the *reverse* or opposite of an opposing claim be argued?

Example: A proposed expressway through a city is claimed to help traffic, but it also could make traffic worse by encouraging more people to drive to the city.

Supporting Good Reasons

Good reasons are essential ingredients of good arguments, but they don't do the job alone. You must support or verify good reasons with evidence. Evidence consists of hard data or examples or narratives or episodes or tabulations of episodes (known as *statistics*) that are seen as relevant to the good reasons that you are putting forward. To put it another way, a writer of arguments puts forward not only claims and good reasons but also evidence that those good reasons are true. And that evidence consists of examples, personal experiences, comparisons, statistics, calculations, quotations, and other kinds of data that a reader will find relevant and compelling.

How much supporting evidence should you supply? How much evidence is enough? That is difficult to generalize about; as is usual in the case of rhetoric, the best answer is to say, "It depends." If a reader is likely to find one of your good reasons hard to believe, then you should be aggressive in offering support. You should present detailed evidence in a patient and painstaking way. As one presenting an argument, you have a responsibility not just to *state* a case but to *make* a case with evidence. Arguments that are unsuccessful tend to fail not because of a shortage of good reasons; more often, they fail because the reader doesn't agree that there is enough evidence to support the good reason that is being presented.

If your good reason isn't especially controversial, you probably should not belabor it. Think of your own experiences as a reader. How often do you recall saying to yourself, as you read a passage or listened to a speaker, "OK! OK! I get the point! Don't keep piling up all of this evidence for me because I don't want it or need it." However, such a reaction is rare, isn't it? By contrast, how often do you recall muttering under your breath, "How can you say that? What evidence do you have to back it up?" When in doubt, err on the side of offering too much evidence. It's an error that is seldom made and not often criticized.

When a writer doesn't provide satisfactory evidence for a because clause, readers might feel that there has been a failure in the reasoning process. In fact, in your previous courses in writing and speaking, you may have learned about various fallacies associated with faulty arguments: faulty definitions, faulty analogies, hasty generalizations, faulty causal arguments (the so-called *post hoc fallacy*), name calling, red herrings, and so forth.

Strictly speaking, there is nothing false about these so-called logical fallacies. The fallacies most often refer to failures in providing evidence; when you don't provide enough good evidence to convince your audience, you might be accused of committing a fallacy in reasoning. You will usually avoid such accusations if the evidence that you cite is both *relevant* and *sufficient.*

Relevance refers to the appropriateness of the evidence to the case at hand. Some kinds of evidence are seen as more relevant than others for particular audiences. For example, in science and industry, personal testimony is seen as having limited relevance, while experimental procedures and controlled observations have far more credibility. Compare someone who defends the use of a particular piece of computer software because "it worked for me" with someone who defends it because "according to a journal article published last month, 84% of the users of the software were satisfied or very satisfied with it." On the other hand, in writing to the general public on controversial issues such as gun control, personal experience is often considered more relevant than other kinds of data. The so-called Brady Bill, which requires a mandatory waiting period for the purchase of handguns, was named for President Ronald Reagan's press secretary, James Brady, who was permanently disabled when John W. Hinckley, Jr., made an assassination attempt on the president in 1981. James Brady's wife, Sarah, effectively told the story of her husband's suffering in lobbying for the bill.

Sufficiency refers to the amount of evidence cited. Sometimes a single piece of evidence, a single instance, will carry the day if it is especially compelling in some way—if it represents the situation well or makes a point that isn't particularly controversial. More often, people expect more than one piece of evidence if they are to be convinced of something. Convincing readers that they should approve a statewide computer literacy requirement for all high school graduates will require much more evidence than the story of a single graduate who succeeded with her computer skills. You will likely need statistical evidence for such a broad proposal.

If you anticipate that your audience might not accept your evidence, face the situation squarely. First, think carefully about the argument you are presenting. If you cannot cite adequate evidence for your assertions, perhaps those assertions must be modified or qualified in some way. If you remain convinced of your assertions, then think about doing more research to come up with additional evidence. If you anticipate that your audience might suspect you have overlooked or minimized important information, reassure them that you have not and deal explicitly with conflicting arguments. Another strategy is to acknowledge explicitly the limitations of your evidence. Acknowledging limitations doesn't shrink the limitations, but it does build your credibility and convinces your audience that alternatives have indeed been explored fully and responsibly. If you are thinking of your reader as a partner rather than as an adversary, it is usually easy to acknowledge limitations because you are looking not for victory and the end of debate but for a mutually satisfactory situation that might emerge as a result of the communication process that you are part of.

Deciding Which Good Reasons to Use

Asking a series of questions can generate a list of because clauses, but even if you have plenty, you still have to decide which ones to use. How can you decide which points are likely to be most persuasive? In choosing which good reasons to use in your arguments, consider your readers' attitudes and values and the values that are especially sanctioned by your community.

When people communicate, they tend to present their own thinking—to rely on the lines of thought that have led them to believe as they do. That's natural enough, since it is reasonable to present to others the reasons that make us believe what we are advocating in writing or speech. People have lots in common, and it is natural to think that the evidence and patterns of thought that have guided your thinking to a certain point will also guide others to the same conclusions.

But people are also different, and what convinces you might not always convince others. When you are deciding what because clauses to present to others, therefore, try not so much to recapitulate your own thinking process as to influence the thinking of others. Ask yourself not just why you think as you do but also what you need to convince others to see things your way. Don't pick the because clauses that seem compelling to you; pick those that will seem compelling to your audience.

It might be easy to choose arguments that are compelling for your readers if you belong to the same community. If you work for the same organization as your readers or if you belong to the same discipline, you have probably learned to value the same things that your readers do. To test whether your arguments are likely to appeal to your intended readers, consult them while you are writing or ask someone to take the position of one of your readers and review your argument when you have completed a draft. Before you commit your arguments to a final draft, do something to get feedback from your reader or a surrogate, and you will almost surely find the places in your argument that leak. You must find and fix those leaks if your argument is going to float instead of sink. We will talk more about analyzing and taking into account your readers' attitudes and values in the next chapter.

 *James Q. Wilson*

Just Take Away Their Guns

James Quinn Wilson (1931–) is a professor of management at UCLA who is well known as a social theorist and an authority on criminal justice and human morality. He is the author or coauthor of several books, including *Varieties of Police Behavior* (1968), *Thinking about Crime* (1975), *Crime and Human Nature* (1985), *Understanding and Controlling Crime: Toward a New Research Strategy* (1986), *Police Performance and Case Attrition* (1987), *Bureaucracy: What Government Agencies Do and Why They Do It* (1991), *The Moral Sense* (1993), and *Moral Judgment: Does the Abuse Excuse Threaten Our Legal System?* (1997).

According to Christopher Jencks, writing in the *New York Review of Books*, Wilson became "probably the most influential single writer on crime in America." From his early writings on police behavior to his recent books that argue that common moral patterns underlie all human cultures, Wilson has presented highly original thinking about our justice system and our society. "Just Take Away Their Guns," published in the *New York Times* in 1994, exemplifies why Wilson is a frequent member of presidential panels and task forces on crime.

James Q. Wilson

1   The president wants still tougher gun control legislation and thinks it will work. The public supports more gun control laws but suspects they won't work. The public is right.

2   Legal restraints on the lawful purchase of guns will have little effect on the illegal use of guns. There are some 200 million guns in private ownership, about one-third of them handguns. Only about 2 percent of the latter are employed to commit crimes. It would take a Draconian, and politically impossible, confiscation of legally purchased guns to make much of a difference in the number used by criminals. Moreover, only about one-sixth of the handguns used by serious criminals are purchased from a gun shop or pawnshop. Most of these handguns are stolen, borrowed or obtained through private purchases that wouldn't be affected by gun laws.

3   What is worse, any successful effort to shrink the stock of legally purchased guns (or of ammunition) would reduce the capacity of law-abiding people to defend themselves. Gun control advocates scoff at the importance of self-defense, but they are wrong to do so. Based on a household survey, Gary Kleck, a criminologist at Florida State University, has estimated that every year, guns are used—that is, displayed or fired—for defensive purposes more than a million times, not counting their use by the police. If his estimate is correct, this means that the number of people who defend themselves with a gun exceeds the number of arrests for violent crimes and burglaries.

4   The available evidence supports the claim that self-defense is a legitimate form of deterrence. People who report to the National Crime Survey that they defended themselves with a weapon were less likely to lose property in a robbery or be injured in an assault than those who did not defend themselves. Statistics have shown that would-be burglars are threatened by gun-wielding victims about as many times a year as they are arrested (and much more often than they are sent to prison) and that the chances of a burglar being shot are about the same as his chances of going to jail. Criminals know these facts even if gun control advocates do not and so are less likely to burgle occupied homes in America than occupied ones in Europe, where the residents rarely have guns.

Some gun control advocates may concede these points but rejoin that the 5
cost of self-defense is self-injury: Handgun owners are more likely to shoot themselves or their loved ones than a criminal. Not quite. Most gun accidents involve
rifles and shotguns, not handguns. Moreover, the rate of fatal gun accidents has
been declining while the level of gun ownership has been rising. There are fatal
gun accidents just as there are fatal car accidents, but in fewer than 2 percent of
the gun fatalities was the victim someone mistaken for an intruder.

Those who urge us to forbid or severely restrict the sale of guns ignore these 6
facts. Worse, they adopt a position that is politically absurd. In effect, they say, "Your
government, having failed to protect your person and your property from criminal
assault, now intends to deprive you of the opportunity to protect yourself."

Opponents of gun control make a different mistake. The National Rifle Asso- 7
ciation and its allies tell us that "guns don't kill, people kill" and urge the Government to punish more severely people who use guns to commit crimes. Locking
up criminals does protect society from future crimes, and the prospect of being
locked up may deter criminals. But our experience with meting out tougher sentences is mixed. The tougher the prospective sentence the less likely it is to be imposed, or at least to be imposed swiftly. If the Legislature adds on time for crimes
committed with a gun, prosecutors often bargain away the add-ons; even when
they do not, the judges in many states are reluctant to impose add-ons.

Worse, the presence of a gun can contribute to the magnitude of the crime 8
even on the part of those who worry about serving a long prison sentence. Many
criminals carry guns not to rob stores but to protect themselves from other
armed criminals. Gang violence has become more threatening to bystanders as
gang members have begun to arm themselves. People may commit crimes, but
guns make some crimes worse. Guns often convert spontaneous outbursts of
anger into fatal encounters. When some people carry them on the streets, others will want to carry them to protect themselves, and an urban arms race will
be underway.

Our goal should not be the disarming of law-abiding citizens. It should be to re- 9
duce the number of people who carry guns unlawfully, especially in places—on
streets, in taverns—where the mere presence of a gun can increase the hazards
we all face. The most effective way to reduce illegal gun-carrying is to encourage
the police to take guns away from people who carry them without a permit. This
means encouraging the police to make street frisks.

The Fourth Amendment to the Constitution bans "unreasonable searches 10
and seizures." In 1968 the Supreme Court decided (Terry v. Ohio) that a frisk—
patting down a person's outer clothing—is proper if the officer has a "reasonable
suspicion" that the person is armed and dangerous. If a pat-down reveals an object that might be a gun, the officer can enter the suspect's pocket to remove it. If
the gun is being carried illegally, the suspect can be arrested.

The reasonable-suspicion test is much less stringent than the probable- 11
cause standard the police must meet in order to make an arrest. A reasonable

suspicion, however, is more than just a hunch; it must be supported by specific facts. The courts have held, not always consistently, that these facts include someone acting in a way that leads an experienced officer to conclude criminal activity may be afoot; someone fleeing at the approach of an officer; a person who fits a drug courier profile; a motorist stopped for a traffic violation who has a suspicious bulge in his pocket; a suspect identified by a reliable informant as carrying a gun. The Supreme Court has also upheld frisking people on probation or parole.

12   Some police departments frisk a lot of people, but usually the police frisk rather few, at least for the purpose of detecting illegal guns. In 1992 the police arrested about 240,000 people for illegally possessing or carrying a weapon. This is only about one-fourth as many as were arrested for public drunkenness. The average police office will make *no* weapons arrests and confiscate *no* guns during any given year. Mark Moore, a professor of public policy at Harvard University, found that most weapons arrests were made because a citizen complained, not because the police were out looking for guns.

13   It is easy to see why. Many cities suffer from a shortage of officers, and even those with ample law-enforcement personnel worry about having their cases thrown out for constitutional reasons or being accused of police harassment. But the risk of violating the Constitution or engaging in actual, as opposed to perceived, harassment can be substantially reduced.

14   Each patrol officer can be given a list of people on probation or parole who live on that officer's beat and be rewarded for making frequent stops to insure that they are not carrying guns. Officers can be trained to recognize the kinds of actions that the Court will accept as providing the "reasonable suspicion" necessary for a stop and frisk. Membership in a gang known for assaults and drug dealing could be made the basis, by statute or Court precedent, for gun frisks.

15   And modern science can be enlisted to help. Metal detectors at airports have reduced the number of airplane bombings and skyjackings to nearly zero. But these detectors only work at very close range. What is needed is a device that will enable the police to detect the presence of a large lump of metal in someone's pocket from a distance of 10 or 15 feet. Receiving such a signal could supply the officer with reasonable grounds for a pat-down. Underemployed nuclear physicists and electronics engineers in the post-cold-war era surely have the talents for designing a better gun detector.

16   Even if we do all these things, there will still be complaints. Innocent people will be stopped. Young black and Hispanic men will probably be stopped more often than older white Anglo males or women of any race. But if we are serious about reducing drive-by shootings, fatal gang wars and lethal quarrels in public places, we must get illegal guns off the street. We cannot do this by multiplying the forms one fills out at gun shops or by pretending that guns are not a problem until a criminal uses one.

Getting Started on Your Draft

Before You Start Writing Your Draft

1. Pick one of the issues from the list you made in chapter 1 as a possible candidate. Then write in one sentence your position on this issue. You can change the statement later if you need to, but at this point, you need to know whether you can write a paper using this statement as your thesis.

2. Use the questions on pp. 43–44 to help you think of as many reasons as you can. List your reasons as because clauses after your claim—for example, "Smoking should be banned on campus *because* nonsmokers are endangered by secondhand smoke."

3. When you finish listing your reasons, put checks beside the strongest ones.

4. What evidence do you have to support your strongest reasons? Do you have any facts, statistics, testimony from authority, or personal observations to back up the reasons? Make notes besides your reasons.

5. List as many reasons as you can against your claim. For example, "Smoking should not be banned on campus *because* the risk of second-hand smoke is minimal if smokers go outside and *because* it would discourage or even prevent smokers from working or going to school on campus." Think about how you are going to answer the arguments against your position.

6. Think about who is going to read your argument. How much will they know about the issues involved? Where are they likely to stand on these issues? Will they define the issues the same way you do? On what are they most likely to agree and disagree with you?

Writing Your Draft

Some people write best from detailed outlines; others write from notes. Try making some notes about your beginning, middle, and end to get you started and to give you a sense of where you're headed.

1. **The beginning.** How much do you need to explain the issue before making your claim? How can you get off to a fast start? What can you do to convince your reader to keep reading? Do you need to establish that there's a problem that your paper will address? Are you answering a specific argument by someone else?

2. **The middle.** If you have more than one reason, which reason do you want to put first? Most of the time, you want your strongest reason to be up front or else at the end. Group similar arguments together. Weaker arguments might go in the middle. Next, you have to think about how you are going to bring in the evidence that you have. If you have only one reason, the evidence will make or break your argument. Finally, you need to think about where you are going to acknowledge opposing viewpoints and how much space you need to give to countering those viewpoints. If you think most of your readers are going to think differently than you, then you need to spend a lot of time anticipating and refuting objections to your claim.

3. **The ending.** Endings are always tricky. Simply stating your claim again isn't the best way to finish. The worst endings say something like "In my essay, I've said this." Is there a summarizing point you can make? Some implication you can draw? Another example you can include that will sum up your position? If you are writing a proposal, your ending might be a call for action.

 # Chapter 3

Thinking More about Your Audience

What Exactly Is an Audience?

The audience is the most important concern in any kind of persuasion—from advertising to the kind of extended written arguments that you write in college. It's important to think in advance about your audience because it pays off when you write. But what exactly is an audience?

Often, the answer is easy to supply. In those cases, *audience* refers to the person or people who actually hear an oral communication or who actually read a written one. Audience denotes the real consumers of communications. The idea of a *real audience* is usually a concrete reality for people who are speaking, because those audiences are actually, visibly present at the scene. When real audiences are present in the flesh, they are hard to ignore. In fact, you do so at your own risk, for audiences who are lost or confused by an oral presentation can make their discomfort known by body language ("If this speech doesn't end soon, I'm going to scream!" their bodies say) or by their verbal responses ("Excuse me, but I'm really confused by what you just said"). Sometimes, the audiences for written communications can be almost as real (and just as responsive) as the ones who take in a verbal performance, especially if you are writing to people whom you know well or who work closely with you. The real audience for this book is certainly immediate to the people who are writing it. The authors are aware of you—the flesh-and-blood student with a real name, a real presence, a student like the ones we work with every semester. And the authors know that you are likely to respond in real ways to what you read.

When the term *audience* is used in this book, then, it most often refers to the real audience. But there is also another way of thinking about audience, another way in which you are the audience for this book: The authors had to imagine you reading while they were composing the chapters. In this sense, an audience can be an imaginary concept in the mind of the writer, not just a real, flesh-and-blood presence. You have this sense of audience whenever you think about someone later reading what you are writing as you write. In fact, from the point of view of the writer, it does not even matter whether the person you imagine reading eventually does read what you write. What is important is that this imaginary reader helps you to think about the reasons and supporting evidence you need to write your argument. When you have very little sense of who will eventually read what you write, this imaginary reader becomes especially important.

The goal of this chapter is to help you make the audience in your mind a concrete, useful concept, whether or not you know the real people who will ultimately read what you write. Real audiences really exist, and you can think about them in productive ways. But even if your real audience doesn't have a concrete presence for you, you can make audience a creative concept in your mind as you write. Whether the audience is a real presence or something in the mind of the writer finally might not make much difference.

One last point about the meanings of *audience*. Before the chapter ends, you will be introduced to a third way of thinking about audience. You will learn that audience can also be a textual presence—an element on the pages that you write, a position that you invite your reader to occupy. In the last section of the chapter, you will meet the *audience in the text,* a more or less fictional character that you can create in your work to help you connect with your readers.

Readers Do More Than Absorb Information

To imagine an audience for what you write, think about what readers actually do when they read. Most people are not very aware of how they read because reading is almost like breathing. They have done it so often for so long that they are hardly conscious of how they do it. Think for a moment about the following examples:

- A third grader brings his mother a flower he has picked from the yard and a note that says "I love you Mom." Earlier in the day, he was bouncing a ball against the hearth in the living room and broke a lamp. His mother reads the note and realizes that he is trying to gain her forgiveness. She thanks him politely and, even though she is still mad about the lamp, hugs him.

- A psychologist finds a reference to an article in a scholarly journal that pertains to her area of research. When she looks up the article in the library, she quickly scans the introduction to learn exactly what question is being investigated. Because she has read many similar articles, she knows where to find what she is looking for. She flips to the "Discussion" section to find out what conclusions the author has drawn and then turns back to the "Methods" and "Results" sections. She decides that the experiment being reported does not test what it claims to test. Later, when she writes a review of research in her field, she criticizes the experiment.

■ A developer of desert land decides to use the contest gimmick to attract customers. Later, a college student, among many others on a mailing list, receives a card telling him that he has won a new car just for visiting El Rancho Estates. The student has a friend who responded to a similar notice, only to find out that the new car was a toy. He throws the card in the trash.

■ A financial analyst who works for a large New York holding company reads the annual financial statement of a small bank in Vermont. Her company may be interested in acquiring the bank. She notices a particularly high amount of deposits in comparison to outstanding loans. She turns to the list of depositors to learn more about why so much money is deposited in the rural bank. On the basis of her review of bank documents, she decides that the bank has the potential for increased profits, and she writes a report recommending that the bank be purchased.

These examples suggest that we rely on a great deal more than what is on the page when we read. The mother understood that the note "I love you Mom" really meant something like "Don't be mad at me any more." In the same way, the college student determined that the announcement that he had just won a contest was a gimmick to get him to visit the real estate development. We don't read just by decoding the words on the page. We read by connecting what's on the page with what we know about the world. The numbers that the financial analyst looked at were meaningless by themselves. They became meaningful when she connected them with what she knew about banks.

Reading is often represented as if people were machines that decode characters on the page. But people don't function like machines when they read. They are more like artists who turn a sketch into a painting. They transform a plan into a particular form by filling in gaps and imagining a background. They are not passive receivers. They infer motives, make judgments, debate points, and sometimes write responses.

Readers Begin with Purposes

Although people rarely think about why they read, they don't read randomly. They read to cope with the everyday concerns of life—filling out car insurance forms, doing income tax, finding out whether the warranty is still good on the CD player that just quit working. People pick up a magazine to relax after supper, flipping through the pages until a title catches their interest, then perhaps reading a paragraph or two and skipping on unless something motivates them to keep reading. Even the most casual kinds of reading, such as reading a stop sign, happen because people have a goal: to drive safely from one place to another. People read differently for different purposes.

Readers Begin with Expectations

One's purpose for reading and knowledge of how people write provide one with certain expectations when one begins to read. The psychologist knows that reports of experiments are usually organized in four parts. She expects to find the specific question being investigated at the end of the "Introduction" section and the conclusions in the "Discussion" section. The college student knows that much of his mail is junk mail. He opens each unfamiliar letter with the expectation that it might attempt to sell him something. He scans each letter for some suggestion of purpose. Expectations change as people read. The financial analyst adjusted her plan for reading the bank's documents when she noticed an unusually high ratio of deposits to outstanding loans.

Readers Compose as They Read

People read by fitting what they know with what is written on the page. The financial analyst predicts how much money the Vermont bank is likely to make in the future on the basis of her knowledge of similar-sized banks. The mother interprets her son's note to mean more than it says because she knows the situation that prompted it. People read by inferring authors' intentions, by predicting what will come next, and by comparing what they read with what they know. As people read, they create a world using the clues the writer gives. When they read for pleasure—say, a science fiction novel—they are willing to imagine a world where people can be shrunk to microscopic size and where travel beyond the speed of light is possible. But if they read for other purposes, they also create worlds. The psychologist traces the author's assumptions about reading and then bases her evaluation of the experiment on those assumptions. She imagines that the author should have done a different kind of experiment to investigate the question.

Readers React to What They Read

People do not just take in information when they read. They carry on an internal conversation with writers, sometimes agreeing with what they say, sometimes disagreeing. People react to what they read. The psychologist takes a stand on the article she reads based on whether the author's assumptions are similar to her own. The college student evaluates his mail, rejecting deceptive attempts to sell him something he doesn't want through a contest gimmick. Readers often take actions based on what they read, extending from a mother hugging her son to a national outcry following the publication of *Silent Spring* discussed in chapter 1 that led to the banning of DDT.

Constructing Your Readers

Thinking of your readers as active participants in what you are writing rather than passive receivers helps you to determine what you need to do to hold up your end of the bargain. You know a lot about what readers do because you too are a reader. But sometimes, people don't use this knowledge when they write.

Who Will Read Your Argument?

Many times, you know exactly who you are writing for. If you write a letter to a close friend, you know that only your friend will read it. You and your friend know the same people, so you don't have to explain who they are. In the workplace, you sometimes write memos making arguments to people you know almost as well as close friends. You don't have to fill them in on the background of the issue because you know they are familiar with the subject. Such audiences called **simple audiences.**

Other times, your real audience might consist of many individuals, but you can conceive of them as a simple audience because their knowledge is very similar. If you write an article for a journal in your field, you can assume that your readers are familiar with the terms and concepts in that field. Although the people who are reading the journal are different individuals, they are similar in their interest in and knowledge about a particular field.

In other situations, the issue of audience is much more complicated. Take as an example the financial statement from the small bank in Vermont that was mentioned talked about in the previous section. Many different people might read that statement for different reasons—officers of the bank, other employees, shareholders, government regulatory officials, financial analysts, and potential investors in the bank. This kind of complex audience—a group of people who read for different reasons—is a **multiple audience.** Multiple audiences are often very difficult to write for.

In writing arguments to multiple audiences, you will have to take into account differing levels of knowledge about your subject among your potential readers and differing attitudes about that subject. Before you begin writing, think carefully about all the people who might read your argument and then analyze what they know and don't know about your subject and what their attitudes toward your subject and you are likely to be.

What Does Your Audience Already Know—and Not Know?

Critical to your argument is your audience's knowledge of your subject. If they are not familiar with the background information, they probably won't understand your argument fully. If you know that your readers will be unfamiliar with your subject, you will have to lay the groundwork of background information before attempting to convince them of your position. A good tactic is to tie your new information with what your readers already know. Comparisons and analogies can very helpful in linking old and new information.

Another critical factor is your audience's level of expertise. How much technical language can you use? For example, if you are writing a proposal to put high-speed Internet connections into all dormitory rooms, will your readers know the difference between a T1 line and a T3 line? The director of the computation center should know the difference, but the vice president for student affairs might not. If you are unsure of your readers' knowledge level, it's better to include background information and explain technical terms. Few readers will be insulted, and they can skip over this information quickly if they are familiar with your subject.

What Are Your Audience's Attitudes toward You?

Does your audience know you at all, either by reputation or from previous work? Are you considered your reader's equal, superior, or subordinate? How your audience regards you will affect the tone and presentation of your message. Does your audience respect you and trust you? What can you include in your presentation to build trust? In many cases, your audience will know little about you. Especially in those circumstances, you can build trust in your reader by following the advice on ethos, to be discussed in chapter 4.

What Are Your Audience's Attitudes toward Your Subject and toward What You Want to Say?

People have prior attitudes about controversial issues that you must take into consideration as you write or speak. Imagine, for instance, that you are preparing an argument for a guest editorial in your college newspaper advocating that your state government provide parents with choices among public and private schools. You will argue that the tax dollars that now automatically go to public schools should go to private schools if the parents so choose. You have evidence that the sophomore-to-senior dropout rate in private schools is less than half the rate of public schools. Furthermore, students from private schools attend college at nearly twice the rate of public school graduates. You intend to argue that one of the reasons private schools are more successful is that they spend more money on instruction and less on administration. And you believe that school choice speaks to the American desire for personal freedom.

It's unlikely that everyone on your campus will agree with your stand. How might the faculty at your college or university feel about this issue? The administrators? The staff? Other students? Interested people in the community who read the student newspaper? What attitudes toward public funding of private schools will they have before they start reading what you have to say? How are you going to deal with the objection that because many students in private schools come from more affluent families, it is not surprising that they do better?

Even when you write about a much less controversial subject, you must think carefully about your audience's attitudes toward what you have to say or write. Sometimes, your audience may share your attitudes; other times, your audience may be neutral; at still other times, your audience will have attitudes that differ sharply from your own. If possible, you should anticipate these various attitudes and act accordingly. You should show awareness of the attitudes of your audience, and if those attitudes are very different from yours, you will have to work hard to counter them without insulting your audience. It's not just a particular attitude that you have to address but also a set of assumptions that follow from that attitude. The next section will include more about identifying assumptions that follow from attitudes.

An even more difficult situation is when your audience is indifferent to what you write. You feel very strongly that your college or university should have a varsity gymnastics team, but most people on campus are indifferent to the issue. The first task, then, is to get your readers engaged in your subject. Sometimes, you can begin by using a particularly striking example to get your readers interested. Another tactic is to add visuals—illustrations, charts, or tables—to catch your readers' attention.

Why People Reach Different Conclusions from the Same Evidence

Some people think that if the facts of an issue are accurately described, then all reasonable people should come to similar conclusions about what course of action should be followed. As you get older, however, you discover that your friends and other people whom you respect often don't agree with your conclusions even when you all agree on the facts. Arguments would be easy to write if reasonable people considered the same facts and came to the same conclusions.

But often they don't. Why do reasonable people look at the same facts and come to different conclusions? Let's look at an example.

One set of facts that has caused great concern is the spread of AIDS among young people. A fifth of the people now living with AIDS are in their twenties. Because the incubation period for the disease can be as long as ten years, many contracted AIDS when they were teenagers. Because of the AIDS epidemic, many parents, politicians, clergy, and school board officials are engaged in a debate over whether condoms should be given out to high school students without fees and without parents' consent. In some high schools, condoms are being distributed in school clinics if parents give their consent. In other cities and communities, school boards have voted down proposals to distribute condoms.

The AIDS epidemic is of particular concern in New York City, which has just 3 percent of the nation's thirteen- to twenty-one-year-old population but 20 percent of the nation's AIDS cases for that age group. On November 26, 1991, after almost two years of public controversy, New York City became the first city in the country to make condoms available to students in its 120 high schools.

Let's take a look at how different viewpoints were argued in the condom debate in New York City. The first article, "Clinic Visit" by Anna Quindlen, appeared on the editorial page of the *New York Times*. The second article, "Condom Sense," was first printed as an unsigned editorial in *Commonweal*, a magazine that has a largely Catholic readership. The author's knowledge of the religious and moral values that the Catholic community holds in common shapes the rhetorical strategy. For example, the author does not define morality because he or she can assume an agreed-upon definition.

> **Quindlen, Anna. "Clinic Visit."** *The New York Times* **21 Feb. 1991, sec A: 19.**
>
> There are two examining rooms, a nurse practitioner and the three pediatricians who alternate days. There is a social worker and a health educator. The psychiatrist comes on Fridays.
>
> Welcome to the clinic at Martin Luther King Jr. High School. You can check your old notions of the school nurse and the kid with the phony stomachache at the door. Most of the students have no family physician and no insurance coverage. Here they can get treatment for their asthma, their acne or their depression. Dr. Alwyn T. Cohall, who runs 3 of the city's 17 school-based clinics, says they've taken care of everything from a splinter to a stab wound. The happiest thing they ever do is a physical for a kid going to college.
>
> There's a questionnaire for patients, and to read it is both a delight, because it was clearly written by someone

who knows adolescents, and a sorrow, because it was written by someone who knows what it's like to be young in 1991. Questions range from "If you were alone on an island, who would you want to visit you?" to "Have you ever been in any trouble with the police?" and "Did you ever try to kill yourself?" There's a poignancy to finding the section on thumb-sucking just after the one on sex. Adolescence is that point in life when, like some mythological creature, we are half one thing, half another. Teenagers think of themselves as adults; parents think of them as kids.

Which brings us to condoms.

Ah, condoms, this year's gnashing-of-teeth issue. Put the idea of teenagers and sex together, and you have two things: reality and controversy. The Chancellor proposes providing condoms to New York City high school students, and he is accused of promoting promiscuity and usurping the essential role of parents. I believe in the essential role. Parents should give their children accurate information about sex. They should discuss their own standards of morality, their ideas of right and wrong. They should let their kids know that they are always available to talk and, more important, to listen.

It's just that they don't. Some great wall rises between parents and children on this issue, a wall that is only scaled by the stalwart. Partly this is because while parents are saying "no, no," adolescent hormones are saying "yes, yes." And partly it is that parents only want to listen to what they want to hear.

Adult authority often is missing.

The doctors at the clinic deal with what is: adolescents who need no permission from the Chancellor, the doctor or anyone else to begin sleeping together. The girl who got the notice that she was positive for the AIDS virus before she got her diploma. The girl who spent three weeks in the hospital being treated for kidney failure caused by secondary syphilis. AIDS has gotten most of the publicity in the condom debate. But one in four sexually active teenagers will get a sexually transmitted disease before high school graduation, and reducing that figure is one reason Dr. Cohall would like to dispense condoms to his patients.

Teens are sexually active regardless.

Condoms reduce AIDS and STDs.

The staff at the clinic have lots of problems as compelling as this one. They have to keep in touch with the kids who are depressed and the ones with drug problems. They need to send pregnant young women to good prenatal care programs. They'd like to be able to prescribe contraceptives for those girls who want them, but for now they refer them to a hospital clinic and hope that they go. Despite abstinence counseling and family planning services, they have a hard time keeping pregnancy tests in stock.

The school clinic requires a parental consent form, and the form allows parents to cross out any services that they don't want their child to receive. Only about 5 percent of the parents do. Dr. Cohall says this is the refrain: "I wish my kid wasn't having sex, but . . . "

His work is the "but." But keep him alive. Keep her from getting pregnant. Keep them all from getting sterile because of some disease. The staff at the clinic do what parents should do: They listen, and they inform, and they try to make the kids hear themselves, hear what they're really saying about how they feel. They deal with what is.

What is is that young men and women are getting sick, even dying, because of unprotected sex. And we can help prevent that. Abstinence, if you can sell it. A condom, if you cannot. To doom the young before they've even shed the chrysalis of adolescence because you disapprove of their behavior is the triumph of pride over charity and self-righteousness over sense. In this clinic, where the staff greet their patients with a hug, where the problems are so enormous, it seems both mean-spirited and shortsighted.

"Condom Sense." *Commonweal* 13 Sept. 1991: 499.
"You can play with them," reads a New York subway ad picturing teenagers gleefully playing volleyball with an inflated condom.

"Don't play around without them. Use a condom," it clinches its point. The clever word play delivers a message about preventing AIDS, but not the one that New York teenagers need to hear. Instead, the merry punsters at New York City's Health Department seem to encourage premature—and possibly lethal—sexual activity among the young while disinviting serious thinking about the dangers AIDS actually presents. The Health Department is not alone.

This past winter New York Schools Chancellor Joseph A. Fernandez pushed a condom distribution plan through the school board with the help of Mayor David Dinkins as part of a utilitarian approach to combating the spread of AIDS among sexually active adolescents. To insure the program's effectiveness, neither parental consent nor notifica-

Margin notes: Teens have rights to their bodies. / The community is responsible for teens' bodies. / Body integrity is prior to moral integrity.

tion will be required. According to the experts, parents only scare students away. Nor will the schools require counseling as part of its condom distribution program. Presumably that too might scare students away. Condoms will be available in New York City high schools later this fall.

As the subway poster and the school board's decision demonstrate, something vital has been lost in the city's approach. That vital something is morality, and "moral" questions about sexual behavior. This is a policy that deethicizes sexual behavior precisely where sexual responsibility is most needed. What, after all, is the likely result of trying to modify sexual behavior without reference to concepts of moral responsibility? Volleyball seems to be the answer.

It's hard to believe the chancellor and his advisors have asked themselves how dispensing condoms along with textbooks can possibly shape the most intimate of human relations. Would they expect students to make themselves accountable if similar minimal expectations were applied to school work? Or to obtaining a driver's license? Could a high school field a sports team if students were simply issued uniforms and told to play the games as they saw fit? It is as if Mr. Fernandez reasons that survival during a drought depended on providing each individual with his or her own well-digging equipment. Survival in such desperate circumstances depends on more compelling forms of cooperation. Thus excluding parents from the school condom program has to be among the most self-defeating aspects of the policy. And there are others.

Mr. Fernandez argues that counseling or guidance is unnecessary: "People at any age have ready access to condoms at supermarkets and drugstores without the benefit of an educational or counseling component." (Let us leave aside the questions about why contraceptive services are being added to an overburdened school system if condoms are so readily available—as they are, and often for free.) More important, if someone is too thoughtless to buy condoms at a drugstore, what chance is there that he will bother to obtain a condom at school? Or that he or she would have the resolve to actually use a condom at the crucial moment? Indeed, the logic of Mr. Fernandez's argument suggests that the more responsible plan would have been to introduce supervised sex into the school system. If the children are going to have sex whether we think it proper or not, shouldn't we provide as safe an environment as possible? The city's unwillingness to go that far (we hope) demonstrates how the seemingly straightforward logic of the chancellor's argument conceals, rather than illuminates, the social and moral questions at stake.

The condom policy implicitly reduces sexual relations to a mechanical and nearly uncontrollable biological urge. It is this absence of a sense of human dignity—something adolescents, especially those who are poor, feel intensely in a society that already marginalizes them in countless ways—that lies at the root of this moral and sexual agnosticism. In an effort to make condom distribution matter-of-fact and therefore palatable, proponents present its case in a way that empties sex of meaning and moral consequence. Condoms and sexual information of all kinds are easily available, yet the tragic consequences of AIDS and other sexually transmitted diseases, of teen-age childbearing, and of sexual crime are increasingly with us, suggesting that sexual behavior is not so amenable to "common sense" and rationalized expectations as those with a penchant for social engineering would have us believe.

Condoms don't reduce AIDS and STDs.

But the problem goes still deeper. The condom plan's illusory practicality is symptomatic; a policy that medicalizes the social and moral question of adolescent sex is a way of avoiding more troubling realities. For example, it encourages us to continue to ignore the poverty and family breakdown that lie at the heart of destructive sexual behavior among many adolescents. AIDS is increasingly a disease of the urban poor, especially intravenous drug users and their sexual partners. Preventing the spread of AIDS among these adolescents is a question of influencing complex behavior and of understanding human motivation and the wellsprings of moral accountability.

Teens are sexually active because adults do not teach moral behavior.

In subordinating sexual morality to the technology of contraception, the condom-distribution plan naively hopes to address human sexual life with the cause-and-effect logic of a vaccination procedure. Sex doesn't work that way. Indeed, in this context, the medicalization of sexual life dehumanizes it by removing it from the context of family life and the necessary ballast afforded the young by tradition and community values.

Authority figures can influence teens.

Parents are responsible for teens' bodies.

Protecting and promoting, rather than undermining, the authority of the family is essential in fostering the kind of moral responsibility that will keep young people alive in these circumstances. Adolescent sexual behavior is not a blind force of nature. It is shaped and driven by many different cultural values—and at this time many of them are frankly exploitative. The school board's condom plan subtly absolves children of moral responsibility exactly where it should insist upon it. It establishes a premature adolescent autonomy and choice without examining what is being chosen. Self-reliance and self-discipline are essential qualities of maturity. Giving condoms to teen-agers because we have despaired of influencing their sexual decision making announces the board's enormous failure of moral and psychological imagination and tragically undermines the dignity of those it hopes to protect. Adolescents desperately want more, not less, expected of them.

Moral integrity is prior to bodily integrity.

"Clinic Visit" and "Condom Sense" agree about the facts: Many high school students are sexually active, and teenage AIDS cases are increasing at an alarming rate. From these facts, however, the articles move in different directions. The author of "Condom Sense" argues that providing condoms will aggravate the problem; the author of "Clinic Visit" argues that providing condoms will alleviate the problems.

The reason that the articles move in different directions is because the authors have different attitudes and different assumptions. These assumptions provide the links between evidence and claim. It takes some close analysis to identify these assumptions, but once they are laid out, it becomes clear how two very different positions can be constructed from the same evidence.

How Different Assumptions Produce Different Claims from the Same Evidence

Evidence: Many high school students are sexually active and at risk of AIDS.

Claim 1: Providing condoms will help to alleviate the problem.

Claim 2: Providing condoms will make the problem worse.

(continued)

First Assumption

Claim 1: Adult authority figures might not exist or might not have influence.

Claim 2: Authority figures do exist in teens' lives and can influence behavior.

Second Assumption

Claim 1: Teens are sexually active regardless.

Claim 2: Teens are sexually active because adults do not teach moral behavior.

Third Assumption

Claim 1: Using condoms reduces AIDS and STDs because they make sex safe.

Claim 2: Using condoms increases the risk of AIDS and STDs because they promote sexual activity and aren't 100 percent effective.

Fourth Assumption

Claim 1: Teens have the right to control own bodies.

Claim 2: Parents have the right to control teens' bodies.

Fifth Assumption

Claim 1: The community is responsible for teens' bodies.

Claim 2: The parents or family are responsible for teens' bodies.

Sixth Assumption

Claim 1: Body integrity is prior to moral integrity.

Claim 2: Moral integrity is prior to bodily integrity.

Creating Your Readers

So far in this chapter on audience, you have been encouraged to think about your real audiences—the actual individuals who will read your arguments. But at the beginning of the chapter, you were also told that another kind of audience would be discussed before the chapter ends: the audience not *of* the argument but *in* the argument—the audience in the text.

What is the audience in the text? This is a rather difficult but important concept. First, consider an example—a short poem called "Spring and Fall: To a

Young Child," written around 1880 by Gerard Manley Hopkins, a Jesuit priest who died in Dublin in 1889. The speaker in the poem is addressing a young child, "Margaret," who is crying in a sense of loss at the sight of "Goldengrove unleaving"—the sight of beautiful autumn leaves falling off the trees in front of her and turning into melancholy late November "leafmeal" (bits of leaves):

> Margaret, are you grieving
> Over Goldengrove unleaving?
> Leaves, like the things of man, you
> With your fresh thoughts care for, can you?
> Ah! As the heart grows older
> It will come to such sights colder
> By and by, nor spare a sigh
> Though worlds of wanwood leafmeal lie;
> And yet you weep and know why.
> Now no matter, child, the name:
> Sorrow's springs are the same.
> Nor mouth had, no nor mind, expressed
> What heart heard of, ghost guessed:
> It is the blight man was born for,
> It is Margaret you mourn for.

Who is the audience of this poem? Despite its title and the presence of "Margaret" in the poem, "Spring and Fall" wasn't really written for a young child at all. Children cannot understand poetry this complicated (indeed, it might be hard for you to understand parts of it). The theme of the poem—mutability (the idea that humans will all turn into leafmeal one day and had best remember that!)—isn't exactly an idea that young children are ready for. The real audience is adults who have grown older, adults whom Hopkins wants to remind that what is truly important in life is the certainty of death. "Margaret" serves as the **audience in the text**—a fictional character created by the author to aid him in making his rhetorical point. Think of it this way: Hopkins creates in his poem a sort of miniature drama, complete with characters (Margaret and the speaker) and action (the leaves falling, the tears, the speaker's sermon). The real readers eavesdrop on and observe this created drama for the author to achieve his rhetorical purpose: to remind readers, in a sort of sermon, about their ultimate end.

What does all this have to do with argument? All writing, believe it or not, can be seen as a sort of verbal drama akin to "Spring and Fall." It has fictional speakers just as this poem has a speaker; it has fictional listeners just as this poem has its Margaret; and it has verbal action. Sometimes the fictional listeners are overtly present, like young Margaret. An open letter that is published in a newspaper is one such example; the letter is addressed to a particular person but is really intended for all the readers of the paper. The *Wall Street Journal* once published an open letter from the economist Milton Friedman to President Reagan's drug czar, William Bennett, that began "Dear Bill" and contained other references to Bennett; yet the letter was really an argument addressed to the readers of the *Journal*. If Friedman wanted to write to Bennett, he would have mailed him a letter rather than publish it in the *Wall Street Journal*. (The letter, with Bennett's response, is reprinted on pages 184–188.) Another example is Martin Luther King, Jr.'s famous "Letter from Birmingham Jail." King's letter begins "To My Fellow Clergymen" and then seems to address those clergymen as "you" throughout the course of the letter. But the letter wasn't really addressed to the clergymen, or King would not have published it in several public places. The clergymen served as the audience in the text, but the real audience was the general public whose support King sought for the civil rights movement.

You can make these strategies work for you. When you write an argument, it's important first to think about what you want your readers to do. If you want to change their attitude, you will have to work hard to influence them with good reasons. But if you want them to take some action, you should give some thought to the kind of role you imply for your reader. You might want to say specifically to your readers that if they share your beliefs about a certain subject—for example, the importance of clean water in the streams and lakes of your city or town—then they should be willing to vote for strict zoning and pollution laws and to pay for the cost of enforcing them.

From The Fiske Guide to Colleges 1993
Marlboro College

The Fiske Guide to Colleges is a guide to more than three hundred U.S. colleges. It attempts to offer an insider's perspective by soliciting information from currently enrolled students, who describe the strengths and weaknesses of the colleges they attend. *The Fiske Guide* gives some of the usual statistics about colleges but also tries to convey a sense of what a school is really like. The profile of Marlboro College in the 1993 edition of *The Fiske Guide* paints a somewhat bleak picture of campus life, yet Marlboro College chose to send out the description with materials recruiting prospective students. Why do you think Marlboro College chose to sent out this portrait of itself, warts and all?

1   As opposed to most people who go to Vermont's Green Mountains expecting relaxation, Marlboro students go expecting plenty of challenging academic work. Marlboro's highly individualized approach to the liberal arts puts every one of its

275 students to the test. The college requires self-motivated students, able to conduct original research and develop their own plans of curriculum. Finally, students must defend what they have learned during their four years at Marlboro to a committee of two faculty members and a visiting expert before they graduate. To be sure, Marlboro is a school that values quality over quantity.

Positioned atop a small mountain, surrounded by maples and pines and with   2
a gorgeous view of southern Vermont, Marlboro certainly has physical beauty on its side. The school was founded just after World War II when returning GIs renovated an old barn as the college's first building. Today, a cluster of modern and New England farmhouse-style buildings, many with passive solar heating, sit proudly in the middle of the 400-acre campus located on hilly farmland. "I can't imagine a more pastoral setting; at the end of the road, at the edge of a mountains," gushes one student.

Marlboro students must pass a clear-writing requirement (20 pages, no less)   3
by the end of their freshman year. After that hurdle, they don't even take courses in the traditional sense. The cornerstone of a Marlboro education is the Plan of Concentration, which is developed independently by each student. Juniors and seniors "on plan" take most coursework in one-on-one tutorials with the faculty sponsors. Seniors present their thesis or project to their faculty sponsors, who are backed up by outside examiners. The administration boasts that by bringing in these outside examiners from "the best Eastern colleges and universities," Marlboro has created its own little accountability system, assuring that neither students nor faculty at this isolated institution will be cut off from the most current academic thinking. Marlboro's flexibility should not be confused with academic flabbiness, though. Grades are an integral part of the evaluation process, professors are stingy with A's, and most students work hard. Self-motivation is a must, although it doesn't always come easy at first. "Study habits range from intense to indolent," a Russian literature student says. "Most students take it easy early on, pursuing a broad range of studies. As graduation comes near, upperclassmen are increasingly consumed by the completion of their plan." Academic pressure is high, but not in the usual way. "Marlboro students don't compete against each other, they compete with themselves," one student explains. Says another, "It's pretty obvious you haven't read the assignment when there's an hour-long discussion with only two other people in the class."

Luckily, procrastination is not much of a temptation since there is little to do   4
evenings atop the mountain but curl up in front of one of the nonworking fireplaces in Marlboro's library and study. The library, which holds only 57,000 titles, is operated on the honor system where students sign out their own books 24 hours a day. Ditto for the computer center, which is tiny but probably has as many computers per student as MIT.

As for the established academic offerings themselves, the main limitation is   5
the lack of variety inevitable at such a small school. Marlboro offers good instruction in literature, history, science, and languages (including Latin and Greek). The World Studies Program, the most popular major, is highly praised by students

and administration alike and has a strong reputation outside the school. In conjunction with the School for International Training, it provides an eight-month professional internship and/or study experience abroad. Natural sciences have recently become quite popular, and the facilities are benefiting from the largest grant Marlboro has ever received—$400,000 from the Howard Hughes Medical Institute. As for the social sciences, sociology, anthropology, and political science are applauded, but philosophy is not highly recommended. Because each subject is taught by only one or two professors, a personality conflict may mean problems with a whole department; the departure of one faculty member can cripple a program. Students point out, however, that since they may freely pursue their intellectual interests wherever they lead, and have the "chance to become the local expert," smallness does not place real limits on the possibilities for study.

6   Marlboro is completely run by a New England town-meeting style of government that involves the whole student body and faculty in every aspect of policy-making. It is, in the words of a history student, "as democratic as any college can be." Students can veto the faculty members on hiring and retention decisions, and it takes a two-thirds vote of the faculty to override them. As in ancient Athens, however, pure democracy can have its problems. Once the town meeting voted to bar smoking in the dining hall during meals. The debate had gone on for weeks, but the actual vote "required a keg to secure a quorum."

7   Marlboro's 275 students come mostly from middle-class suburban homes, and one administrator says that the school tends to attract not Ivy League types but their nonconformist siblings (both older and younger—the average age is 23). In the 1960s and early 1970s the dominant tone of the college was communal and nonmaterialistic, and some of today's students retain the fierce liberalism of yesteryear. One student goes so far as to say, "The idea of 'studying' business is repulsive to most of Marlboro's students and faculty." Nevertheless today's prevailing conservative winds have not left the campus untouched. One denizen reports, "Legs go unshaven, though less so with each passing year." But the widespread tendency to wear black makes campus activities resemble sprightly funerals. A photography major adds that while "some students wear suits and ties, others wear pajama pants and T-shirts." Minority enrollment has been embarrassingly low in recent years, but the administration is quite proud of its program to recruit and support poor rural students from within Vermont. What Marlboro students do share, in addition to their independent spirit, is a distaste for "unnecessary pomposity" and a suspicion of "form-filling education." Many of these students find they can't even handle Marlboro's nonconformist stance, and about 20 percent of each freshman class will not be back the next year. Whether they last or not, the college, which is need-blind in its admissions policy, assembles a "workable" financial package for those in need, but don't look for any merit or athletic handouts here.

8   The dorms, mostly coed, are small (about 12 to 20 students each), but rooms are large. Housing is based on credits, so freshmen have triples, sophomores have doubles, and upperclassmen have singles. "All the dorms have a very warm, homey feel to them—a far cry from the sterile dorms of larger colleges," says a photogra-

phy student. Additional housing is available, and highly desired, in eight cottages about 10 minutes on foot from campus. The community of off-campus dwellers is relatively large but well integrated into campus life. Most live 20 minutes away in Brattleboro and shuttle to and from campus in a school van. Boarders gather for home-cooked meals in a converted barn, where the food is wholesome and plentiful but still provides "inherent excuses for leftovers." Students say the best meals tend to coincide with trustee meetings and parent weekends.

Students don't much care for the actual town of Marlboro, which has "about 800 people, a post office, two inns, and a general store." But Brattleboro offers drama, films, and restaurants and is a fascinating spot in itself—"a combination of local working-class counterculture holdovers from the '60s and affluent patrons of the summer music festival." As you may have guessed, there are no Greek organizations at Marlboro, but there is at least one organized activity on campus each weekend as well as several that are spontaneous; snowball fights by the library are a particularly serious business. The annual Apple Fest attracts alumni, and on Community Work Day, students and faculty take a break from classes and work on manual projects around the campus. "Marlboro College is the kind of place where on a Saturday night someone will bring music to the Student Center, and there will suddenly be a party," one man explains. And a literature major notes that "most parties have a lot of dancing." Although drinking is not a huge deal here, alcohol is easily obtained by underage students. Because most of the drinking takes place on campus, people do not drink and drive. A "pretty extensive" freshman orientation program involves trips, tours, and even square dancing.

A wide-ranging program of coed sports for novices and experts—soccer, basketball, volleyball, and even hackeysack—offers plenty of excuses to drop the books for an afternoon. Sports are student-arranged, so they change yearly, but the "incredibly dynamic" outing club ensures plenty of opportunities to enjoy the local wilderness, including hiking and cross-country skiing on runs that radiate from the center of campus. Excellent downhill skiing is only a few minutes' drive away. Intercollegiate competition is, to say the least, low key, and so for the most part it is limited to volleyball and soccer against other alternative colleges and to cross-country and downhill skiing, where Marlboro holds its own against Ivy competitors.

The smallness of the college community is a mixed blessing. It's difficult to be forgotten or lost here, and students who are in distress will frequently be sought out by a faculty member or dean and offered help. But while students will undoubtedly find professors who are interested in their activities, they may also find that everyone else is curious, too. "People tend to know a lot about people, due just to the small number and the size of their mouths," warns one talked-about student.

"The Community," as students call it, provides an exciting alternative to typical colleges for students following a different tom-tom. The president, who came to the woods after a quarter century as an editor for *Newsweek* magazine, is determined to increase public awareness of what the school has to offer, and he has plenty of young ambassadors ready to help. "It's small, and on a human scale," one junior writes of Marlboro, "but diversified beyond imagination."

Getting Started: Writing for Particular Audiences

1. Write a letter to the editor of your campus newspaper arguing that your college or university (A) should emphasize computer education OR (B) has placed too much emphasis on technology and should encourage more face-to-face education.

   If you choose A, here are some points you might think about:

   - Technology will be increasingly involved in how we create, communicate, store, and use knowledge.

   - Computers offer access to vast amounts of information and to people around the world.

   - Nearly every occupation that requires a college education requires extensive use of computers.

   If you choose B, here are some other points you might think about:

   - Technology is a means to an end, not an end in itself; therefore, emphasizing technology neglects what is at the heart of education.

   - Computers are expensive and divert money from other programs.

   - Occupations in the future will require people who can adapt quickly to change, not people who are trained in the use of specific technologies.

2. Rewrite your letter for junior high school students, persuading them that (A) gaining expertise in using computers will be essential for their later education OR (B) gaining a solid general education is more important than learning how to use computers.

3. Rewrite your letter for the governor of your state, urging him or her to take leadership. If you don't know your governor's views on education, assume for the moment that he or she is very much in favor of students going to school over the Internet and doesn't believe in building more campuses or hiring more faculty.

4. Analyze the changes you made when you rewrote the letters. Did you change any reasons? Did you provide different background? How did you adjust the style? What other changes did you make?

Chapter 4

The Style of Arguments

Facts Alone Do Not Persuade

Chapter 1 explained how *Silent Spring* became an influential book that shaped thinking about the environment in the United States. Rachel Carson was not the first person to warn against the excessive use of pesticides, nor was she the first to urge that people think of the environment as a unified system in which changing one part means affecting the others. But she engaged her readers as no scientific writer on the environment had done before. She had good reasons to support her contentions, but the way she wrote also stirred her readers into action.

Part of the brilliance of *Silent Spring* is that Carson didn't let the facts speak for themselves. In the following two paragraphs, she makes a simple point that insect populations are held in check by nature. Notice how she illustrates this broad principle with a personal example:

> No one knows how many species of insects inhabit the earth because there are so many yet to be identified. But more than 700,000 have already been described. This means that in terms of the number of species, 70 to 80 percent of the earth's creatures are insects. The vast majority of these insects are held in check by natural forces, without any intervention by man. If this were not so, it is doubtful that any conceivable volume of chemicals—or any other methods—could possibly keep down their population.
>
> The trouble is that we are seldom aware of the protection afforded by natural enemies until it fails. Most of us walk unseeing through the world,

unaware of its beauties, its wonders, and the strange and sometimes terrible intensity of the lives that are being lived about us. So it is that the activities of insect predators and parasites are known to few. Perhaps we many have noticed an oddly shaped insect of ferocious mien on a bush in the garden and been dimly aware that the praying mantis lives at the expense of other insects. But we see with understanding eye only if we have walked in the garden at night and here and there with a flashlight have glimpsed the mantis stealthily creeping upon her prey. Then we sense something of the drama of the hunter and the hunted. Then we begin to feel something of that relentlessly pressing force by which nature controls her own.

Carson turned a dull point into a fascinating observation. She was keenly aware that the facts by themselves are not persuasive. She knew that she had to appeal to the heart as well as the mind. Her task wasn't simply to get people to feel sorry for animals that were killed by pesticides. She wanted people to think about nature differently. She wanted people to think of themselves as part of the natural world, and she wanted her readers to share her own great curiosity about nature. Convincing her readers that massive poisoning of insects meant also poisoning ourselves was a way to get people to think about ecology.

Let's take a look at a more recent book that also makes an argument that goes against the grain of popular thinking: *Eat Fat* by Richard Klein. Klein is a professor of comparative literature at Cornell University who grew tired of writing just for other professors and decided to write for a broad audience on a topic that was close to his heart: being overweight. *Eat Fat* became a brilliant success, enjoying rave reviews and selling many copies. Klein begins by observing that no nation is more obsessed with being thin than the United States. Consumers spend $33 billion dollars a year on weight loss. But the results of all this money and self-denial are largely negative. People in the United States are the fattest people on the earth, at least among developed nations. Fashion models keep getting thinner to the point of looking like victims of starvation, but nearly half of U.S. women wear size 14 or larger, and about 32 percent wear size 16 or larger. Americans continue to gain weight at an astounding rate, adding 10 percent to their bulk on the average from 1984 to 1996, a time when health consciousness was never higher and when Americans dieted more and exercised more than they ever had in their history. But almost all their good efforts were doomed to failure. Out of 100 people who went on diets, 96 were even fatter three or four years later.

Richard Klein takes a position contrary to what most of us believe. He thinks that maybe the fact that Americans are getting fatter isn't really failure, that there may be good reasons why so many people are getting fatter. Furthermore, he argues that maybe this is a good thing rather than a bad thing. He begins by analyzing our hatred of fat. He says that there are three primary motives for people's desire to be thin. First, they believe that fat is ugly. Although this attitude is less than a hundred years old, it is constantly reinforced by the images of beautiful people that pervade the media. Second, people believe that fat is unhealthy. The medical, diet, and insurance industries have all promoted the idea that being thin is healthier and that thin people live longer. Third, people believe that fat weighs them down. Thinner people are seen as sexier, faster, and more agile—better suited for the fast-paced lifestyle of Western nations.

For each of these beliefs, Klein offers good reasons to think otherwise. Fat has not always seemed so disgusting to Americans. Indeed, a hundred years ago, fat signified health and well-being. People wanted to gain weight, and books were written telling them how to become plump. The turn of the century brought the so-called Banquet Years, marked by feasts on every occasion. One of the biggest eaters was President William H. Taft, who weighed over 300 pounds at his inauguration in 1908.

To question the attitude that fat is unhealthy, Klein notes that the spread of dieting has often led to less-healthy people, causing eating disorders in children as young as nine years of age, not to mention thousands of teenagers and adults. Furthermore, dieting has exactly the opposite effect of its purpose; it makes people fatter after a few years. Apparently, when the body is deprived of something it wants, it finds ingenious methods of satisfying those cravings. Evidence from research studies suggests that the human body has a certain level of fat that it tries to maintain. When someone cuts down on fat, the body may overreact and make fat more efficiently, thus causing the person to blow up rather than slim down. And contrary to the belief that thin people are sexier, Klein cites several studies showing that fat people are more sexually active.

Nevertheless, Klein is well aware that he is not going to convince many people with good reasons that appeal to the intellect. The problem (and opportunity) that Klein faces in defending fat is people's attitude toward it. Nearly everyone in the United States believes down deep that being fat is bad. Klein writes, "It's easy in our society to love thin, but hard to achieve it. It's easy to be fat today, but hard to love it." He continues:

> In our culture, fat is evil. Eating it or wearing it, feeding it or bearing it is a sign of some moral deficiency. Aesthetically, physically, and morally, fat is a badge of shame. A visible sign that in crucial areas of our life we have failed to be all we could be. An inescapable source of disappointment, of sadness and guilty self-contempt—of unrelenting shame.

President William Howard Taft is an exemplar of the "Banquet Years" in the late nineteenth and early twentieth centuries, when fat was viewed as healthy. As late as the 1950s, the image of the glamorous beauty included showing off a full figure. In the 1960s and continuing today, thinness became a prerequisite for elegance, an ideal young women sometimes have sought to unhealthy extremes.

William Howard Taft

Marilyn Monroe

Gwyneth Paltrow

Klein's task of arguing a position that people should not only accept fat but come to believe that fat is beautiful seems too ridiculous even to consider. After all, Americans have been taught all their lives to loathe fat.

So what do you do when you are in a very difficult rhetorical situation like the one into which Klein puts himself? Klein has an ingenious strategy, and he's up front about what he is attempting. He writes:

> My fundamental purpose, the whole aim of this book, summed up in its title, is not to convince but to charm you. By that I don't only mean to please you or seduce you into accepting my arguments, in the common sense of charm; I mean as well something more literal, more concrete: this book aims to work like a charm, to cast a spell by conjuring a spirit—a compelling voice, repetitive, monotonous, as if from another world, that says over and over EAT
>
> FAT.

Klein aims to persuade not through appealing to the reader's intellect but through the power of his voice. His voice makes the reader want to keep reading. And a reader who keeps reading at least grants the possibility that there are other attitudes toward fat besides the one that dominates in U.S. culture. Maybe the reader even admits that people in the United States would be a little happier if they weren't so obsessed with fat. If this happens, Klein has been successful.

In chapter 1, there was a discussion of how Aristotle recognized that good reasons that appeal to the intellect (logos) is only one strategy for effective arguments. He maintained that an audience has to view a speaker as trustworthy and reliable if they are to consider seriously the speaker's argument. Thus, an effective speaker has to seem credible to the audience through the effects of what Aristotle called ethos. Aristotle also recognized that appeals to emotions, values, and beliefs play important roles in effective arguments. He classified these appeals as pathos. Appeals to emotions, values, and beliefs often get downplayed in college writing courses, especially in the sciences and social sciences. But Rachel Carson knew that dry scientific argument would not move the government to ban DDT. And Richard Klein understood from the beginning that he would have to use alternative appeals, that is, he would have to win his readers by his witty style, his knowledge of history, and his shrewd observations about modern culture. Much can be learned from their tactics.

Ethos: Creating an Effective Persona

You have probably noticed that many times in the course of reading, you get a very real sense of the kind of person who is doing the writing. Even if you have never read this person's writing before, even if you really know nothing about the actual person behind the message, you still often get a sense of the character and personality of the writer just by reading. How you respond to the message to some extent depends on how you respond to the person who delivers it. The term *ethos* refers to the persuasive value associated with this person that is created in the text. People sometimes use the term *persona* to distinguish the narrator—the voice in the text—from the real author. You have encountered a great number of created personas in your reading. Sometimes it is obvious that the narrator is not the author; for example, Huckleberry Finn is a created persona to be distinguished from the real author, Mark Twain. Mark Twain, the pen name used by Samuel Clemens, is also a kind of persona. Clemens did public lecture tours adopting the Mark Twain personality, performing the equivalent of today's standup comedy. But in fact, every piece of writing is delivered by a created character, a persona, who may or may not have much in common with the real author.

In March 1997, scientists at the Oregon Regional Primate Research Center held a press conference to announce that they had successfully cloned two rhesus monkeys from early stage embryos. They took a set of chromosomes from cells in a primitive monkey embryo and inserted them into egg cells from which the original DNA had been removed. These embryos were then implanted in the wombs of host mothers using in vitro fertilization techniques. The monkeys were born normally and are expected to live as long as twenty years. Donald Wolf, a senior scientist at the center, called the cloning a major breakthrough, since it would remove some of the uncertainties in animal research that might have been attributed to genetic differences among animals.

Other people were greatly alarmed by the cloning of the monkeys that followed closely the announcement of the successful cloning of sheep. President Bill Clinton called the research "troubling" and immediately banned any federal funding for experiments that might lead to the cloning of human beings. The U.S. Congress organized hearings that began in March 1997 to examine the implications of cloning research.

Following are two examples of letters sent to the House Science Subcommittee on Technology following the hearings. What persona did the writer of each of the following letters create?

Rep. Connie Morella, Chairperson
House Science Subcommittee on Technology
2319 Rayburn House Office Building
Washington, DC 20515

Dear Representative Morella:

I am pleased to see among members of Congress great concern that humans should not be cloned. What perplexes me is the lack of protest against cloning animals. "Repulsive," "repugnant," "offensive"- -scientists and politicians alike have used these words to describe human cloning experiments, but these adjectives should also be invoked to describe cloning experiments on animals.

There are both ethical and scientific reasons to oppose the cloning of animals. Animals are simply not commodities with whose genetic material we can tamper in pursuit of human ends. M. Susan Smith, director of the Oregon Primate Research Center, where Rhesus monkeys were cloned from embryo cells, says that we should be glad that scientists will now need to use "only" 3 or 4 animals instead of 20 or 30. But Smith and other proponents of animal experimentation really just don't get it. What about the 3 or 4 beings who will suffer and die in experiments? We don't bargain with lives- -3 or 40- -it's their use in experiments that's wrong.

Smith and other scientists justify their work by stating that genetically identical monkeys will help research into AIDS, alcoholism, depression and other illnesses. Scientists can clone a million monkeys, but they still won't be good models for human disease. It is not genetic variability that limits the effectiveness of animal experimentation- -it's that the physiology of animal species differs. Animals are not "little humans," and there's no way that researchers can clone themselves around that reality.

At the recent Congressional hearings on the ethics of cloning, testimony was heard from the following: the director of National Institute of Health, the largest funding agency of animal experimentation in the country; the head of Genzyme Transgenics Corporation, a company that seeks to profit from genetically manipulated animals; a representative from the US Department of Agriculture, which is interested in the potential of cloning animals for food; Smith of Oregon Primate Research Center; and an ethicist who declared (and numerous exposes of animal experiments refute) that we do not permit research that is cruel to animals in our society.

There was a voice missing from this panel biased in favor of animal cloning: someone to represent the animals, whose lives and interests are so readily dismissed. We all need to speak up for them now and demand legislation to ban all cloning experiments.

Sincerely, Helen Barnes

Rep. Connie Morella, Chairperson
House Science Subcommittee on Technology
2319 Rayburn House Office Building
Washington, DC 20515

Dear Representative Morella:

I cannot believe you actually pretended to have a hearing on animal cloning
and only invited people in favor of cloning. Why didn't you invite someone to
speak for the animals? What a waste of our tax dollars! You should be passing
laws against cloning instead of trying to justify it.

Don't you understand that the monkeys are being cloned to be killed?
Thousands of monkeys have died in research on cancer and AIDS, and we're
still no closer to finding cures. Don't you see that such research is useless?
It's not that difficult to figure out. Monkeys are not people. It doesn't matter
if they have identical genes or not.

We see what's happening. This is another example of government protecting
big business over the interests of the people. The only people who will benefit
from cloning animals are the big executives of the high-tech companies and a
few scientists who will make big profits.

Haven't you read the polls and noticed that the great majority of Americans
are opposed to cloning? You'll find out how we feel when you have to run
for reelection!

                    Sincerely, Ed Younger

Both letters contain the same major points, and both are passionate in demanding legislation to end cloning of animals. Both assert that cloning monkeys for research purposes is wrong because it lacks scientific and ethical justification. But they stand apart in the ethos of the writer.

The writer of the first letter, Helen Barnes, attempts to establish common ground by noting that nearly everybody is opposed to the cloning of humans. Barnes makes a bridge to her issue by noting that the terms used for human cloning—*repulsive, repugnant, offensive*—should also be used for the cloning of animals. She urges Representative Morella to look at monkeys as beings rather than genetic material for the use of researchers. She points out the absence of any voices opposed to the use of monkeys for experiments at the hearings on cloning. She takes a strong stand at the end, but she uses "we," inviting Representative Morella to join her.

The writer of the second letter, by contrast, is confrontational from the outset. Ed Younger accuses Representative Morella of stacking the deck by inviting only proponents of cloning to the hearing. He insinuates that she is stupid if she doesn't realize the cloned monkeys will be killed and that the use of animals for testing has not produced cures for diseases such as cancer and AIDS. He suggests that she is a dupe of high-tech companies by taking their side. He ends with a threat to vote her out of office. His persona is clearly that of angry citizen.

Representatives often receive more than a thousand letters, faxes, and emails each day, and they have to deal with letters from angry people all the time. Usually, staff members answer the mail and simply tally up who is for and against a particular issue. Often, the reply is a form letter thanking the writer for his or her concern and stating the representative's position. But sometimes, representatives personally write detailed answers to letters from their constituents. Imagine that you are Representative Morella and you have to answer these two letters. Ed Younger's persona makes it difficult to say more than "I appreciate hearing your opinion on this issue." Helen Barnes's persona leaves open the possibility of an exchange of ideas.

People make judgments about you that are based on how you represent yourself when you write. Sometimes the angry voice is the one to present if you believe that your readers need a wake-up call. However, most people don't like to be yelled at. Just as you can change your voice orally when the situation calls for it— just as you can speak in a friendly way, in an excited way, or in a stern way in different circumstances—so too you should be able to modulate your voice in writing, depending on what is called for. Some important factors are the following:

- Your relationship with your audience (your voice can be less formal when you know someone well or when you are communicating with people in the same circumstances than when you are communicating with a relative stranger or with someone above or below you in an organization)
- Your audience's personality (different people respond sympathetically to different voices)

- Your argument (some arguments are more difficult to make than others)
- Your purpose (you may take a more urgent tone if you want your readers to act immediately)
- Your genre (arguments in formal proposals usually have a different voice from arguments in newspaper sports and opinion columns)

Advice on Argument from Benjamin Franklin's *Autobiography*

"There was another bookish lad in town, John Collins by name, with whom I was intimately acquainted. We sometimes disputed, and very fond we were of argument, and very desirous of confronting one another. Which disputatious turn, by the way, is apt to become a very bad habit, making people often extremely disagreeable in company, by the contradiction that is necessary to bring it into practice. Besides souring and spoiling the conversation, it is productive of disgust and enmities where you may have occasion for friendships. I had caught it by reading my father's books of disputes about religion. Persons of good sense, I have observed, seldom fall into it, except lawyers, university men, and men of all sorts that have been bred at Edinburgh."

Choosing an Appropriate Voice

In November 1998, voters in Minnesota elected a new governor to replace the retiring incumbent. They chose among three candidates: St. Paul Mayor Norm Coleman, who was credited with revitalizing a city that had been in decline; state attorney general Hubert H. Humphrey III, son of a former vice president, who won a $6 billion lawsuit against the tobacco industry; and Jesse "The Body" Ventura, the 6'4", 250-pound former professional tag-team wrestling champion and movie actor featured in the Arnold Schwarzenegger movie *Predator.* At one debate, Coleman and Humphrey wore the usual dark suits, but Ventura came dressed in black jeans, a camouflage shirt, and the Australian bush hat with the snakeskin band that he had worn in *Predator.*

Ventura had only a sixth of the budget of each of his rivals, but he made his ads count. In one televised ad, Ventura made his point about not taking campaign money from special interests by using action figures. When the Evil Special Interest Man doll held out a dime, the Ventura doll rebuked, "I don't want your stupid money." In another, Ventura wore only a pair of shorts and sat in the pose of Rodin's *The Thinker.* After a voice-over listed reasons to elect him,

Jesse "The Body" Ventura celebrates at the People's Inauguration in Minneapolis, January 1999.

Ventura looked up, smiled, and winked. No politician winks. His opponents called his campaign a joke, but on election day, they discovered that the joke was on them. Ventura pulled off one of the biggest upsets in recent U.S. politics.

Although his opponents did not take him seriously until the end of the campaign, Ventura recognized that many Minnesotans wanted a change from politics as usual. His opponents, while well qualified, were short on charisma and came across as symbols of politics as usual. By contrast, Ventura seemed to be a down-to-earth, straightforward antipolitician. His persona carried through in the debates and in interviews with reporters. When a reporter asked about his qualifications, Ventura replied, "I can do the job. It's not like transplanting kidneys."

Ventura taught his opponents a simple lesson: There is more than one way to make an argument. Although most of the time, people listen more carefully to a serious, rational voice, sometimes that voice seems boring and even insincere. Ventura's opponents could accuse him of being overly simplistic, but the voters recognized that at the very least, Ventura was being honest with them.

Arguments that are totally predictable quickly lose their effectiveness. If you use the same strategy all the time—introduce your points, make your points, and summarize your points—you will get the job done, but you might not convince anyone who doesn't think the same way you do already. People who write about complex issues don't expect to convert everyone to their way of thinking with a few paragraphs. It's enough to both register a point of view and get their readers to think a little bit differently. And like Jesse Ventura, they can have some fun along the way too.

In the September 24, 1987, issue of *Rolling Stone,* P. J. O'Rourke published "LSD: Let the Sixties Die" in response to a Sixties revival that was going on at the time. (A similar revival occurred in 1997–1998, and we'll no doubt see the Sixties return again in 2007–2008.) O'Rourke wasted no time letting his readers know how he felt about the revival:

> There's a stench of patchouli oil in the air. The overrated old Grateful Dead have a hit record. Hemlines are headed up. Beatle bangs are growing out. People are saddling their children with goofy names. The peace symbol—footprint of the American chicken—is giving the spray-paint industry a bad name again. Oh, God! The Sixties are coming back.
>
> Well, speaking strictly for this retired hippie and former pinko beatnik, if the Sixties head my way, they won't get past the porch steps. I've got a twelve-gauge, double-barreled duck gun chambered for three-inch Magnum shells. Any Sixties come around here, they'll be history. Which, for chrissakes, is what they're supposed to be.

O'Rourke goes on to make fun of the excesses of the Sixties, using the language of the Sixties. Slang that was popular in the Sixties—"can you dig it?," "the whole riff," "pick up on the heavy vibes," "if you know where I'm coming from"—now sounds silly. Other phrases, such as "Wow, man, which way to the bummer tent?" remind us that all wasn't peace and love at the big rock concerts.

Through the first half of his argument, O'Rourke uses satire to point out that many Sixties fads were ridiculous, much of its music was bad, and the acceptance of widespread drug use harmed many young people. But he didn't stop there. He next says, "Even if we wanted to, we couldn't recreate the Sixties now. We just don't have what it takes any more. First of all, there aren't any politicians left worth killing." The focus of his satire shifts subtly from the Sixties to the Eighties. Of young people, he writes, "And too many of today's college students are majoring in Comparative Greed and Advanced Studies in Real-Estate Arts." He also jabs his own generation, which used to shun possessions.

Near the end, O'Rourke gives his piece one more twist: "There was another bad thing about the Sixties, all those loopy beliefs—Karma, Krishna, Helter Skelter, participatory democracy, and all that." It's startling to find "participatory democracy" in that list of dismissed fads, but that's exactly O'Rourke's point. Thus, it's not until the end that O'Rourke chooses to make his implicit claim: that Sixties revivals are bad not just because they celebrate vacuous fads such as bell-bottom pants and psychedelic music but also because they reduce what is worth recovering from the Sixties to fad status. But if O'Rourke would have advanced his claim in such a straight-up way, he would have come off like the career politicians who ran against Jesse Ventura. Re-

Demonstration in Washington, D.C., May 1970

member that O'Rourke was writing for the readers of *Rolling Stone*. Sometimes, you don't want to wear a suit when you argue.

Being aware of your options in creating a voice when you write is one of the secrets of arguing successfully. Before those options are described for a specific argument, a little background for the case in point will be useful. In June 1989, the Supreme Court ruled in *Texas* v. *Johnson* to uphold the First Amendment right to burn the U.S. flag as symbolic political speech. An outraged Congress approved the Flag Protection Act of 1989, but the Senate voted down an amendment to the Constitution. After the Flag Protection Act became law, there were many protests against it. Some protesters were arrested, but the courts ruled that the Flag Protection Act was unconstitutional. Pressure built to get a flag protection amendment into the Constitution, and legislation was introduced for such an amendment in the 1995, 1997, and 1999 sessions of Congress.

You have decided to write an argument arguing that flag burning should be protected as free speech. You think that people could find better ways to protest than by burning the flag, but nonetheless, you think they still should have that right. When you start researching the issue and look at the text of laws that have been passed against flag burning, you discover that the laws are very vague about defining what a flag is. You realize that people could be arrested and put in prison for cutting a cake with an image of the flag in the icing at a Fourth of July picnic.

You decide that examining definitions of the U.S. flag is a great way to begin your paper because if the flag cannot be defined, then you have a good argument that attempts to ban burning of the flag are doomed to failure. Congress cannot pass an amendment against something that it cannot accurately define. You look up the U.S. Code about the flag that was federal law from 1968 to 1989, when it was overturned in the Supreme Court case of *Texas* v. *Johnson*. It reads:

> *Whoever knowingly casts contempt upon any flag of the United States by publicly mutilating, defacing, defiling, burning, or trampling upon it shall be fined not more than $1,000 or imprisoned for not more than one year, or both.*
>
> *The term "flag of the United States" as used in this section, shall include any flag, standard, colors, ensign, or any picture or representation of either, or of any part or parts of either, made of any substance or represented on any substance, of any size evidently purporting to be either of said flag, standard, color, or ensign of the United States of America, or a picture or a representation of either, upon which shall be shown the colors, the stars and the stripes, in any number of either thereof, or of any part or parts of either, by which the average person seeing the same without deliberation may believe the same to represent the flag, standards, colors, or ensign of the United States of America.*

You think the definition in the second paragraph is ridiculous. It could apply to red and white striped pants or almost anything that had stars and was red, white, and blue. But the question is how to make the point effectively in your analysis. Here are three versions of an analysis paragraph that would come after you quote the above law:

Version 1

The language of the 1968 law, passed in the midst of the protest over the Vietnam War, demonstrates the futility of passing laws against flag burning. Congress realized that protesters could burn objects that resembled the American flag and evade prosecution so they extended the law to apply to anything "the average person" believed to represent the flag. The great irony was that the major violators of this law were the most patriotic people in America, who put flags on their cars and bought things with images of flags. When they threw away their flag napkins, they desecrated the flag and violated the law.

Version 2

The 1968 law against flag burning is yet another example of why the Washington bureaucrats who love big government always get it wrong. They see on TV something they don't like- -protesters burning a flag. So they say, "Let's pass a law against it." But for the law to have teeth, they realize that it has to be far reaching, including every imagined possibility. So they make the law as broad as possible so the police can bust the heads of anyone they want to. The attempt to ban flag burning shows how people with good intentions take away your liberties.

Version 3

"Wait a second!" you're probably saying to yourself. "Any number of stars? Any part or parts of either? On any substance? Or a picture or representation?" You bet. Burning a photo of a drawing of a three-starred red, white, and blue four-striped flag would land you in jail for a year. I'm not making this up. Do you still trust them to define what a flag is? I don't.

You can hear the differences in voices of these paragraphs. The first is the modulated voice of a radio or television commentator, appearing to give a distanced and balanced perspective. The second is the voice of an angry libertarian, asserting that the government that governs best is the one that governs least. The third is the voice of Comedy Central or the alternative press, laughing at what government tries to do. Once again, the point is not which one is most effective, because each could be effective for different audiences. The point is to be aware that you can take on different voices when you write and to learn how to control these voices.

 ## Strong Beginnings

Stephen Covey begins his international best-seller, *The Seven Habits of Highly Effective People,* with this sentence: "In more than 25 years of working with people in business, university, and marriage and family settings, I have come in contact with many individuals who have achieved an incredible degree of outward success, but have found themselves struggling with an inner hunger, a deep need for personal congruency and effectiveness and for healthy, growing relationships with other people." The first sentence tells you a lot about why the book became a best-seller. In one sentence, Covey establishes his own credentials and sets out the central issues that the book addresses. He also accomplishes the two things you have to do before you can get anyone to consider your claims and good reasons. You first have to convince your readers that what you want to talk about is worth their time to read. Next, you have to convince them that you know enough to be worthy of their attention.

By starting out with "25 years of working with people in business, university, and marriage and family settings," Covey establishes his ethos as the voice of experience. In the main part of the sentence, Covey poses in a subtle way the problem the book addresses: "I have come in contact with many

(continued)

individuals who have achieved an incredible degree of outward success, but have found themselves struggling with an inner hunger." He could have said something like "Many people who are well off are still unhappy," but that's not quite his point. He sets out the problem as a contrast: Many people who have achieved outward success struggle with an inner hunger. But what does *inner hunger* mean? Covey finishes the sentence by defining *inner hunger*—"a deep need for personal congruency and effectiveness and for healthy, growing relationships with other people"—in a grammatical construction called an **appositive.** You've heard appositives frequently on newscasts. Broadcasters use appositives to sum up or describe the significance of an event in sentences such as "Today, the prime ministers of India and Pakistan signed a treaty concerning disputed territory in Kashmir, an agreement that will help to ease building tensions between the two countries."

So far so good. But what exactly does Covey mean by "a deep need for personal congruency and effectiveness" and "healthy, growing relationships"? Those concepts are abstract, and if Covey is going to keep his potential readers, he must make those concepts relate to those readers. The primary readers for *The Seven Habits of Highly Effective People* presumably are people who already work for corporations and organizations. Therefore, Covey follows with a series of examples his clients have related to him:

> I've set and met my career goals and I'm having tremendous professional success. But it's cost me my personal and family life. I'm not even sure I know myself and what's really important to me. I've had to ask myself—is it worth it?
>
> I've started a new diet—for the fifth time this year. I know I'm overweight, and I really want to change. I read all the new information, I set goals, I get myself all psyched up with a positive mental attitude and tell myself I can do it. But I don't. After a few weeks, I fizzle. I just can't seem to keep a promise I make to myself.
>
> I'm busy—really busy. But sometimes I wonder if what I'm doing will make any difference in the long run. I'd really like to think there was meaning in my life, that somehow things were different because I was here.

Evidently readers recognized themselves in these examples. The sales of *The Seven Habits of Highly Effective People* remain strong a decade after it was first published.

Covey offers a lesson about strong beginnings. Even if you don't have twenty-five years of experience on a particular subject, you can still get off to a fast start. Establish your subject, your voice, and what's at stake for your readers right away, and there's a good chance your readers will stick with you.

Pathos: Appealing to Your Reader's Values

The chapter on audience discussed how to take into account your audience's attitude toward you and your argument as you develop your content. *Pathos* also is audience-oriented and attitude-oriented; it refers to appeals to your audience's most basic, heartfelt attitudes and values.

Sometimes, pathos is defined (and dismissed) simply as an unsubtle appeal to your audience's barely controllable emotional side. You know that your reader fears something, loves something, or despises something, and you somehow tie your argument to those feelings. Critics of advertising in general and of television advertising in particular contend that advertisers depend on purely emotional arguments when they connect automobiles with achieving success or depict drinking beer as part of a happy social life, when insurance ads are associated with scare tactics, or when a new movie is promoted through sexually suggestive scenes. Because in Western culture, the emotions are often associated with the instinctive and irrational and subconscious—with the so-called animal side of human beings—pathos seldom gets much respectful attention in argument. Most people in academic disciplines and the professions, especially the sciences and engineering, never want to be accused of making bald-faced emotional arguments like the ones you see on television. Therefore, it is not surprising that arguments in most academic writing are presented as sober and reasonable, avoiding overt appeals to an audience's subconscious instincts and emotions.

Then again, there is nothing necessarily irrational about the emotions. As many of the old *Star Trek* episodes with Mr. Spock show, emotions make people human just as much as reason does. There's nothing irrational or unreasonable about an argument that "Our city should attend to its solid waste problems because we want our children to live in safe, healthy, and attractive communities," even if there are emotional values latent in that argument. As that statement also illustrates, there is also probably no such thing as a purely emotional argument—an argument that totally bypasses reason. Even a beer ad on television that depicts men as moronic beach bums and women as brain-dead bikini-clad bodies has an implicit argument with a claim: "If you drink our beer, you'll have more fun."

Appealing to emotions is not necessarily a bad strategy, but pathos is a broader concept than simply appealing to emotions. The example claim, "Our city should attend to its solid waste problems because we want our children to live in safe, healthy, and attractive communities," illustrates that there is another way to think about pathos. Think of pathos as an appeal to the most basic values held by your audience. Pathos carries emotional values because it refers to the values that people hold so dearly that they don't think about them very much and don't question them very often—values such as the importance of safety and security, freedom and personal liberty, loyalty and friendship, equal opportunity and fairness. If your claim is "Interstate highways in urban areas should have concrete dividers placed in the median to prevent vehicles from skidding across the median into oncoming traffic," you have made a logical, matter-of-fact statement. But this argument carries pathetic overtones because safety is one of most basic values. Indeed, it might be a good strategy to begin with an example of a tragic head-on collision that might have been prevented if all urban interstate highways had concrete dividers on their median strips.

Pathos fails in argument when the linkage isn't clear. The linkage in TV ads is often absent. Many ads imply that the user of the product will be attractive to the opposite sex, younger, or happier, but how these changes are supposed to happen is never made clear. Using pathos is not a shortcut to making an effective argument.

 ## Strong Endings

Endings are often the toughest part of a work to write. The easy way out is to repeat what you have said earlier. If you're writing a PhD dissertation, summarizing your conclusions is a good way to end. But if your argument is relatively short—the equivalent of three or four double-spaced pages—then you should hope that your readers have not forgotten your main points by the time they get to the end. Instead, think of a way to end that will be emphatic rather than sleep inducing. Here is how Anne Marie O'Keefe concluded an argument against the use of drug testing by employers ("The Case against Drug Testing," *Psychology Today* [June 1987]: 36–38):

> Civil libertarians claim that as long as employees do their work well, inquiries into their off-duty drug use are no more legitimate than inquiries into their sex lives. Then why has drug testing become so popular? Perhaps because it is simple and "objective"—a litmus test. It is not easily challenged because, like the use of lie detectors, it relies on technology that few understand. It is quicker and cheaper than serious and sustained efforts to reduce illegal drug use, such as the mass educational efforts that have successfully reduced cigarette smoking. And finally, while drug testing may do little to address the real problem of drug use in our society, it reinforces the employer's illusion of doing something.
>
> Apparently some employers would rather test their employees for drugs than build a relationship with them based on confidence and loyalty. Fortunately, there are employers, such as Drexelbrook Engi-

neering Company in Pennsylvania, who have decided against drug testing because of its human costs. As Drexelbrook's vice president put it, a relationship "doesn't just come from a paycheck. When you say to an employee, 'you're doing a great job; just the same, I want you to pee in this jar and I'm sending someone to watch you,' you've undermined that trust."

O'Keefe's next-to-last paragraph answers the question, If drug testing is so bad, then why do so many employers require it? Her last paragraph concludes her article with a positive example rather than restating what she has said before. An example, an additional point, a quotation, or a call to action is a good alternative to a bland summary in the final paragraph.

The Language of Arguments

So far, this chapter has focused on language as a means of creating a voice when you write, but voice is just one way to discuss style in arguments. Just as a personal style reflects all that a person does—the way she dresses, the way she talks, her personality—so too does style in argument. At the most fundamental level, style in argument begins with language—the words and sentences that the writer selects and assembles. Paying close attention to the words you use and how you put sentences together can pay big dividends for you as a writer.

Advertisers have long understood the critical role that words play in persuading people. The writers of advertising copy are well aware that the average American is exposed to over three thousand ads a day and that such oversaturation has made people cynical about ads. Advertisers have to be clever to get our attention, so ads often use the tactics of poets and comedians. Words in ads often use puns and metaphors to draw our attention to the products they promote. A watch ad runs with the banner "Every second counts." An ad for a coffeemaker asks, "Who better to handle his ugly mug in the morning?" A plastic wrap ad shows two chicken legs under the headline "Stop our legs from drying out." A used car ad appears under the words "Born again."

But it is not just clever plays on words that do the work in the language of advertising. We often find words in ads that do not make much sense at first reading. For example, a Nikon camera ad displays in big bold letters, "It's a stealth bomber with fuzzy dice." Calling a camera a "stealth bomber with fuzzy dice" is an example of metaphor. **Metaphor** is a Greek term that means "carry over," which describes what happens when you encounter a metaphor. You carry over the meaning from one word to another. Metaphor is but one kind of **figurative language.** Also common in advertising are **synecdoche,** in which the part is used to represent the whole (a hood ornament represents a car), and **metonymy,** in which something stands for something else with which it is closely associated (using flowers to represent a product's fresh scent).

There are other kinds of figurative language, but the main idea is that meanings are transferred from one word or phase to another. How this transfer works is more complicated. If we encounter an unfamiliar metaphor such as the stealth bomber example, we do our best to make sense of what the writer means. Most metaphors, however, are much more familiar and don't force us to put forth much mental effort. Think of all the clichés you hear daily: Clichés are the spice of life, the bread and butter of any conversation, the greatest things since sliced bread, the . . . well, you get the picture. Time flies when you're having fun, and we could keep writing clichés like there's no tomorrow, but there's no use flogging a dead horse. Clichés at some point in their past were original metaphors, but through repeated use, their attention-grabbing power has worn out.

Shakespeare used his knowledge of how figurative language works to great effect in his sonnets, in which, again and again, he sets up a cliché, such as comparing his love to a summer day in *Sonnet 18,* only to subvert that cliché by carrying over other meanings. He says that his love is more temperate and more lovely than a summer's day, but more important, a summer day is closely followed by autumn and winter: "A summer's lease hath all too short a date." If beauty lasts for only a day, then it's not desirable. Shakespeare turns the cliché of comparing one's lover to a summer's day inside out.

What meanings, then, is the reader supposed to carry over from "stealth bomber with fuzzy dice" to a Nikon camera? Cameras don't have wings, wheels, jet engines, or bomb bays, nor are they covered with fake fur. The advertisers didn't want the reader to work too hard, so they put in fine print at the bottom their interpretation of the metaphor: "The technology of a serious camera. The spontaneity of a point-and-shoot. Now you don't have to choose between the two."

Metaphors are but one way in which advertisers exploit the associations many words carry in addition to their literal meanings. Many ads are sexually suggestive. A moisturizing cream ad announces: "Shed your inhibitions." An ad for an online shopping service tells us to "Go naked to the mall." A whiskey ad in an outdoor magazine states: "Get in touch with your masculine side." Nowhere are the associative meanings of words more carefully considered than in the discourse of politics. Politicians sprinkle their speeches with positive words referring to themselves and their party, words such as these:

change, opportunity, truth, moral, courage, reform, prosperity, crusade, children, family, debate, candid, humane, pristine, liberty, commitment, principle, unique, duty, precious, care, tough, listen, learn, help, lead, vision, success, empower(ment), citizen, activist, mobilize, dream, freedom, peace, rights, pioneer, proud/pride, building, preserve, flag, children, environment, reform, eliminate strength, choice/choose, fair, protect, confident, incentive, hard work, initiative, common sense, passionate

In referring to their opponents, they use words such as these:

decay, failure, crisis, destructive, destroy, sick, pathetic, lie, bureaucracy, betray, shallow, endanger, coercion, hypocrisy, radical, threaten, waste, corruption, incompetent, destructive, impose, self-serving, greed, ideological, insecure, pessimistic, excuses, intolerant, stagnation, corrupt, selfish, insensitive, status quo, shame, disgrace, punish, cynicism, cheat, steal, abuse of power

Saying good things about yourself and bad things about your opponents is characteristic of all politicians. The key to winning most elections is to get the positive associations linked to the candidate you are supporting and the negative associations linked to the opponent.

Some people denounce the language of advertising and politics as being corrupted with bias. Although it is unfortunate that much advertising and political discourse does involve outright deception, to expect such language to be completely objective and free of bias is unrealistic. With the exception of purely functional words such as *the, to,* and *for,* all words carry various meanings and associations that they have picked up in the larger culture and individual experience. The word "Mom," for example, brings associations of your own mother and how motherhood is understood in your culture.

On controversial topics, be aware of the associated meanings of key terms. The hotter the topic, the stronger the associations; therefore, the words that are used in the debate over abortion tend to be heavily laden with associated meanings. This can be illustrated by looking at two articles that concern the issue of abortion. The first article, "Abortion, Ethics, and the Law" by Claudia Wallis, was published in *Time* magazine. Although *Time* does include editorials by guest columnists that take particular stands on controversial issues, this article comes from the news sections and is a presumably objective report on the legal status of abortions.

The second article, "New Questions—Same Old Debate" by John Cavanaugh-O'Keefe, was published in *America,* a magazine that is sympathetic to and associated with the Roman Catholic Church. The article is labeled "Op Ed," an abbreviation for "opinion editorial," indicating that the author will take a stance on an issue. Because the article was written to appear in *America,* the author also makes certain assumptions about his readers. He takes for granted that they are opposed to abortion, and he assumes that they are familiar with recent battles over doctrine within the Roman Catholic Church.

As you read, notice exactly how each author refers to abortions.

Wallis, Claudia. "Abortion, Ethics, and the Law." *Time* 6 July, 1987: 82.

The juxtaposition of these two images [hospital staff members attempting in one instance to save a premature baby while in another aborting a fetus a few weeks younger] has long preoccupied people on both sides of the abortion debate. If medicine can save the life of an immature fetus, how can society allow the termination of an advanced pregnancy? When does the constitutional obligation to protect a potential citizen begin? How are the fetus' interests weighted against the mother's right to liberty and privacy?

Cavanaugh-O'Keefe, John. "New Questions–Same Old Debate." *America* 25 April, 1987: 335.

I asked students all over the Berkeley campus: "If I could tell you where an innocent person was scheduled to be killed, would you do anything about it?" Most said "Yes." When I explained that I was talking about Planned Parenthood in Oakland, most disagreed that unborn babies are "persons" and refused to act. Fair enough, though distressing. But what about those millions of people who profess to believe that unborn children are members of the human family? What is their response? Their answer too is "No." Is it possible to justify that refusal? How?

During the 1960's, police in all major cities learned to arrest protesters and demonstrators with whom they agreed. How often we heard the sleepy response, "Just doing my job." Fair enough. But today, "rescue teams" enter abortion clinics, block access to the suction machines and refuse to leave. We insist that our actions are not "protests" but are, in fact, rescue missions. When police officers prepare to haul us out, we state that our simple presence inside the operating rooms is the sole remaining protection for children, and that removing us is cooperating in abortion. All is ready for execution. We point at the suction machines, at the abortionists and at the waiting room where mothers are seated nervously, and we ask to be left in peace.

It seems clear to the rescue teams that arresting and removing them is cooperation in abortion. If the police refuse to arrest, nobody dies. If they make arrests, children die. Their actions are necessary, though not sufficient, to kill those children at that location with that machine.

The *Time* article is about a controversial subject but is written in a noncontroversial way. Its purpose is more to inform than to persuade; therefore, the reader's role is that of an interested person who wants to be informed about current issues. The article steers away from the unpleasant details. It uses phrases such as "termination of an advanced pregnancy." *Termination* is a noun formed from the verb *terminate.* There is an action. Someone terminates, and something is terminated. But the reader doesn't get the gory details. The role for the implied reader in this article is a distant one from the actual circumstances. Instead, the focus is on the broad issues.

The author of the editorial in *America,* John Cavanaugh-O'Keefe, wishes to overturn the present situation. He recognizes that the struggle over a woman's right to an abortion is a struggle over meanings. What Wallis calls an "immature fetus," Cavanaugh-O'Keefe calls an "innocent person," "unborn babies," "unborn children," "children," and a "member of the human family." Cavanaugh-O'Keefe says that it is regrettable that some people do not classify a fetus as a person, but he is not concerned with convincing them that abortion is morally wrong. Instead, he addresses those readers who agree with him that abortion is wrong. He sets out a hypothetical example in which police who believe that abortion is morally wrong are asked to arrest protesters at an abortion clinic. If the police follow orders, they will make the arrests. If they follow their beliefs, then they will refuse to make the arrests and perhaps be subject to disciplinary action for refusing to obey orders. Cavanaugh-O'Keefe poses the moral dilemma directly: "If the police refuse to arrest, nobody dies. If they make arrests, children die." The moral dilemma that he presents is a call for action.

The contrast between the Wallis and Cavanaugh-O'Keefe articles illustrates another principle about style: Effective style is closely correlated to purpose. Wallis is writing an informative article, so her style is more distanced. Cavanaugh-O'Keefe is writing a persuasive editorial that is a call to action, so his style is much more direct with the focus on people. He is saying to his readers that if they believe they believe abortion is wrong, then they should be trying to do something to stop abortions.

 Christopher Hitchens

Scenes from an Execution

An Englishman by birth and educated at Oxford, Christopher Hitchens (1949–   ) is a prominent political journalist who now lives in Washington, D.C. He works as a columnist for *The Nation* and *Vanity Fair,* where "Scenes from an Execution" appeared in 1998. He has also written a dozen books on subjects ranging from Britain's plundering of the Parthenon to the perceptions that British and Americans have of each other. When asked why he decided to come to the United States, Hitchens replied, "I wanted to know if it was really true that it was the land of opportunity, of democracy, and individual liberty. My conclusion was that, at least as compared to the ancien régime under which I had been brought up, it was."

"Scenes from an Execution" describes Hitchens's experience of witnessing the September 1997 execution of Samuel Lee McDonald at the state prison in Potosi, Missouri. Hitchens expresses outrage about the routine way the death penalty is administered in the United States, but he uses a voice that is at times humorous. For example, he is surprised at how simple it is to witness an execution and writes, "It's really quite easy to book an appointment with death, and see for yourself your tax dollars at work." Why do you think he adopts a light tone about such a serious subject?

Christopher Hitchens

1   Last May 22, Larry Wayne White was executed by lethal injection in Huntsville, Texas. As a celebrated double murderer, he attracted few mourners and only a thinly attended vigil of death-penalty opponents. I've been spending a fair amount of time in and around death row in the past few years, and two aspects of White's terminal experience caught my attention. First, he was turned off at six P.M. so that the event was more within the manageable compass of business and working hours. No midnight dramas. Strictly routine. Second, he asked for a last cigarette and was refused it by the prison authorities. (This, sir, is a nonsmoking facility. Our policy is one of zero tolerance.)

2   They call it gallows humor for a reason. You may laugh at death all you like, but only on the recognized condition that you allow death the concluding cackle. Kingsley Amis, a man of a deep, awed respect for the Grim Reaper, once wrote:

Death has got something to be said for it:
There's no need to get out of bed for it;
Wherever you may be,
They bring it to you, free!

3   And passing from the absurd to the near sublime, Yeats wrote of an Irish airman who "foresaw" his own death: "I know that I shall meet my fate / Somewhere among the clouds above."

4   The two verses share an ineluctable element of the random and the uncertain. "*Wherever* you happen to be," "*Somewhere* among the clouds above." Our whole existence as a species is made unique by our absolute foreknowledge of death combined with our complete ignorance of its timing.

5   So here is our paradox. Nothing is more predictable and more certain than death, and nothing is less predictable and less certain. Two classes of people are exempt from this rule: those who plan their own deaths, and those who are sentenced to be "put to death."

Most "advanced" countries in the world have abolished capital punishment. In   6
order to be a fully signatory nation of the Council of Europe, for example, you
have to show that you have wiped it from your book of statutes. The very first act
of the Constitutional Court of liberated South Africa was to abolish the penalty of
death. Russia, which is applying to join the Council of Europe, has pledged the
abolition of capital punishment. And in the diminishing group of countries which
claims, with the United States, the right to life and death over the citizen, the
Japanese practice a peculiar protocol. They don't notify either the family or the
condemned of the time or the date. If you are the leading actor in this little drama
your cue comes without warning. A cell door opens all of a sudden, and a group
of strangers is standing there. And then you jump—to a conclusion.

This policy strikes many people as barbarous, which it most certainly is. But, like   7
other similar barbarities, it may have its origin in a vague humanitarianism. Dos-
toyevsky wrote that if, in the last moment before a man's execution, he were given
the alternative of passing the rest of his life on the summit of a bare rock he would
choose the rock with gratitude. Some methods of punishment were so ghastly and
so elaborate that even the clearly worded U.S. Constitution could only prohibit
them with a shudder as "cruel and unusual." The guillotine, a symbol of horror to
Albert Camus, was originally installed by the French Republic as a swift and ten-
der alternative to the wheel and the fire. In keeping a man uncertain of the time
of his own death, the Japanese are bizarrely and ironically preserving his status as
a human being—ignorant of the biggest date he's ever scheduled to make.

This is a country rather short on irony and long on euphemism, so here I am in   8
Potosi, Missouri, in a brightly lit barracks in the Ozark Mountains, to keep a bu-
reaucratic appointment with death. Somewhere in the bowels of this building is
a man who knows the very hour of his own terminus, and who has known it for
a while.

   Samuel Lee McDonald, a burly, balding black man a few months older than   9
myself, is tonight in the ticklish position of being the retiring dean of Missouri's
death row. On May 16, 1981, in the parking lot of a convenience store, he shot an
off-duty policeman. Officer Robert Jordan had no idea that this evening was to be
the one booked for his death. So far from that, he had taken his 11-year-old
daughter to buy "treats" for the weekend, and she was the one who had to watch
while McDonald shot her father down. And then, as he lay on the ground, blasted
him again. Jordan got off several shots himself, two of which hit McDonald. The
assailant had to be nursed back to life so that the process of putting him to death
could get properly under way.

   Every feasible appeal has now been exhausted—this is all happening on the   10
night and morning of September 23–24, 1997—and McDonald has had a "date
certain" since July. The American execution drama used to make a special feature

of the last-minute reprieve, the phone call from the governor to the death cell and all the rest of it. (At Parchman prison farm in Mississippi, where I once went to talk to someone who was about to be gassed, they still wait a ritual extra few minutes after midnight because, according to unshakable death-house folklore, Chief Justice Earl Warren actually did once call and was told he was just a tad too late.) But in these increasingly unsentimental times, the cry is all for taking the uncertainty out of the procedure. The U.S. Supreme Court, in a number of recent rulings, has effectively allowed states to lower a boom after which not even the production of fresh evidence can save you. "Get on with it" is the slogan. Are the clotted and clogged death rows a national embarrassment? Well, then, let's expedite the business!

11   As a consequence, it's really quite easy to book an appointment with death, and see for yourself your tax dollars at work. Missouri calls itself the "Show Me State." The jaunty motto appears on the license plates, which, it just occurs to me, are manufactured in the prison system. The Missouri Department of Corrections sent me a form, which asked me my Social Security number and arrest record and all that, and also inquired in a friendly way why I had asked to see an execution in Missouri. I did not reply, "Because Missouri is executing somebody almost every week this month, so I won't have to hang about." I replied, "Because this is a major policy debate and because Missouri is in Middle America and because it's the 'Show Me State.' " They said, Come right on down.

12   As a designated "state's witness" I was instructed to appear no later than a certain hour on a cold and rainy night. Buzzed in to the interior, I was placed in a room with coffee and doughnuts and overfriendly officials. They did everything they were supposed to do, like giving me the full menu of the condemned man's traditional last meal ("Rib-eye steak, fried shrimp, catfish fillet, Texas toast, French fries, two eggs over easy, and a Coke"). Too *physical* somehow. Too gross and fleshly. Also, I couldn't help recalling Rickey Ray Rector, the man executed by Governor Clinton during the 1992 New Hampshire primary. So gravely impaired and lobotomized was he that, when they came to take him away, he explained that he was leaving a wedge of pecan pie "for later." Laid upon the gurney, he helped them find a vein for the IV because he thought they were doctors come at last to cure him.

13   Like a majority of capital-punishment states these days, and like the new federal execution "facility" in Terre Haute, Indiana, which I have toured (and which might have the honor and distinction of killing Timothy McVeigh), Missouri now employs the lethal-injection method, first used in the Lone Star State in 1982. This is supposed to be more tranquil and predictable and benign than the various forms of burning, shooting, strangling, and gassing that in the past have squeezed themselves through the "cruel and unusual" rubric. It looks and feels—to the outsider at least—more like a banal medical "procedure." Here's what's supposed to

happen, as the supervisors gently and patiently explain. A few hours before the appointment, the "inmate"—as he is still called—is offered a sedative shot. This is seldom refused. At the midnight hour, once attached to a gurney or medical trestle, he is given a dose of sodium pentothal, which induces unconsciousness. This is swiftly rammed home, as it were, by a shot of pancuronium bromide, which causes cessation of respiration. A final chaser of potassium chloride immobilizes the heart.

As with the increased practice of "doing" the condemned in batches, in remote prisons and in working hours, this medicalized "putting down" is designed to leach the drama and agony out of the business: to transform it into a form of therapy for society and "closure" for the perp. In Arkansas last January, three men were executed by clinical injection in one night. State corrections officials explained un-ironically that this (a) was cheaper and (b) made for a great saving in wear and tear on staff emotions. "By doing these together," said spokeswoman Dina Tyler, "you only have to make that climb once to get mentally prepared to do this. I think everybody gets a little tense." I think so, too. But I also think that efforts to smooth or remove all that tension are unlikely to be crowned with success. Why, even that night in Arkansas there was a glitch. Kirt Wainwright, one of the three men in the execution queue—they choose the order by prison number—did get himself a brief last-minute stay. Clarence Thomas's clerk called from the Supreme Court. The justices deliberated for an hour. Mr. Wainwright lay strapped to a gurney for this period, with a needle in his arm. Sixty minutes of that and then Justice Thomas called to say they could press the plunger after all. Talk about your stress factor! 14

There have been some extraordinary scenes in these lethal-injection parlors. Tubes and needles have come adrift. In the execution of former heavy intravenous "users," agonizing periods of time have elapsed in the search for a usable blood vessel. (Rickey Ray Rector underwent what the authorities brusquely termed a "cutdown" as his arm was laid open to find a vein.) The American Medical Association considers it unethical for its members to take part, so the work is often farmed out to inadequately trained corrections personnel. As a result, thicker and heavier layers of denial and obfuscation have already begun to encrust this new, pristine, hygienic, pain-free system. Let me tell you what I saw when Samuel Lee McDonald, No. CP 17 in the Potosi correctional facility, was kicked off the planet in your name this past fall. 15

The time came when the smiling officials and amiable spokespersons could do no more for the state-witness contingent, and we were delivered into the domain of the mirthless ones with the big keys on the big belts. Escorted through various blindingly lit yards and along massively secure corridors (the other inmates still get to enjoy the traditional "lockdown" on execution nights), we were ultimately led into the lethal chamber itself. Here, a most grotesque and unexpected proscenium 16 had been erected. Mr. McDonald was concealed on the far side of a thick glass window, which was covered first by a rather frail and delicate venetian blind and second by an ordinary curtain. On either flank of the peep-show-size window stood two amazingly butch guards, almost absurdly motionless and impassive in their heavy equipment, each holding the end of a tiny cord in a hamlike fist. As they waited for the order to tug on the dainty strings and unveil the set, I was assailed by a powerful sensation of voyeuristic indecency. There was something camp and wrong and over-rehearsed about it—the result of an ill-considered attempt to impose primness and decorum on something obscene. There was something else, too. It took me a little while to "get" it. It was the moment in *Great Expectations* when Magwitch is put back in the prison hulk:

> *No one seemed surprised to see him, or interested in seeing him, or glad to see him, or sorry to see him, or spoke a word. . . . Then, the ends of the torches were flung hissing into the water, and went out, as if it were all over with him.*

17   Snuffed, in fact. That was the word for what I then witnessed. Radiating the most professional indifference imaginable, the huge warders pulled the small strings, and the blinds opened and rose. Through the narrow window we could discern Samuel McDonald, already lying on the gurney, covered to his chin by a sheet, as if all "prepped" and ready for the physician. He was looking urgently at the opposite window, behind which stood his friends and family and lawyer to the number of about six. A third window shielded the family of Officer Robert Jordan. McDonald was speaking hurriedly but inaudibly, yet was perhaps lip-readable by his own team. At 12:02 A.M., he stopped talking. It was as if he'd suddenly gagged or hiccupped, and given a slight arch of his back, as the pentothal—delivered by remote control from offstage—hit him. The one thing this hopeless, helpless splutter didn't resemble, even with the greatest permissible metaphorical strain, was "a moment of truth." A robotic voice from somewhere announced that we had duly witnessed the first injection. The next two were counted out loud, but there was no visible impact. So when the robot voice assured us that the McDonald-shaped form was now "deceased," we had to take the statement on trust. That was it. From gurney to slab in three moves. Hustled out quickly, I heard someone say, "Sam McDonald bought the farm. E-I-E-I-O." Even the most spotless scaffold must have its jester.

18   Back in the coffee-and-doughnut section, we were introduced to some of Officer Jordan's male relatives. They were black also, which made them as conspicuous in this part of Missouri (if not in this jail) as Sam McDonald had been. They spoke beautifully and with gravity and bearing, though with that slight constriction and constraint that you sometimes notice when people are employing a script that is not quite their own. Neologistic words like "closure" did not, I could easily see, form part of their daily vernacular. Nonetheless, when they said they had been

praying for McDonald and his family and knew what they were going through and bewailed the appalling length of time that everything had taken, they were genuine and—it seemed to me—rather baffled. It's the done thing to feature the victim's family at trials and at executions these days; this after all is a populist and "feeling" epoch. But I had the slight suspicion that, for this family, revenge was sour or perhaps tasteless.

That of course is presumptuous of me. Otherwise, though, I can be confident in stating that the entire enactment involves a series of unintended consequences. As a state's witness, I was supposed to sign a book saying that everything had been kosher. It was, by definition, too late for that. What if I didn't think so and wouldn't sign? The shrug I got in response only proved that we were, all of us, spending an off night in Absurdistan. For example, who *was* that announcing the chemical hits? Was it a doctor? And why the curtain and the blind before the first injection? "The curtains are to preserve staff anonymity. The EKG is monitored by a physician." Make what you will of that. As in "A Hard Rain's A-Gonna Fall" so in the United States of Therapy: "The executioner's face is always well hidden."   19

Did McDonald have any last words, and if so, what were they, please? Official face consults official cue card. "The inmate's last words were: 'Tell my brothers to be strong.' " Oh, come *on*. I was there. He was talking for very much longer than that, and more animatedly. And why were we not permitted to hear what he said? A final address was the privilege of the condemned even in the Dark Ages. Every attempt, in other words, to make this "procedure" more rational, more orderly, and more hygienic succeeded only in calling attention to something that I'm now firmly convinced is inescapable—namely, that it's irrational, random, and befouled and bemerded with residues of ancient cruelty and superstition. They can deny it's cruel, they can certainly make it less unusual, but they are still stuck with the task of running a premeditated state killing: Big Government at its worst. (When the French finally abolished the guillotine in 1981 they did so on the noble grounds that "It expresses a totalitarian relationship between the citizen and the state.")   20

CP 17 was in effect Samuel McDonald's lottery number. I had myself (I am rather disgusted to admit it now) drawn him out of a hat, feeling that I could no longer ride the long train of argument about the death penalty if I kept on getting off before the last stop. I had deliberately not interested myself in his case. I was just surfing the capital-punishment Web, soliciting an invitation to a beheading in a country that seeks the solace of execution almost daily. But if you have seen someone snuffed, choked off and put down, you are almost bound to feel a certain curiosity. It seemed only polite to inquire what had brought us together.   21

Five days after his 17th birthday, McDonald had enlisted in the United States Army and been promptly sent off to Vietnam. There he earned a Good Conduct Medal, a Vietnam Service Medal, a Vietnam Combat Service Medal, a Combat   22

Infantryman Badge, and two Overseas Service Bars. But he also lost his nerve and his moral center of gravity. At one point during the Tet offensive, he was cut off behind Vietcong lines for five panic-stricken days. On another occasion, he saw almost three-quarters of his company become casualties of war in a single engagement. In his own opinion, he became a killer, if not a murderer. In the course of sweeping a village for "unfriendlies," he heard a sound he didn't care for and machine-gunned an old woman and an infant. Narcotics were his means of escape.

23   I spoke to his attorney, Richard Sindel, who is your typical overworked and under-recognized capital-punishment pro bono local hero. There's one of these in every state of the union, which isn't anything like enough in these days of photo-op executions on election eve. He showed me the court transcript, where McDonald's former platoon commander, Douglas Falek, had turned up to testify on his behalf and had indeed eloquently done so—but in the absence of a jury. An impressive stable of medical men and psychiatrists, including the reigning experts in the field of Post-Vietnam Stress Disorder, had him down as a classic case. In deciding for death, judges and juries are supposed to consider the elements such as premeditation, mental condition, and depraved indifference to human life. In this instance, the jury was denied the information with which to do so. A small break, said Sindel, and his client would have gone to long-term confinement but not to death row. Is it impossible to imagine an arrangement whereby he'd have gone to rehab *before* being turned loose, howling and neurotic and war-torn, onto the streets? Don't be such a bleeding heart. Get with the program.

24   "The program" is that lottery I mentioned. In spite of a well-publicized decline in the murder rate in New York City, the number of murders and murderers in the United States continues to be many, many times greater per capita than for any comparable country. (And certainly, by the way, for any comparable country that has abolished the death penalty.) There are approximately *one hundred thousand* convicted murderers stockpiled in the American prison system. If they were all to to be executed, the country would become charnel house: a saturnalia of eye for eye and tooth for tooth. So, instead, a certain number are selected for the ultimate vengeance and the severest sanction. You can make the procedure as ponderous and pedantic as is humanly possible. You can build in so many "safeguards" and "reviews" that the process will be lengthened until it's tantamount to torture. But this will only emphasize what you most desire to conceal—the fact that you are running a game of chance with a crooked wheel.

25   In effect, nobody who is not from the losing classes has ever been thrust into a death cell in these United States. Clinton Duffy, the warden of San Quentin who supervised 90 executions, once tersely described the penalty as "a privilege of the poor." You could say, without much of a stretch, that Samuel Lee McDonald drew a fairly low lottery number on the day his mother bore him. That is not to relieve

him of his responsibility. But it is not to forget our own either. There are many strong arguments against the very principle of capital punishment, which any intelligent person can deploy, and which I like to think I could deploy conclusively in another article. But it is the *practice*, not the principle, that has been making the most converts lately, and making these converts among the very people who are supposed to administer the business.

"From this day forward," wrote former Supreme Court justice Harry Blackmun in 1994,   26

> *I no longer shall tinker with the machinery of death. For more than twenty years I have endeavored—indeed I have struggled—along with a majority of this Court, to develop procedural and substantive rules that would lend more than the mere appearance of fairness to the death penalty endeavor. Rather than continue to coddle the Court's delusion that the desired level of fairness has been achieved and the need for regulation eviscerated, I feel morally and intellectually obligated to concede that the death penalty experiment has failed.*

When I went to Parchman prison farm in Mississippi that time, to see the last   27
hours of Edward Earl Johnson, I asked to meet the warden. Parchman is the most feared prison in the whole of the former Confederacy, and did not earn its reputation by accident, so I wasn't expecting to run into any fancy liberals. But it did seem to me that the warden, Donald Cabana, was undergoing some distress of mind. Now he has resigned from the prison service and written an extraordinary book entitled *Death at Midnight: The Confession of an Executioner,* in which he "comes out" as a convinced foe of the penalty. I tracked him down at the University of Southern Mississippi, where abolitionists don't grow on trees, even if some people wish they dangled from them. "Christopher," he said, "it's bingo personified. Except that the odds change drastically with your geographical location, your jury pool, your . . . " He didn't need to add race or class or education level.

All right then, what about the victims and what about society's right to be   28
firm? The family members I met at Potosi were concerned above all else with how long it had taken to get justice, if that's what they had indeed ended up getting. Fifteen years is certainly a long time to wait. Speed it up? Be aware of what you may be asking for: an increase in the velocity of the lottery wheel. But between 1973 and the present, we know of *seventy-three* documented cases where innocent people were found on death row and released. Before me is a brilliant and haunting article from the 1995 *Boston University Law Review,* written by Stephen Bright and Patrick Keenan. Its title, "Judges and the Politics of Death: Deciding Between the Bill of Rights and the Next Election in Capital Cases," is a fair guide to its contents. In most states of the union which employ the death penalty, judges are subject to re-election. The effect upon the judicial process is the same as upon the electoral and political processes. There are, as Clinton proved in the Rickey

Ray Rector case, poll driven executions in this country. The contrast between the vulgarity and populism of that and the supposed clinical detachment of the lethal injection is a repellent one. (It's the supporters of capital punishment, in other words, and not its opponents, who rely upon emotion.) Norman Mailer and Phil Donahue have both proposed that executions be either public or televised, so that the voters can be faced with what they are demanding. They, too, are trying to be ironic. The fact is that the crowd already plays more of a role than anyone cares to admit. The lottery affects, and is affected by, even the people who don't play in it.

29   In my time, I have seen people die and be killed, in sickness and in warfare. I have watched children being born, and I'm morally certain that I once even watched a child being conceived. I would, in principle and in very different degrees, be prepared to see any of that again. It's all, in a manner of speaking, part of life. But I feel permanently degraded and somewhat unmanned by the small part I played, as a complicit spectator, in the dank and dingy little ritual that was enacted in that prison cellar in Missouri. The medical butchery of a helpless and once demented loser, the descendant of slaves and a discarded former legionary of the Empire, made neither society nor any individual safer. It canceled no moral debt. It was a creepy, furtive, and shameful affair, in which the participants could not decently show their faces or quite meet one another's eye. I don't know that I shall ever quite excuse myself, even as a reporter and writer who's supposed to scrutinize everything, for my share in the proceedings. But I am clear on one thing. Death requires no advocates. It is superfluous to volunteer for its service. Those who argue "for" it are missing the point. Edna St. Vincent Millay hit on the truth long before Justice Blackmun and Donald Cabana. "I shall die," she wrote in her poem *Conscientious Objector,* "but that is all that I shall do for Death." Me, too.

Steps in Writing a Rhetorical Analysis

1. **Find an argument that you either strongly agree with or strongly disagree with.** You can find arguments on the editorial pages of newspapers; in opinion features in magazines such as *Time, Newsweek,* and *U.S. News and World Report;* in magazines that take political positions such as *National Review, Mother Jones, New Republic, Nation,* and the online journal *Slate;* and on the Web sites of activist organizations (for a list of some of these organizations, see www.yahoo.com/Society_and_Culture/Issues_and_Causes/). Letters to the editor and online news-

group postings probably won't work for this assignment unless they are long and detailed.

2. **Analyze the structure of the argument.** First, number the paragraphs; then, on a separate page, write a sentence summarizing each of the paragraphs. Where is the main claim located? Underline it. What are the reasons offered in support of the claim? Put stars beside those. Are any opposing positions considered? If so, put O's beside those.

3. **Analyze the language and style of the argument.** Make a list of the key words in the argument. Which are controversial? Are the key terms adequately defined? Are any metaphors or other figurative language used in the argument? Does the writer use "I" or "we," or does he or she speak from a distanced viewpoint? How would you characterize the writer's style? Is it formal or informal? Is it serious, humorous, or satirical?

4. **Analyze the ethos.** How does the writer represent himself or herself? Does the writer have any credentials to be an authority on the topic? Do you trust the writer? Why or why not?

5. **Analyze the logos.** Where do you find facts and evidence in the argument? What kinds of facts and evidence does the writer present: Direct observation? Statistics? Interviews? Surveys? Secondhand sources such as published research? Quotes from authorities?

6. **Analyze the pathos.** For whom do you think the argument was written? Are there any places where the writer attempts to invoke an emotional response? Where do you find appeals to shared values with the audience? You are a member of that audience, so what values do you hold in common with the writer? What values do you not hold in common?

7. **Assess the overall effectiveness of the argument.** How successful is the argument overall? What two or three things are most important in making it effective or ineffective.

8. **Write a draft.**

   - *Introduction:* Describe briefly the argument you are analyzing including where it was published, how long it is, and who wrote it. If the argument is on an issue that is unfamiliar to your readers, you may have to supply some background.

   - *Body:* Use you assessment of the overall effectiveness of the argument as your starting point. Then show how the writer is effective or ineffective using your analysis in steps 2–6. Remember that you don't want to present your analysis as a list. Instead, determine what factors most contribute to the argument's success or lack of success, and make those factors the focus.

- *Conclusion:* Do more than simply summarize what you have said. You might, for example, end with an example that typifies the argument. You don't have to end by either agreeing or disagreeing with the writer. Your task in this assignment is to analyze the strategies the writer uses.

9. Take your draft through the revision steps in chapter 15.

Part II

Some Types of Arguments

Options for Arguments

Imagine that you bought a new car in June and you take some of your friends to your favorite lake over the Fourth of July weekend. You have a great time until, as you are heading home, a drunk driver—a repeat offender—swerves into your lane and totals your new car. You and your friends are lucky not to be hurt, but you're really mad because you believe that repeat offenders should be prevented from driving, even if that means putting them in jail. You also remember going to another state that had sobriety checkpoints on holiday weekends. If such a checkpoint had been at your lake, you would still be driving your new car. You live in a town that encourages citizens to contribute to the local newspaper, and you think you could get a guest editorial published. The question is, how do you want to write the editorial?

You could tell your story about how a repeat drunk driver endangered the lives of you and your friends. You could argue for a national standard definition of driving while intoxicated (DWI) as .08 percent blood alcohol content level instead of the present situation, in which the definition of DWI varies from state to state. You could compare the treatment of drunk drivers in your state with the treatment of drunk drivers in another state. You could cite statistics that drunk drivers killed 16,000 people in 1997, a figure that was down from previous years but still represented a lot of needless deaths. You could evaluate the present enforcement of drunk driving laws as unsuccessful or less than totally successful. You could propose taking vehicles away from repeat drunk drivers and forcing them to serve mandatory sentences. You could argue that your community should have sobriety checkpoints at times when drunk drivers are likely to be on the road.

You're not going to have much space in the newspaper, so you decide to argue for sobriety checkpoints. You know that they are controversial. One of your friends in the car with you said that they are unconstitutional because they involve search without cause. However, after doing some research to find out whether they are defined as legal or illegal, you learn that on June 14, 1990, the U.S. Supreme Court upheld the constitutionality of using checkpoints as a deterrent and enforcement tool against drunk drivers. But you still want to know whether most people would agree with your friend that sobriety checkpoints are an invasion of privacy. You find opinion polls and surveys going back to the 1980s that show 70–80 percent of those polled support sobriety checkpoints. You also realize that you can argue by analogy that security checkpoints for alcohol are similar in many ways to airport security checkpoints that protect the passengers. You decide you will finish by making an argument from consequence. If people who go to the lake with plans to drink a lot know in advance that there will be checkpoints, they will find a designated driver or some other means of safe transportation, and everyone else will also be a little safer.

The point of this example is that people very rarely set out to define something in an argument for the sake of definition, compare for the sake of comparison, or adopt any of the other ways of structuring an argument. Instead, they have a purpose in mind, and they use the kinds of arguments that are discussed in part II—most often in combination—as means to an end. Most arguments use multiple kinds of approaches and multiple sources of good reasons. Proposal arguments in particular often analyze a present situation with definition, causal, and evaluative arguments before advancing a course of future action. The advantage of thinking explicitly about the structure of arguments is that you often find other ways to argue. Sometimes you just need a way to get started writing about complex issues.

An even greater advantage of thinking explicitly about specific kinds of arguments is that they can often give you a sequence for constructing arguments. Take affirmative action policies for granting admission to college as an example. No issue has been more controversial on college campuses during the last ten years. But what exactly does *affirmative action* mean? You know that it is a policy that attempts to address the reality of contemporary inequality based on past injustice. But injustice to whom and by whom? Do all members of minorities, all women, and all people with disabilities have equal claims for redress of past injustices? If not, how do you distinguish among them? And what exactly does affirmative action entail? Do all students who are admitted by affirmative action criteria automatically receive scholarships? Clearly, you need to define affirmative action first before proposing any changes in the policy.

Since affirmative action policies have been around for a few years, next you might investigate how well they have worked. If you view affirmative action as a cause, then what have been its effects? You might find, for example, that the percentage of African-Americans graduating from college dropped from 1991 through 1998 in many states. Furthermore, affirmative action policies have created a backlash attitude among many whites who believe, rightly or wrongly, that they are victims of reverse racism. But you might find that enrollment of minorities at your university has increased substantially since affirmative action policies were instituted. And you might come across a book by the then-presidents of Princeton and Harvard, William G. Bowen and Derek Bok, entitled *The Shape of the River: Long-Term Consequences of Considering Race in College and University Admissions,* which examines the effects of affirmative action policies at twenty-eight of the nation's most select universities. They found that African-American graduates of elite schools were more likely than their white counterparts to earn graduate degrees and to take on civic responsibilities after graduation.

With a definition established and evidence collected, you can move to evaluation. Is the goal of achieving diversity through affirmative action admissions policies a worthy one because white people enjoyed preferential treatment until the last few decades? Or are affirmative action admissions policies bad because they continue the historically bad practice of giving preference to people of certain races and because they cast into the role of victims the people they are trying to help? When you have a definition with evidence and have made an evaluation, you have the groundwork for making a recommendation in the form of a proposal. A proposal argues what "should" or "must" be done in the future.

Even though types of argument are distinguished in part II, they are closely linked parts of a whole. Though each type of argument can stand alone, they always involve multiple aspects. If you are clear in your purpose for your argument and have a good sense of the knowledge and attitudes of the people your argument is aimed toward, then the types of arguments you want to use will often be evident to you.

Chapter 5

Definition Arguments

You don't get very far in an argument without having to do some defining. Even arguments that don't appear at first even to be arguments often require some definitional sorting. In a chapter from *Travels with Lizbeth,* his account of wandering homeless around the country with his dog Lizbeth, Lars Eighner describes how he survived by finding the necessities of daily life in Dumpsters. Before going into detail about the practical art of Dumpster diving, he finds it necessary to define what he does for a living:

> Long before I began Dumpster diving I was impressed with Dumpsters, enough so that I wrote to Merriam-Webster research service to discover what I could about the word *Dumpster.* I learned from them that is is a proprietary word belonging to the Dempster Dumpster company. Since then I have dutifully capitalized the word, although it was lowercased in almost all the citations Merriam-Webster photocopied for me. Dempster's word is too apt. I have never heard these things called anything but Dumpsters. I do not know anyone who knows the generic name for these objects. From time to time I have heard a wino or hobo give some corrupted credit to the original and call them Dipsy Dumpsters.
>
> I began Dumpster diving about a year before I became homeless.
>
> I prefer the word scavenging and use the word scrounging when I mean to be obscure. I have heard people, evidently meaning to be polite, use the word foraging, but I prefer to reserve that word for gathering nuts and berries and such, which I do also according to the season and the opportunity. Dumpster diving seems to me to be a little too cute and, in my case, inaccurate because I lack the athletic ability to lower myself into the Dumpsters as the true divers do, much to their increased profit.

I like the frankness of the word scavenging, which I can hardly think of without picturing a big black snail on an aquarium wall. I live from the refuse of others. I am a scavenger. I think it a sound and honorable niche, although if I could I would naturally prefer to live the comfortable consumer life, perhaps—and only perhaps—as a slightly less wasteful consumer, owing to what I have learned as a scavenger.

This passage might strike you as an odd introduction to a chapter written by a homeless person about how to live off what other people throw away. Eighner starts off by noting that Dumpster is a proprietary name, just like Coca-Cola, owned by a company and must by law be capitalized in print. Then he goes on to distinguish scavenging from *scrounging, foraging,* and *Dumpster diving.* The first question one might ask after reading this passage is, what difference does the definition make? So what if Eighner doesn't actually dive into the dumpster? *Dumpster diving* sounds more interesting than *scavenging.* The alliteration makes it fun to say, just like the official name, Dempster Dumpster. *Scavenging* sounds like a more technical, almost academic term. So why go for the big word when the more colorful *Dumpster diving* is available?

Notice too that while Eighner's writing is fresh and vivid, it also uses some fairly conventional ways of defining. One is to refer to the dictionary and distinguish one's own definition from the dictionary definition. Another is to use the **etymology** of the word being defined, that is, the linguistic derivation of the word. Eighner points out the source of the term *Dumpster* as a way of clarifying it, just as someone defining *the ideal university* might refer to the etymology of the word *university* to achieve his or her aim. (The word *university* derives from the late Latin word *universitas,* meaning "a society or guild," suggesting that the ideal university has something to do with community and with the aggregations of experts that one would associate with medieval guilds. More remotely, the term comes from two Latin words meaning "one" and "turn"—perhaps associated with unifying many sources of knowledge into a whole.)

In the rest of the chapter, Eighner explains how one can live by sorting through Dumpsters. He observes that many people will occasionally find something they want in a Dumpster, but only a select few will regularly eat out of a Dumpster. He gives a lot of street-savvy advice: "Candy . . . is usually safe if it has not drawn ants." He then goes on to differentiate scavengers from *divers,* who tend to collect things out of Dumpsters that they have no use for, and *can scroungers,* who are typically winos looking for enough aluminum to exchange for cheap alcohol. Eighner takes only what he needs. Thus, Eighner creates a definition by classifying kinds of interactions between people and Dumpsters. **Classification** is one of the primary tactics of defining. He thus also distinguishes Dumpster diving from things that are not Dumpster diving, for another way of clarifying a definition is to distinguish what you are talking about from things that are similar. In other words, *distinguish the term you are defining from what it is not.*

Still, it seems hardly worth the bother of defining *scavenging* in relation to *Dumpster diving* and *can scrounging* if Eighner is only trying to differentiate himself from pack rats and winos. He would not go to so much effort unless he were after something more important, a question raised by the book itself: Why would someone this intelligent who writes this well choose to be homeless and live off what he can find in Dumpsters? Eighner answers this question at the end of the chapter:

> Many times in our travels I have lost everything but the clothes I was wearing and Lizbeth. The things I find in Dumpsters, the love letters and rag dolls of so many lives, remind me of this lesson. Now I hardly pick up a thing without envisioning the time I will cast it aside. This I think is a healthy state of mind. . . . I think this is an attitude I share with the very wealthy—we both know there is plenty more where what we have came from. Between us are the rat-race millions who nightly scavenge the cable channels looking for they know not what.
>
> I am sorry for them.

It turns out that Eighner is making an argument with his definition of a scavenger: "that some things are not worth acquiring" and that "mental things are lived longer than . . . material things." He suggests that we are all scavengers, but only a few are wise enough not to get caught up in the possessions they can only temporarily own. So the definition matters a great deal after all. Besides the straight-from-the-pavement philosophy that Eighner offers, he also demonstrates that dictionary definitions don't take us very far when an entire argument hinges on issues of definition.

Not every definition can be made by classifying, explaining etymologies, or saying what something is not; and even when you can define in those ways, the result may not be particularly effective. Take a definition of democracy. It's easy enough to come up with a junior high civics class type of definition where you discuss the kinds of democracy or contrast democracy with dictatorship or monarchy (i.e., show what it is not). It would also be easy to define democracy by offering its etymology; the term comes from the Greek works *demos* ("people") and *krateein* ("to rule")—literally, "rule by the people." But during World War II, when E. B. White, a writer working for *The New Yorker,* was asked to define democracy, here's what he wrote:

> We received a letter from the Writers' War Board the other day asking for a statement on "The Meaning of Democracy." It presumably is our duty to comply with such a request, and it is certainly our pleasure.
>
> Surely the Board knows what democracy is. It is the line that forms on the right. It is the don't in don't shove. It is the hole in the stuffed shirt through which the sawdust slowly trickles; it is the dent in the high hat. Democracy is the recurrent suspicion that more than half of the people are right more than half the time. It is the feeling of privacy in the voting

booths, the feeling of communion in the libraries, the feeling of vitality everywhere. Democracy is the letter to the editor. Democracy is the score at the beginning of the ninth. It is an idea which hasn't been disproved yet, a song the words of which have not gone bad. It's the mustard on the hot dog and the cream in the rationed coffee. Democracy is a request from a War Board, in the middle of the morning in the middle of a war, wanting to know what democracy is.

White made his definition not by etymology or classification but by using **examples.** Instead of writing that democracy has no privileged class, White wrote "It is the line that forms on the right." Instead of saying "democracy includes the right of free speech," White wrote "Democracy is the letter to the editor." White makes these abstract ideas concrete and memorable by using commonplace examples.

Definitions that you don't think much about often turn out to have big consequences for some people. When you get a great job after college and decide to buy a sport utility vehicle (SUV), it might not make much difference to you whether your new SUV is defined as a truck or a car. But it makes a big difference to the manufacturers of SUVs. Trucks have different emissions control standards from cars; therefore, they do not have to meet the same strict pollution standards. The manufacturers will have fewer design headaches and make more money if they can define your new SUV as a truck.

Two very important principles operate when definitions are used in arguments. First, people make definitions that benefit their interests. You learned very early in life the importance of defining actions as accidents. Windows can be broken from being careless, especially when you are tossing a ball against the side of the house, but if it happened by accident, well, accidents just happen (and don't require punishment). Second, most of the time when you are arguing from a definition, your audience will either have a different definition in mind or be unsure of the definition. Your mother or father probably didn't think breaking the window was an accident, so you had to convince mom or dad that you were really being careful but the ball just slipped out of your hand. It's your job to get them to accept your definition.

In a far more famous example, the stakes were much higher. From 1957 until his assassination in April 1968, Martin Luther King, Jr., served as president of the Southern Christian Leadership Conference, an organization of primarily African-American clergymen dedicated to bringing about social change. King, who was a Baptist minister, tried to put into practice Mahatma Gandhi's principles of nonviolence in demonstrations, sit-ins, and marches throughout the South. During Holy Week in 1963, King led demonstrations and a boycott of downtown merchants in Birmingham, Alabama, to end racial segregation at lunch counters and discriminatory hiring practices. On Wednesday, April 10, the city obtained an injunction directing the demonstrations to cease until their legality could be argued in court. But after meditation, King decided, against the advice of his associates, to defy the court order and proceed with the march planned for

Martin Luther King, Jr.

Good Friday morning. On Friday morning, April 12, King and fifty followers were arrested. King was held in solitary confinement until the end of the weekend, allowed neither to see his attorneys nor to call his wife. On the day of his arrest, King read in the newspaper a statement objecting to the demonstrations signed by eight white Birmingham clergymen of Protestant, Catholic, and Jewish faiths, urging that the protests stop and that grievances be settled in the courts.

On Saturday morning, King started writing an eloquent response that addresses the criticisms of the white clergymen, who are one primary audience of his response. But King intended his response to the ministers for widespread publication, and he clearly had in mind a larger readership. The clergymen gave him the occasion to address moderate white leaders in the South as well as religious and educated people across the nation and supporters of the civil rights movement. King begins "Letter from Birmingham Jail" by addressing the ministers as "My Dear Fellow Clergymen," adopting a conciliatory and tactful tone from the outset but at the same time offering strong arguments for the necessity of acting now rather than waiting for change. A critical part of King's argument is justifying not obeying certain laws. The eight white clergymen ask that laws be obeyed until they are changed. Here's how King responds:

> You express a great deal of anxiety over our willingness to break laws. This is certainly a legitimate concern. Since we so diligently urge people to obey the Supreme Court's decision of 1954 outlawing segregation in the public schools, at first glance it may seem rather paradoxical for us consciously to

break laws. One may well ask: "How can you advocate breaking some laws and obeying others?" The answer lies in the fact that there are two types of laws: just and unjust. I would be the first to advocate obeying just laws. One has not only a legal but a moral responsibility to obey just laws. Conversely, one has a moral responsibility to disobey unjust laws. I would agree with St. Augustine that "an unjust law is no law at all."

Now, what is the difference between the two? How does one determine whether a law is just or unjust? A just law is a man-made code that squares with the moral law or the law of God. An unjust law is a code that is out of harmony with the moral law. To put it in the terms of St. Thomas Aquinas: An unjust law is a human law that is not rooted in eternal law and natural law. Any law that uplifts human personality is just. Any law that degrades human personality is unjust. All segregation statutes are unjust because segregation distorts the soul and damages the personality. It gives the segregator a false sense of superiority and the segregated a false sense of inferiority. Segregation, to use the terminology of the Jewish philosopher Martin Buber, substitutes an "I-it" relationship and ends up relegating persons to the status of things. Hence segregation is not only politically, economically and sociologically unsound, it is morally wrong and sinful. Paul Tillich has said that sin is separation. Is not segregation an existential expression of man's tragic separation, his awful estrangement, his terrible sinfulness? Thus it is that I can urge men to obey the 1954 decision of the Supreme Court, for it is morally right; and I can urge them to disobey segregation ordinances, for they are morally wrong.

Martin Luther King's analysis of just and unjust laws is a classic definitional argument. Definitional arguments take this form: *X is a Y if X possesses certain criteria that differentiate it from other similar things in its general class.* According to King, a **just law** possesses the criteria of being consistent with moral law and uplifting human personality. Just as important, King sets out the criteria of **unjust law,** when X is not a Y. Unjust laws have the criteria of being out of harmony with moral law and damaging human personality. The criteria are set out in because clauses: *X is a Y because it has criteria A and B.* The criteria provide the link between X and Y:

$$X \longleftarrow LINK\ (because) \longrightarrow Y$$

1954 Supreme Court   ⟵—— LINK *(because)* ——⟶ just law prohibiting
decision   │   school segregation

                         1) consistent with moral law

                         2) uplifts human personality

The negative can be argued in the same way:

Segregation laws ◄──── LINK (because) ───► unjust law
|
1) inconsistent with moral law
2) degrades human personality

An extended definition like King's is a two-step process. First you have to determine the criteria of Y. Then you have to argue that X has these criteria. If you want to argue that housing prisoners in unheated and non-air-conditioned tents is cruel and unusual punishment, then you have to make exposing prisoners to hot and cold extremes one of the criteria of cruel and unusual punishment. The keys to a definitional argument are getting your audience to accept your criteria and getting your audience to accept that the case in point meets those criteria. King's primary audience was the eight white clergymen; therefore, he used religious criteria and cited Protestant, Catholic, and Jewish theologians as his authority. His second criterion about just laws uplifting the human personality was a less familiar concept than the idea of moral law. King therefore offered a more detailed explanation drawing on the work of Martin Buber.

But King was smart enough to know that not all of his potential readers would put quite so much stock in religious authorities. Therefore, he follows the religious criteria with two other criteria that appeal to definitions of democracy:

Let us consider a more concrete example of just and unjust laws. An unjust law is a code that a numerical or power majority group compels a minority group to obey but does not make binding on itself. This is *difference* made legal. By the same token, a just law is a code that a majority compels a minority to follow and that it is willing to follow itself. This is *sameness* made legal.

Let me give another explanation. A law is unjust if it is inflicted on the minority that, as a result of being denied the right to vote, has no part in enacting or devising the law. Who can say that the legislature of Alabama which set up that state's segregation laws was democratically elected? Throughout Alabama all sorts of devious methods are used to prevent Negroes from becoming registered voters, and there are some counties in which, even though Negroes constitute a majority of the population, not a single Negro is registered. Can any law be enacted under such circumstances be considered democratically structured?

King expands his criteria for just and unjust laws to include four major criteria, and he defines both by classifying and by giving examples.

Segregation law ◄—— *LINK (because)* ——► unjust law

  1) inconsistent with moral law
  2) damages human personality
  3) applies to minority group but not
     majority group that made the law
  4) made by a body that was not
     democratically elected

King's "Letter from Birmingham Jail" draws much of its rhetorical power from its reliance on a variety of arguments that are suited for different readers. An atheist could reject the notion of laws made by God but could still be convinced by the criteria that segregation laws are undemocratic and therefore unjust. King understood that his most powerful arguments were definitional arguments. It is a lesson that is generally true: *Definition arguments are the most powerful arguments.*

To make definitional arguments work, often you must put a lot of effort into identifying and explaining your criteria. You must convince your readers that your criteria are the best ones for what you are defining and that they apply to the case your are arguing. King backs up his assertion that Alabama's segregation laws in 1963 were unjust because the Alabama legislature was not democratically elected by pointing to counties that had African-American majorities but no African-American voters.

 Scott McCloud

Setting the Record Straight

Scott McCloud is the pseudonym of Scott Willard McLeod, who was born in Boston in 1960 and graduated from Syracuse University in 1982. After a short stint in the production department at DC Comics, he quickly became a highly regarded writer and illustrator of comics. His works include the ten-issue series *Zot!* (1984–1985), *Destroy!!* (1986), and the nonfiction *Understanding Comics: The Invisible Art* (Northampton, MA: Tundra, 1993), from which this selection is taken.

Understanding Comics is a brilliant explanation of how comics combine words and pictures to achieve effects that neither words nor pictures can do alone. At the beginning of the book, McCloud finds it necessary to define what comics are and are not before he can begin to analyze the magic of comics. Notice how he has to refine his criteria several times before he has an adequate definition.

IN LESS THAN A *YEAR*, I BECAME *TOTALLY* **OBSESSED** WITH COMICS! I DECIDED TO BECOME A *COMICS ARTIST* IN *10th GRADE* AND BEGAN TO *PRACTICE, PRACTICE,* **PRACTICE!**

I FELT THAT THERE WAS SOMETHING *LURKING* IN COMICS... SOMETHING THAT HAD *NEVER BEEN DONE.*

SOME KIND OF *HIDDEN* **POWER!**

BUT WHENEVER I TRIED TO *EXPLAIN* MY FEELING, I FAILED *MISERABLY.*

COMIC BOOKS?! HA! HA! HA!

BUT IT-- BUT IT'S-- BUH...

SURE, I REALIZED THAT COMIC BOOKS WERE USUALLY *CRUDE, POORLY-DRAWN, SEMILITERATE, CHEAP, DISPOSABLE KIDDIE FARE*--

--BUT--

THEY DON'T *HAVE* TO BE!

THE *PROBLEM* WAS THAT FOR *MOST PEOPLE,* THAT WAS WHAT *"COMIC BOOK"* **MEANT!**

DON'T GIMME THAT *COMIC BOOK* TALK, BARNEY!

IF PEOPLE FAILED TO *UNDERSTAND* COMICS, IT WAS BECAUSE THEY DEFINED WHAT COMICS COULD BE *TOO* **NARROWLY!**

A *PROPER DEFINITION,* IF WE COULD *FIND* ONE, MIGHT GIVE *LIE* TO THE STEREOTYPES--

--AND SHOW THAT THE *POTENTIAL* OF COMICS IS *LIMITLESS* AND *EXCITING!*

THIS IS WHERE OUR JOURNEY *BEGINS.*

[Scott McCloud observes that the problem is finding a definition that is broad enough to cover the many different kinds of comics but not so broad to include anything that is not comics. A comic book is a physical object, but what exactly is *comics*?]

THE ARTFORM--THE *MEDIUM*--KNOWN AS COMICS IS A *VESSEL* WHICH CAN HOLD ANY *NUMBER* OF *IDEAS* AND *IMAGES*.

THE *"CONTENT"* OF THOSE IMAGES AND IDEAS IS, OF COURSE, UP TO *CREATORS*, AND WE ALL HAVE DIFFERENT *TASTES*.

≈GLUG≈
≈GLUG≈

PTUI!!!

≈GAAK≈
≈WHEEEEZ≈
≈KAF! KAF!≈
GLUGH-GGH...

≈ahem≈

THE *TRICK* IS TO NEVER MISTAKE THE *MESSAGE*--

--FOR THE *MESSENGER*.

COMICS

AT ONE TIME OR ANOTHER VIRTUALLY *ALL* THE GREAT MEDIA HAVE RECEIVED *CRITICAL EXAMINATION*, IN AND OF *THEMSELVES*.

WRITTEN WORD

MUSIC

VIDEO

THEATRE

VISUAL ART

FILM

BUT FOR *COMICS*, THIS ATTENTION HAS BEEN *RARE*. *

LET'S SEE IF WE CAN HELP *RECTIFY* THE SITUATION.

*EISNER'S OWN *COMICS AND SEQUENTIAL ART* BEING A HAPPY EXCEPTION.

*JUXTAPOSED= ADJACENT, SIDE-BY-SIDE.
GREAT ART SCHOOL WORD.

Meghann O'Connor

Cheerleading Is a Competitive Sport

Meghann O'Connor cheered for four years on both the varsity basketball squad and the competitive squad at Lewisburg (Pennsylvania) Area High School. Her letter is addressed to the Lewisburg Athletic Director, Jim Cotner, who is in charge of funding and practice times and spaces for the sports teams.

November 11, 1998

Dear Mr. Cotner,

1   Imagine individuals propelling their bodies to flip, twist, and turn in ways one did not know was humanly possible. Picture these individuals being hurled into the air, reaching unfathomable heights, and then being safely caught by their own teammates. Feel the excitement in your own being as you watch strength and skill come together to create an awesome display of athleticism. Realize that these individuals are cheerleaders; their sport, cheerleading.

2   Sport? Cheerleading? Many feel that these two words have no business being grouped in the same sentence together. It is a popular stereotype to consider cheerleaders to be a group of screaming girls in short skirts. Because there is no equipment involved, and there are not any playoffs for the cheerleading squads, many support the opinion that cheerleading is far from a competitive sport. However, in the following paragraphs I will explain why cheerleading should be weighed as a competitive sport and be granted the same rights and respect that other athletic teams receive.

3   There is a myriad of rationale as to why cheerleading should be defined as a competitive sport instead of only an activity. One of the most important reasons is because of the fact that cheerleaders do, in fact, compete. The New Merriam-Webster Dictionary defines competition as a **contest, match; *also:* one's competitors.** Cheerleaders from all over the world compete at various levels in many different kinds of competitions. Who do they compete against? They oppose their competitors, of course. How is it, then, that both schools and organizations claim that cheerleading is not a competitive sport? There are local, state, regional, and national competitions for cheerleading squads of all different levels including, Midget, Junior High, Jayvee, Varsity, Coed, All-Star, and Collegiate. A qualified panel of judges rate the cheerleading squads based on a point system and that determines the winners of these competitions. The squad that finishes with the highest total of points will then be declared the winner. There are many different areas that the judges focus on, including the levels of difficulty, creativity, and ath-

letic ability. This type of judging is similar to the panels of judges found in the Olympic Games, such as figure skating and gymnastics. Both of these activities are viewed as competitive sports, so why can cheerleading not be viewed in the same way? When dealing with the issue of pragmatics, it is only sensible to agree with the fact that cheerleading is a competitive sport. To say that competition is not a huge aspect of cheerleading would be incorrect and inaccurate.

Just as other sporting teams practice and prepare for upcoming contests, so do cheerleaders. Football teams sweat on the field. Basketball players run up and down the court. Swimmers race in the pool. Each of these teams practice day in and day out, making sure that their skills are where they should be and that they are prepared for their upcoming competition. Cheerleaders do the same! They practice, sweat, and strive to be the best they can be, just as other teams do. It would be unfair to discredit the time and energy cheerleaders spend preparing for their upcoming contest. Ethically, it is unjust and discriminatory to not give cheerleaders credit where credit is due. Ultimately, they put an equal amount of time into practicing and getting ready for their "games" as the other sporting teams do.   4

Cheerleaders are talented athletes who work hard. If one has ever taken the time to pause on ESPN long enough to watch a National Cheerleading Competition, one would see the great acts of athleticism that are displayed by squads from all different areas and of all different age groups. Coordination and timing are crucial in synchronizing motions and dance movements. Strength is required for the amazing stunts that are built within the routine. Power and grace are necessities in tumbling from one end of the floor to the other. If these aspects are not considered characteristics of an athlete, then what are the components that make up this type of individual? All athletes compete; therefore, since cheerleaders accomplish athletic feats, it is only evenhanded to consider them competitors.   5

Schools who falter in considering cheerleading a competitive game will lag behind what the rest of society is doing. By failing to label cheerleading as a competitive sport, an example of regressiveness is being exhibited. For instance, many high schools, colleges, and universities around the country already group cheerleading in the same category as all other sports. The University of Michigan and Ohio State University provide scholarships for the cheerleaders that attend their universities. If these prestigious institutions of higher education are able to view cheerleading as the competitive sport it truly is, then why cannot all school districts and colleges do the same? Just because it has traditionally been thought that cheerleading is not a sport doesn't mean that this line of thinking has to continue. It will one day be out of date and against the norm to not classify cheerleading as a competitive sport, so it is imperative to make the crucial change now.   6

In opposition to the argument that cheerleading should be considered a competitive sport, there are a few weak points. One of them is the fact that in   7 cheerleading, a team can not win anything such as a district championship. This argument is entirely false because cheerleaders are always up for awards in their competitions. Not only can they win first, second, or third place, at many different levels, but also they can place in other categories as well such as jumping ability, tumbling ability, and how difficult their stunting is.

8   Another breakable claim against the sport of cheerleading is the statement made by Dr. Shaft, who claims that, "Real athletes don't wear skirts." This assertion is absolutely ridiculous. It should not matter at all what the uniforms of the athletes' look like. That is a frivolous and unnecessary aspect of competition and should have nothing to do with the subject at hand. The fact that Dr. Shaft is drawing attention to the cheerleaders' skirts could also be grounds for sexual discrimination. A skirt is a form of clothing for women, and when Dr. Shaft proclaims cheerleading an invalid sport due to the fact that a skirt is worn, it seems as though he is discrediting women's sports in general.

9   Another justification Dr. Shaft has of why cheerleading should not be a sport is because he feels that there are no coaches involved. This is entirely inaccurate. At every level of cheerleading there are coaches who put in just as much time, effort and energy as any other coach of any other sport. These coaches are paid for their hard work and deserve the respect the coaches of other sporting teams receive.

10   My support of the idea that cheerleading should be a competitive sport remains even after hearing the points made by those who oppose me. Cheerleaders compete and spend just as much time practicing as any other team, they display great feats of athletic talent, and by not considering cheerleading a competitive sport, one is ultimately primitive and tardy in their beliefs, due to the increasing number of organizations that are in accordance with my thoughts. How would one feel if he or she spent endless hours planning and preparing for upcoming competitions to only then be told that they do not even participate in a "real" sport? This individual may become extremely discouraged and confused, which are the last emotions any school wants for its active students. By acknowledging the cheerleading squad as competitors, a great deal of self-esteem could rise from each individual member. This cheerleader would feel that they are equal with the other athletes in their school and feel as if they were finally treated on the same level. This "happiness" could become contagious. First, it may spread throughout the squad, causing them to have a sense of belonging to their school. Their renewed spirit would radiate at matches, games, and competitions, which would benefit those who the cheerleaders were supporting. The added confidence felt when the squad performs would not only be beneficial to them but to their organization and all of its members as well. On the subject of aesthetics, their renewed sense of ease and comfort would shine through during practices and competitions, bringing nothing but positive consequences to considering cheerleaders competitive athletes.

11   Our society has made a great deal of progress when dealing with the issues of equality and fairness. To continue on with this tradition, it would only be fair to view cheerleading as a competitive sport.

Steps in Writing
a Definition Argument

If your instructor asks for a topic proposal, use steps 1–4 to guide you in writing the proposal.

1. **Make a definitional claim on a controversial issue that focuses on a key term.** Use this formula: *X is (or is not) a Y because it has (or does not have) features A, B, and C (or more).*

   Examples:

   - Hate speech (or pornography, literature, films, and so on) is (or is not) free speech protected by the First Amendment because it has (does not have) these features.

   - Hunting (or using animals for cosmetics testing, keeping animals in zoos, wearing furs, and so on) is (or is not) cruelty to animals because it has (or does not have) these features.

   - Doctors should be (should not be) allowed to assist patients to die if they are terminally ill and suffering.

   - Displaying pinup calendars (or jokes, inuendo, rap lyrics, and so on) is (is not) an example of sexual harrassment.

2. **What's at stake in your claim?** If nearly everybody would agree with you, then your claim probably isn't interesting or important. If you can think of people who would disagree, then something is at stake. Who argues the opposite of your claim? Why do they benefit from a different definition?

3. **Make your list of criteria.** Write as many criteria as you can think of. Which criteria are necessary for X to be a Y? Which are not necessary? Which are the most important? Does your case in point meet all the criteria?

4. **Analyze your potential readers.** Who are your primary and secondary readers? How does the definitional claim you are making affect them? How familiar will they be with the issue, concept, or controversy that you're writing about? What are they likely to know and not know? Which criteria are they most likely to accept with little explanation and which will they disagree with? Which criteria will you have to argue for?

5. **Write a draft.**

   Introduction:

   - Set out the issue, concept, or controversy.

- Explain why the definition is important.
- Give the background that your intended readers will need.

Body:

- Set out your criteria and argue for the appropriateness of the criteria.
- Determine whether the criteria apply to the case in point.
- Anticipate where readers might question either your criteria or how they apply to your subject.
- Address opposing points of view by acknowledging how their definitions might differ and by showing why your definition is better.

Conclusion:

- Do more than simply summarize what you have said. You can, for example, go into more detail about what is at stake or the implications of your definition.

6. **Take your draft through the revision steps in chapter 15.**

Chapter 6

Causal Arguments

Why has binge drinking greatly increased among college students over the last ten years while the overall percentage of students who drink has remained about the same? Why do some countries have long histories of people of different religious and ethnic backgrounds living together in peace while in other countries people regularly kill each other because of religious and ethnic differences? Why do owners of professional sports teams complain about losing money and then offer multimillion-dollar salaries not only to stars but even to mediocre players? Why is the United States the only major industrialized country not to have a system of national health care? Why do universities in the United States have general education requirements while universities in most of the rest of the world do not, allowing students to take courses only in their major and minor fields? Why have the death rates for some kinds of cancer gone way up in this country (for example, deaths from lung cancer in women increased 438 percent from 1962 to 1992) while the rates for other kinds of cancer went down (deaths from cancer of the cervix dropped 67 percent during the same period)? If meteorologists now have massive amounts of satellite data and supercomputers to crunch the numbers for long-range weather forecasting, why haven't they become much more reliable than the *Farmer's Almanac*?

Besides big questions like the ones above, you also are confronted with little questions of causation in your everyday life. Why did the driver who passed you on a blind curve risk his life to get one car ahead at the next traffic light? Why is it hard to recognize people you know when you run into them unexpectedly in an unfamiliar setting? Why do nearly all kids want the same toy each Christmas, forcing their parents to stand in line for hours to buy them?

Why does your mother or father spend an extra hour plus the extra gas driving to a grocery store across town just to save a few pennies on one or two items on sale? Why do some people get upset about animals that are killed for medical research but still eat meat and wear leather clothing? Why do some of your friends keep going to horror films when they can hardly sit through them and have nightmares afterward?

Life is full of big and little mysteries, and people spend a lot of time speculating about the causes. Most of the time, however, they don't take the time to analyze in depth what causes a controversial trend, event, or phenomenon. But before and after you graduate, you likely will have to write causal arguments that require in-depth analysis. In a professional career you will have to make many detailed causal analyses: Why did a retail business fail when it seemed to have an ideal location? What causes cost overruns in the development of a new product? What causes people in some circumstances to prefer public transportation over driving? What causes unnecessary slowdowns in a local computer network? Answering any of these questions requires making a causal argument, which takes a classic form: *X causes (or does not cause) Y.* The causal claim is at the center of a causal argument. Therefore, to get started on a causal argument, you need to propose one or more causes.

The big problem with causal arguments is that any topic worth writing about is likely to be complex. Identifying causes usually isn't easy. The philosopher John Stuart Mill recognized this problem long ago and devised four methods for finding causes:

1. *The Common Factor Method.* When the cause-and-effect relationship occurs more than once, look for something in common in the events and circumstances of each effect; any common factor could be the cause. Scientists have used this method to explain how seemingly different phenomena are associated. There were a variety of explanations of fire until, in the 1700s, Joseph Priestley in England and Antoine Lavoisier in France discovered that oxygen was a separate element and that burning was caused by oxidation.

2. *The Single Difference Method.* This method works only when there are at least two similar situations, one that leads to an effect and one that does not. Look for something that was missing in one case and present in another—the single difference. The writer assumes that if everything is substantially alike in both cases, then the single difference is the (or a) cause. At the Battle of Midway in 1942, the major naval battle of World War II in the Pacific, the Japanese Navy had a four-to-one advantage over the U.S. Navy. Both fleets were commanded by competent, experienced leaders. But the U.S. commander, Admiral Nimitz, had a superior advantage in intelligence, which proved to be decisive.

3. *Concomitant Variation.* This tongue twister is another favorite method of scientists. If an investigator finds that a possible cause and a possible effect have a similar pattern of variation, then one can suspect that a relationship exists. For example, scientists noticed that peaks in the eleven-year sunspot cycle have predictable effects on high-frequency radio transmission on the earth.

4. *Process of Elimination.* Many possible causes can be proposed for most trends and events. If you are a careful investigator, you have to consider all that you can think of and eliminate the ones that cannot be causes.

For an example of how these methods might work for you, suppose you want to research the causes of the increase in legalized lotteries in the United States. You might discover that lotteries go back to colonial times. Harvard and Yale have been long-time rivals in football, but the schools' rivalry goes back much further. Both ran lotteries before the Revolutionary War! In 1747, the Connecticut legislature voted to allow Yale to conduct a lottery to raise money to build dormitories, and in 1765, the Massachusetts legislature gave Harvard permission for a lottery. Lotteries were common before and after the American Revolution, but they eventually ran into trouble because they were run by private companies that occasionally took off with the money without paying off the winners. After 1840, laws against lotteries were passed, but they came back after the Civil War in the South. The defeated states of the Confederacy needed money to rebuild the bridges, buildings, and schools that had been destroyed in the Civil War, and they turned to selling lottery tickets throughout the nation, tickets which, perhaps ironically, were very popular in the North. Once again, the lotteries were run by private companies, and scandals eventually led to their banning.

In 1964, the voters in New Hampshire approved a lottery as a means of funding education in preference to an income tax or sales tax. Soon other northeastern states followed this lead, establishing lotteries with the reasoning that if people are going to gamble, the money should remain at home. During the 1980s, other states approved not only lotteries but also other forms of state-run gambling such as keno and video poker. By 1993, only Hawaii and Utah had no legalized gambling of any kind.

If you are analyzing the causes of the spread of legalized gambling, you might use the **common factor method** to investigate what current lotteries have in common with earlier lotteries. That factor is easy to identify: It's economic. The early colonies and later the states have turned again and again to lotteries as a way of raising money that avoids unpopular tax increases. But why have lotteries spread so quickly and seemingly become so permanent since 1964, when before that, they were used only sporadically and were eventually banned? The **single difference method** points us to the major difference between the lotteries of today and those of previous eras: Lotteries in the past were run by private companies, and inevitably someone took off with the money instead of paying it out. Today's lotteries are owned and operated by state agencies or else contracted under state control, and while they are not immune to scandals, they are much more closely monitored than lotteries were in the past.

The controversies over legal gambling now focus on casinos. In 1988, Congress passed the Indian Gaming Regulatory Act, which started a new era of casino gambling in the United States. The Foxwood Casino in Connecticut, owned by the Pequot tribe, became a huge money maker—with over $800 million wagered in 1995—and its revenues exceeded those of the Connecticut lottery. Other tribes and other states were quick to cash in on casino gambling. Iowa legalized riverboat gambling in 1989, followed shortly by Louisiana, Illinois, Indiana, Mississippi, and Missouri. As with lotteries, the primary justification for approving casino gambling has been economic. States have been forced to fund various programs that the federal government used to pay for. Especially in states where lottery revenues had begun to sag, legislatures and voters turned to casinos to make up the difference.

Casinos, however, have been harder to sell to voters than lotteries. For many voters, casinos are a NIMBY ("not in my back yard") issue. They may believe that people should have the right to gamble, but they don't want a casino in their town. Casino proponents have tried to overcome these objections by arguing that casinos bring added tourist dollars, benefiting the community as a whole. Opponents argue the opposite: that people who go to casinos spend their money on gambling and not on tourist attractions. The cause-and-effect benefit of casinos to community businesses can be examined by **concomitant variation.** Casino supporters argue that people who come to gamble spend a lot of money elsewhere. Opponents of casinos claim that people who come for gambling don't want to spend money elsewhere. Furthermore, they point out that gambling represents another entertainment option for people within easy driving distance and can hurt area businesses such as restaurants, amusement parks, and bowling alleys. So far, the record has been mixed, some businesses being helped and others being hurt when casinos are built nearby.

Many trends don't have causes as obvious as the spread of legalized gambling. One such trend is the redistribution of wealth in the United States since 1973. From 1950 to 1973, businesses in the United States grew by 90 percent, and the resulting wealth benefited all income classes. Since 1973, however, almost all the growth in wealth has gone to people at the top of the economic ladder. During the 1980s, the incomes of the richest 1 percent of the population grew by 62.9 percent, and the incomes of the bottom 60 percent actually declined. According to *U.S. News and World Report,* in 1996, the richest 1 percent of Americans, with minimum assets of $2.3 million per family, hold 42 percent of all marketable assets, exerting unprecedented influence on the economy. Often-cited statistics are those for the pay of top executives. In 1973–1975, chief executive officers of major corporations made 41 times the pay of the average worker in that corporation. By 1987–1989, the average CEO made 141 times the pay of the average worker; and by 1992–1994, the compensation for the average CEO increased to 225 times that of the average worker.

The increasing divide between the rich and the rest of the people in the United States is well documented, but economists don't agree about the reasons why the U.S. middle class has been increasingly divided into those who are very well off and those who are struggling to keep their heads above water. The explanations that have been given include the tax cuts of 1986, the decline of labor unions, the downsizing of corporations, the increase in corporate mergers, automation, competition from low-wage nations, and simple greed. Although each of these may be a contributing cause, there must be other causes too.

The **process of elimination** method can be a useful tool when several possible causes are involved. The shift in income to the wealthy started before the tax cuts of 1986, so the tax cuts cannot be the only cause. Low-wage nations now produce cheap exports, but the sectors of the U.S. economy that compete directly with low-wage nations make up a small slice of the total pie (about 2 percent). And it's hard to explain why people might be greedier now than in earlier decades; greed has always been a human trait.

In a book published in 1995 entitled *The Winner-Take-All Society,* Robert H. Frank and Phillip J. Cook argue that changes in attitudes help to account for the shifts in wealth since 1973. In an article summarizing their book, published in *Across the Board* (33:5 [May 1996]: 4), they describe what they mean by the winner-take-all society:

> Our claim is that growing income inequality stems from the growing importance of what we call "winner-take-all markets"—markets in which small differences in performance give rise to enormous differences in economic reward. Long familiar in entertainment, sports, and the arts, these markets have increasingly permeated law, journalism, consulting, medicine, investment banking, corporate management, publishing, design, fashion, even the hallowed halls of academe.
>
> An economist under the influence of the human-capital metaphor might ask: Why not save money by hiring two mediocre people to fill an important position instead of paying the exorbitant salary required to attract the best? Although that sort of substitution might work with physical capital, it does not necessarily work with human capital. Two average surgeons or CEOs or novelists or quarterbacks are often a poor substitute for a single gifted one.
>
> The result is that for positions for which additional talent has great value to the employer or the marketplace, there is no reason to expect that the market will compensate individuals in proportion to their human capital. For

these positions—ones that confer the greatest leverage or "amplification" of human talent—small increments of talent have great value and may be greatly rewarded as a result of the normal competitive market process. This insight lies at the core of our alternative explanation of growing inequality.

A winner-take-all market is one in which reward depends on relative, not absolute, performance. Whereas a farmer's pay depends on the absolute amount of wheat he produces and not on how that compares with the amounts produced by other farmers, a software developer's pay depends largely on her performance ranking. In the market for personal income-tax software, for instance, the market reaches quick consensus on which among the scores or even hundreds of competing programs is the most comprehensive and user-friendly. And although the best program may be only slightly better than its nearest rival, their developers' incomes may differ a thousandfold.

Frank and Cook find that technology has accelerated the trend toward heaping rewards on those who are judged best in a particular arena. In the 1800s, for example, a top tenor in a major city such as London might have commanded a salary many times above that of other singers, but the impact of the tenor was limited by the fact that only those who could hear him live could appreciate his talent. Today, every tenor in the world competes with Luciano Pavarotti because opera fans everywhere can buy Pavarotti's CDs. This worldwide fan base translates into big money. In another example, it might not surprise you that in 1992, Michael Jordan reportedly received $20 million for promoting Nike shoes, an amount that was greater than the combined annual payrolls for all six factories in Indonesia that made the shoes. What is new is how other professions have become more like sports and entertainment.

The Winner-Take-All Society is a model of causal analysis that uses the **process of elimination** method. The authors

- describe and document a trend,
- set out the causes that have been previously offered and show why together they are inadequate to explain the trend, and then
- present a new cause, explaining how the new cause works in concert with those that have been identified.

But it's not enough just to identify causes. They must be connected to effects. For trends in progress, such as the growing divide between the rich and the rest in the United States, the effects must be carefully explored to learn about what might lie ahead. Frank and Cook believe that the winner-take-all attitude is detrimental for the nation's future because, like high school basketball players who expect to become the next Michael Jordan, many people entering college or graduate school grossly overestimate their prospects for huge success and select their future careers accordingly:

> The lure of the top prizes in winner-take-all markets has also steered many of our most able graduates toward career choices that make little sense for them as individuals and still less sense for the nation as a whole. In increasing numbers, our best and brightest graduates pursue top positions in law, finance, consulting, and other overcrowded arenas, in the process forsaking careers in engineering, manufacturing, civil service, teaching, and other occupations in which an infusion of additional talent would yield greater benefit to society.
>
> One study estimated, for example, that whereas a doubling of enrollments in engineering would cause the growth rate of the GDP to rise by half a percentage point, a doubling of enrollments in law would actually cause a decline of three-tenths of a point. Yet the number of new lawyers admitted to the bar each year more than doubled between 1970 and 1990, a period during which the average standardized test scores of new public-school teachers fell dramatically.
>
> One might hope that such imbalances would fade as wages are bid up in under-served markets and driven down in overcrowded ones, and indeed there have been recent indications of a decline in the number of law-school applicants. For two reasons, however, such adjustments are destined to fall short.
>
> The first is an informational problem. An intelligent decision about whether to pit one's own skills against a largely unknown field of adversaries obviously requires a well-informed estimate of the odds of winning. Yet people's assessments about these odds are notoriously inaccurate. Survey evidence shows, for example, that some 80 percent of us think we are better-than-average drivers and that more than 90 percent of workers consider themselves more productive than their average colleague. Psychologists call this the "Lake Wobegon Effect," and its importance for present purposes is that it leads people to overestimate their odds of landing a superstar position. Indeed, overconfidence is likely to be especially strong in the realm of career choice, because the biggest winners are so conspicuous. The seven-figure NBA stars appear on television several times each week, whereas the many thousands who fail to make the league attract little notice.
>
> The second reason for persistent overcrowding in winner-take-all markets is a structural problem that economists call "the tragedy of the commons." This same problem helps explain why we see too many prospectors for gold. In the initial stages of exploiting a newly discovered field of gold, the presence of additional prospectors may significantly increase the total amount of gold that is found. Beyond some point, however, additional

prospectors contribute very little. Thus, the gold found by a newcomer to a crowded gold field is largely gold that would have been found by others.

This short example illustrates why causal arguments for any significant trend that involves people almost necessarily have to be complex. Most people don't quit their day job expecting to hit it big in the movies, the record business, or professional athletics, yet people do select fields such as law that have become in many ways like entertainment, with a few big winners and the rest just getting by. Frank and Cook point to the "Lake Wobegon Effect" (named for Garrison Keillor's fictional town where "all children are above average") to give an explanation of why people are realistic about their chances in some situations and not in others. Effective causal arguments move beyond the obvious to get at underlying causes. The immediate cause of the growing income inequality in the United States is that people at the top make a lot more now than they did twenty-five years ago while people in the middle make the same and people at the bottom make less. Those causes are obvious to anyone who has looked at the numbers. What isn't obvious is why those changes occurred.

Another trend that has drawn much commentary is the increase in eating disorders among young Americans between the ages of fifteen and thirty-five. This increase is no surprise, since we live in a society that is obsessed with thinness as sign of success. Nearly everyone at some time is dissatisfied with his or her weight, body shape, or self-image. But again the question is not so much why this trend exists at all, because throughout the history of the United States, people have been concerned about their looks. The issue is why this concern has led to rapidly rising numbers of people with eating disorders. An estimated two million men and women suffer from anorexia nervosa, bulimia, and binge eating disorder.

Anorexia nervosa is a frequent illness among women in college and is on the rise among college-age men. Increasingly younger girls and boys suffer from anorexia, down to ages ten and eleven. In severe cases, people die from starvation. People who suffer from anorexia are emaciated but still perceive themselves as fat and refuse to eat. The causes of anorexia are not clear, but there's little doubt that the equation of physical attractiveness with thinness in our culture contributes to the problem. In 1993, the U.S. Department of Health and Human Services found that 70 percent of normal-weight women want to be thinner and 23 percent of underweight women want to be thinner still.

Some physicians, therapists, and even the popular media blame images of women glamorized in the media as causing the problem. *People* ran a cover story with the headline "Too Fat? Too Thin? How Media Images of Celebrities Teach Kids to Hate Their Bodies" (June 3, 1996). The story pointed to the media treatment of Alicia Silverstone, who as a teenager starred in *The Crush* and *Clueless* and at age nineteen attended the 1996 Academy Awards ceremony having gained five or ten pounds. For her sin of being a normal woman who adds a few pounds during her college years, Silverstone was ridiculed in the tabloid press, which, "noting Silverstone's role in the next *Batman* sequel, blared out lines like 'Batman and Fatgirl' and 'Look Out Batman! Here Comes Buttgirl!' and *Entertainment Weekly* sniped that Alicia was 'more *Babe* than babe.' " Her director in *Batman,* outraged by the mean-spirited treatment of Silverstone, asked, "What did this child do? Have a couple of pizzas?"

A target of criticism for promoting an unhealthy body image in the 1990s was the then skin-and-bones supermodel Kate Moss, who was referred to as "the Waif." *People* ran a story about Kate Moss in 1993 with the headline "Is a dangerous message being sent to weight-obsessed teens?" Certainly, the fashion industry, the movie industry, and images in the popular media influence how we perceive beauty, but it's quite a jump to argue that images of ultrathin models cause anorexia. To argue for direct causation would suggest that people have no power to resist the media or advertising and that we're all media dupes. If it were this simple, then all advertising campaigns would succeed in using images to sell whatever they were pitching. But advertisers know that it's not so simple. People in the United States, especially younger people, are overexposed to advertising and cynical about it. They encounter images that carry an oversupply of meanings from having been seen before in different contexts. Therefore, explaining the causal relationship of images to cultural trends such as the increase in the number of young people who suffer from anorexia is necessarily complex.

Susan Bordo, a philosophy professor at the University of Kentucky, has explored with her students the range of meanings people attach to the slenderness ideal. In her book *Twilight Zones,* she writes about how her students perceive Kate Moss:

> When we admire an image, a kind of recognition beyond a mere passive imprinting takes place. We recognize, consciously or unconsciously, that the image carries values and qualities that "hit a nerve" and are not easy to resist. Their power, however, derives from the culture that has generated them and resides not merely "in" the images but in the psyche of the viewer too. I recently asked my students why they found Kate Moss so appealing. It took them a while to get past 'She's so thin! And so beautiful!' I wanted to know what made her beautiful in their eyes and how her thinness figured into that. Once they began to talk in nonphysical terms, certain themes emerged again and again: She's so detached. So above it all. She looks like she doesn't need anything or anyone. She's in a world of her own, untouchable. Invulnerable. One of my students, who had been struggling unsuccessfully with her bulimia all semester, nearly moved me to tears with her wistful interpretation. 'She looks so cool,' she whispered longingly. 'Not so needy, like me.'
>
> These are not mere projections on the part of my students. The unfocused princess of indifference whom Kate Moss impersonates in fashion photos is also part of the "real" persona created by Moss and those who market her. Her detachment is always emphasized (and glamorized).

"I like doing the [fashion] shows," she told *People* magazine, "but I don't need to at all." The quotation was the apt caption for an image of slouching, blank-faced Moss, cigarette in hand, in a dazed world of her own. Worries about lung cancer? It wouldn't be chic to be concerned about one's health. And although many models admit to smoking in order to hold their weight down, Moss denies that she ever frets over her diet. "It's kind of boring for me to have to eat," she said in an *Esquire* interview. . . .

To the degree that a "message" is being sent by her body, it is not only or primarily about the desirability or attractiveness of being thin. Rather, thinness is a visual code that speaks to young women about the power of being aloof rather than desirous, cool rather than hot, blasé rather than passionate, and self-contained rather than needy. They don't learn to value these qualities, of course, from the images alone.

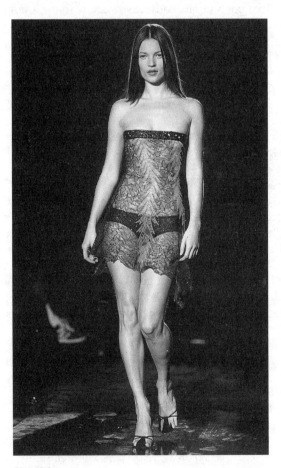

Kate Moss

Bordo's causal argument avoids making a single factor responsible for a complex trend. She discusses how a major cultural figure such as Kate Moss can send a number of different messages. Insightful causal analyses of human trends and events avoid oversimplification by not relying on only one direct cause but instead showing how that cause arises from another cause or works in combination with other causes. Indeed, Frank and Cook have been criticized for placing too much emphasis on the winner-take-all hypothesis.

Another common pitfall in causal arguments that use statistics is mistaking correlation for causation. For example, the FBI reported that criminal victimization rates in the United States in 1995 dropped 13 percent for personal crimes and 12.4 percent for property crimes, the largest decreases ever. During that same year, the nation's prison and jail populations reached a record high of 1,085,000 and 507,000 inmates, respectively. The easy inference is that putting more people behind bars lowers the crime rate, but there are plenty of examples to the contrary. The drop in crime rates in the 1990s remains quite difficult to explain. Others have argued that the decline in SAT Verbal scores during the late 1960s and 1970s reflected a decline in literacy caused by an increase in television viewing. But the fact that the number of people who took the SAT during the 1970s greatly increased suggests that there was no actual decline in literacy but only a great expansion in the population that wanted to go to college.

 *Douglas Rushkoff*

Channel Surfing

Princeton graduate Douglas Rushkoff's (1961–) first book, *Free Rides: How to Get High without Drugs,* was published in 1991, but his career took off in 1994 with the publication of *Cyberia: Life in the Trenches of Hyperspace* and *Media Virus!: Hidden Agendas in Popular Culture.* Rushkoff suddenly became a major interpreter of a technology-inspired culture, a position that put him in high demand as a media consultant. In *Coercion: Why We Listen to What They Say* (1999), Rushkoff investigates how people are subjected to increasingly sophisticated and invisible methods of control. He published his first novel, *Ecstasy Club,* in 1997. In an interview in the online magazine *Spike,* Rushkoff called himself a member of the "hinge" generation, saying, "I'm a translator of what's going on." What's going on in Rushkoff's eyes is largely good. He told the interviewer, "I think our technological progress is our moral progress."

In his recent book, *Playing the Future: How Kids' Culture Can Teach Us to Thrive in an Age of Chaos,* from which this selection is taken, Rushkoff examines the effects on children of growing up with remote controls, computers, video games, and other electronic toys. Channel surfing on television and, more recently, the World Wide Web has been attacked for undermining linear thinking and diminishing children's attention span. Rushkoff counters this causal analysis with his own causal argument. He maintains that children are better prepared to enter new and rapidly changing environments because they can react more quickly, process information faster, and take a wider perspective. See whether you agree with his challenging argument.

1   Just like ocean surfing, the habitual channel surfing of our TV-fixated youth is as lamented by parents as it is valuable to us all as an example of thriving on chaos. Just like the ocean or the man-made cityscape, the modem mediaspace, too, is a chaotic system, and subject to the same laws of dynamics. Better yet, for this same reason the media is surfable. This sport of couch potatoes offers both a lesson in coping with discontinuity and a possible challenge to the status-quo-promoting (and evolution-resisting) linearity of our traditional media.

2   The old style of viewing television involved commitment. We would decide which program we were going to watch, turn the dial on the television set to the network (one of three) for the evening, and passively absorb our programming. And it wasn't called "programming" for nothing. We were a captive audience, relatively unable or at least uninspired to make choices while we watched. We "behaved" like good little school children, and when Walter Cronkite ended his television news broadcasts each evening with a reassuring "And that's the way it is," we had no reason to question him. The TV was our parent and teacher. To shut it off or change the channel in the middle of a program was a deliberate statement of dissatisfaction.

3   With the knowledge that they had a captive audience, programmers and their sponsors were free to persuade us by using linear arguments—by telling stories. Time was on their side, and the instantaneous visual language of the image was still only in its infancy. The highly developed but somewhat infantilizing techniques of public relations were perfected during this era of linear programming, and they all depended on narrative storytelling. Like fables, PR campaigns follow a line of reasoning: (1) here is something you care about; (2) here is a terrible threat to that something; and (3) here is the way to annihilate that threat. We came to America and, with God's help, created a paradise, but the evil, atheist Russians decided to take over the world. They are about to invade—what can we do? Build weapons now.

4   As viewers, we grew used to "staying tuned" for the answers to the world's problems, and by the time the broadcast was over, we knew how to feel, buy, fight, or vote. As children of linear reasoning, we valued the attention span and the ability to draw the correct conclusions from the data presented to us. Of course, we had the announcer to tell us whether our conclusions were in fact correct, and quiz shows with which to practice. It never occurred to us that the shows could be rigged or that the announcer could be just plain wrong.

The introduction of the remote control altered our relationship to the tube   5
forever. We no longer had to make the grand gesture of walking up to the television set and physically rotating a dial in the real, material world in order to change the picture on the screen. (Television viewers of the 1940s and 1950s were further inhibited by their memories of the days of radio, where tuning in a new station was an act that required even greater effort.) Thanks to the remote, a simple channel change no longer signifies rebellion. A tiny motion of the viewer's finger wipes Cronkite's successor's image from the screen, along with his message. The linear argument is broken, and a gap is introduced—for the viewer's weapon against programming is discontinuity.

Dramatic television was even more dependent on linearity for its effective-   6
ness as a persuader and marketer. As Aristotle well understood, drama works by creating and then releasing tension. The structure of such a story is like an arc, rising to a turning point, and then falling again. A successful teleplay will follow a formula analogous to the newscast: (1) create a character we like; (2) put that character in peril; and (3) rescue him. The object of the game, for the programmer, is to generate as much tension as possible—make the situation so horrifically unresolvable that the audience begs for relief. To raise tension, the television dramatist needs to create a pressure cooker. Within this closed system, the captivated audience is led up a linear thread and eventually over the arc of the story. (The occasional commercial break, though a potential lapse in continuity, is bridged as best as possible with an interim cliffhanger. Ideally, the cliffhanger leaves the viewer in wideeyed, anxious suspension, all the more ready to absorb the advertising content.)

In linear drama or news, the audience is only willing to put up with the   7
increase in tension if it knows it is going to be rewarded with a satisfactory conclusion. With the knowledge that they are going to be rescued, viewers allow themselves to be led into great confusion. The more desperate the story gets, the more preposterous the conclusion is allowed to get. If we are driven into tremendous tension, we will accept almost any relief. If the entire Athenian civilization is at risk, then Athena herself can fly in, deus ex machina style, and save the day. If innocent babies are being yanked from their incubators and allowed to die, then an American invasion of Iraq feels justified. We have been brought into tension, and we demand relief. The perpetrators must be identified, the guilty punished, and the innocent somehow bettered by the whole experience. From Aesop's fables to *Dragnet,* whoever gave us relief from the tension was allowed to tell us the moral of the story.

Television, for a time, perpetuated this linear, moralistic worldview—a view   8
sponsored by those who stood to gain most from maintaining public faith in traditional values and allegiances. By the 1960s, however, a few events conspired to change the tube's role from an enforcer of linearity to a promoter of chaos. The Kennedy assassination, for one, cannot be underestimated for its long-term effect on the media public. Culturally, of course, the assassination marked a lapse in the

continuity of our government. Yes, according to protocol Lyndon Johnson assumed his rightful place in the Oval Office, but a term we had collectively set in motion with our votes had been abruptly ended. More insidiously corrosive to our sense of continuity was the way our media deconstructed the moment-to-moment reality of the assassination and its aftermath.

9   The Zapruder film, a watershed event in American television paralleled only by the Rodney King tape and maybe O. J. Simpson's Bronco ride, took an already discontinuous event and broke it down further. We watched, frame by frame, as our president's head flung back, and his wife sprang out of her seat onto the trunk of the limo. Rather than providing us with answers, our news media unintentionally flooded us with questions. Was Jackie escaping the car? Was she reaching for a piece of her husband's brain? Was there only one gunman? Two? A conspiracy? Making matters worse, when the suspected gunman was finally being escorted to his formal and customary arraignment, he was murdered, too! We would get no satisfactory ending. No matter how much tension was generated, relief was nowhere in sight. The discontinuous style in which the information was presented to us, coupled with the overwhelming discontinuity of the event itself, altered our relationship to the image on the set and our image of reality.

10   There were three cultural reactions to this tear in linear reality. Some chose to ignore it completely. These people convinced themselves that even though the Kennedy assassination appeared utterly discontinuous, it was actually a simple and linear event. The assassin got killed a little early, Jackie panicked a bit, the camera footage was blurry, and FBI physicists figured out how a bullet can zigzag back and forth. In the long term this was, perhaps, the most painful path to take. The resignation of Nixon, the end of the cold war, and the development of a postmodern culture has left these people in a state of unimaginably irreconcilable cognitive dissonance. The second reaction was to try to create connections between discontinuous events, even when there were none. These were the conspiracy theorists (we'll be seeing a lot of them in later chapters) who were compelled to create an antiauthoritarian but nonetheless linear explanation for what had happened to their president, nation, and values.

11   The conspiracy theorists were the baby-boomers, who brought us some tremendously positive social transformation. But their problem was that they still believed in the power of authority and value of static moral templates. They staged antiwar protests, civil rights demonstrations, and hippy-yippy revolutions because they saw the incumbent regime's templates as wrong and their own as right. They regarded the president and their teachers as powerful parent figures who needed to be revolted against. Their peculiar style of revolution was to revise the way that lines of continuity were being drawn among inherently discontinuous events. It's like a game of connect the dots. The young baby-boomers wanted to change the numbers on the dots, so that the lines would be drawn in a different order and the picture would come out different. When this form of conspiracy theory works, it yields Woodward and Bernstein's Watergate investigation.

When it seeps out to popular culture, it yields an Oliver Stone movie. All this, again, in reaction to the first incursion of media discontinuity into mainstream social awareness.

But there was a third reaction to the Kennedy crisis—the reaction of children [12] growing up with this assassination as their first presidential memory. To anyone under thirty-five, presidents are, by definition, people who get assassinated. To them, the Zapruder film is a media classic. This generation does not turn to the media for answers, but for questions. They understand that to subject a seemingly linear event to media scrutiny is to break that event down into its component, frame-by-frame segments. It loses its original meaning—or at least the meaning that may have originally been intended. For this younger audience, discontinuous media is not the exception, it is the rule. As a result, they have adopted a social philosophy very different from their predecessors'. They do not work to recombine and reduce the seemingly endless stream of media bits into coherent, unified pictures, and they no longer believe in hard-and-fast answers to the world's problems.

They are comfortable in the disassembled mediascape because they are [13] armed; the first weapon to appear in their arsenal was the remote control. As the media became increasingly chaotic, the remote emerged as the surfboard on which the armchair media analyst could come to reckon with any future attempts to program him back into linearity. The minute he felt the hypnotic pull of story or propaganda, he could impose discontinuity onto the flow by changing the channel. At first, this served as a simple negation of the broadcast reality. Whenever a newscaster says something irritating to the viewer's sensibility, even an Archie Bunker can curse at the screen and change the channel in disgust. Eventually, though, in order to maintain their viewerships, the media dispensed with linearity altogether, and devised new styles and formats to appeal to the channel surfer. They didn't realize what they were doing.

The media's own form of discontinuity, the edit points linking one shot to another, have been around since the films of D. W. Griffith. When film editing was first introduced, moviehouse audiences were baffled by a visual language they did not yet understand. When a film would show a house burning down, then cut to a reaction shot of the homeowner standing outside, the audience had no idea what they were supposed to be looking at. Every edit point was experienced as a break in continuity—a lie. The art of moviemaking was learning how to create stories so compelling and geographies so ordered that the audience could leap the gaps created by each cut. By slowly developing a series of conventions like size of shot, axis, eye-lines, and frame composition, the moviemakers created a language called "film grammar." Anyone who can watch a film and understand what's going on has learned this language of the edited moving image.

Over time and, eventually, to make television more compelling to the remote [15] control viewer, television editors sliced and diced their programming into more rapid-fire segments. Although any film textbook will explain that an audience cannot comprehend a shot with a duration of less than two seconds, and that such rapid-fire editing should be used only for effect, two-second shots and even one-second reactions soon became the norm on television. Like the drips of water coming out of a faucet at an increasing rate, once the speed of edits reached a critical frequency, the linear story just broke apart as the programs reached turbulence. The media chaos this turbulence generated was called MTV.

16   Music television is a celebration of the gaps. The component segments of a rock video fly by too quickly to be comprehended on an individual basis. MTV must be thrashed as if on a skateboard. The texture of the programming is more important than the content. The rapidity of edits produces a new sort of changing image. Just as a regular film is made up of thousands of frames running by so quickly that it creates the illusion of a single moving image, MTV juxtaposes its moving images so quickly and so disjointedly that it creates another level of imagery. This style of rough, disjointed media was precisely the landscape preferred by the channel surfer. It made coercion through traditional, narrative programming techniques impossible, and required that a new language—a language of chaos—be developed. The kids watching MTV learned to speak it like natives.

17   Advertisers had the greatest stake in adopting this language quickly into their repertoire. From watching MTV videos, they learned to make commercials with rapid cuts, screens within screens, and, most important, no linear story. Their products couldn't look like conclusions to a set of propositions but instead needed to nestle themselves within the gaps of an intentionally disjointed set of words and images. Their rapid and disjointed editing style was soon adopted by primetime programmers as well, who developed shows like *Hard Copy, COPS,* and eventually *ER* and *NYPD Blue* (their very titles evoke discontinuity). Now the viewer with his remote was no longer the only one imposing nonlinearity onto television programming. Like a self-deprecating Borscht Belt comedian, the shows were doing it to themselves.

18   It can be argued that these postmodern qualities of television are nothing new. True, cubists, dadaists, situationists, and others have long understood the advantages of cut-and-paste techniques and employed them in their work. Writers from James Joyce to William Burroughs used cut-up language and juxtaposed samples in order to create confusion, resonance, and persuasion in their texts. But never before has such dislocated imagery been in the mainstream. These formerly ingeniously unconventional methods of expression are now absolutely conventional.

19   A few other innovations conspired, so to speak, to make the mediaspace into a full-fledged dynamical system. Cable television, for one, increased the number of channels in the home from about six to over fifty. The number of gaps to be surfed increased accordingly, transforming the mediaspace from a set of streams into an ocean break worthy of championship tube runs. Even more significant, home media like camcorders, video decks, and, later, satellite dishes, public access channels, computers, modems, and networks changed the essential rules of

the mediaspace. Media was no longer something to be passively received. It could be created and, to some extent, broadcast by anybody.

Many media analysts, including myself, have outlined the way our media   20
evolved from a top-down, unidirectional forum into the interactive free-for-all it is today. Some explain how the media used to be "one-to-many," meaning that just a few broadcasters controlled what millions of viewers absorbed, and go on to rejoice that now the media is "many-to-many," because anyone with a modem or camcorder can tell his own stories to the rest of the world through public access television or the Internet. Anyone can feed back to his leaders, thanks to call-in radio or forum-style talk shows and presidential debates. George Bush lost the 1992 election because Clinton could respond better to the demands of the interactive media marketplace.

While all this is true, it is still an oversimplified view of the way our media has   21
reached its current level of complexity. There has always been feedback in politics and government. It has just operated a lot slower than it does today. If a king or president enacted too many policies against the public interest, the people would revolt or elect someone else. Even if the public had been bamboozled by the public relations strategies of the day, eventually, if taxes were too high or war too tragic, they would change things. Consumers' demand still affected the producers' supplies, and governments had to keep their populations contented enough so that they would not rebel. Just the fact that leaders and marketers employed public relations strategies proves that they understood the natural laws of society, however suppressed or delayed the reactions. The introduction of home technology into the mediaspace increased the flow of feedback from the "many" back to the "few." Once enough interactive channels had been put in place, that flow, like the content of television media, reached turbulence.

The watershed event that made us all aware of the media's new turbulence   22
was the Rodney King tape. Even without an Internet to speed our opinions around the globe, one man with a $300 camcorder captured a moment of injustice on tape, and the chaotic nature of the mediaspace spread that tape, like a virus, throughout our culture overnight.

Were the media not already exhibiting the properties of a dynamical system,   23
the Rodney King tape would never have replicated as it did, nor would it have provoked such a violent social upheaval. The format of television had reached turbulent levels and consisted of little more than discontinuous bites of data and imagery. The Rodney King tape could be effortlessly inserted into every newscast, tabloid show, rock video, and even the opening credits of Spike Lee's *Malcolm X.*

Had media technology not reached turbulence, there would not, in all probability, have been a camcorder-ready individual within earshot and camera   24
range of the scene of the beating, nor would there have been such an instantaneously responsive mechanism for the tape's distribution. A television producer, somewhere, may have even decided against airing the potentially incriminating evidence.

25   Had the media not developed into a natural system, capable of responding to our societal needs, the tape would not have caused even a stir. Rodney King would have meant very little if blacks in America weren't already subject to brutality of many kinds. There is a police problem in this country, and there is a race problem in this country. They just aren't being addressed appropriately yet. A media virus like the Rodney King tape will only spread if there is a cultural immune deficiency to the viral code within it. In this way, then, like a true partner in our cultural evolution, the chaotic media serves to promote or at least bring to the forefront the agendas that we need to address.

26   Finally, though, if we as members of the chaotic mediaspace were not equipped to absorb the data flying across our screens, make sense of the postlinear grammar with which it is formatted, and participate in its production as amateur journalists, then our media's ability to promote our cultural evolution would remain totally unrealized.

27   If we couldn't surf the waves of modern media, we would surely drown in them.

28   But the skills we need to develop in order to become adept at surfing channels (and computer networks, online services, the World Wide Web, even our own e-mail messages, for that matter) are the very opposite of what we traditionally valued in a good television viewer. We are coming to understand that what we so valued as an attention span is something entirely different from what we thought. As practiced, an attention span is not a power of concentration or self-discipline in the least, but rather a measure of a viewer's susceptibility to the hypnotic effects of linear programming. The "well-behaved" viewer, who listens quietly, never talks back to the screen, and never changes channels, is learning *what* to think and losing his own grasp on *how* to think. This was a gap-evasive viewing style that ignored the basic reality of a discontinuous mediaspace, helping us convince ourselves that our lives could run smoothly and easily if we simply followed instructions.

29   We see now, though, that the viewing style of our children is actually the more adult. Nearly every essay about kids and television cites the (relatively undocumented) fact that the attention span of our children is decreasing dangerously. In a brochure from the famously progressive Rudolph Steiner/Montessori schools, parents are encouraged to prevent their children from watching any television at all. Even *Sesame Street,* this Luddite document contends, is formatted with so many quick edits that it decreases the attention span. On the contrary, the ability to piece together meaning from a discontinuous set of images is the act of a higher intellect, not a lower one. Moreover, the child with the ability to pull himself out of a linear argument while it is in progress, reevaluate its content and relevance, and then either recommit or move on, is a child with the ability to surf the modem mediaspace. He is also immune to many of the methods of programming and persuasion foisted so easily upon our unsuspecting,

well-behaved viewers. He refuses to be drawn in as a passive, receive-only audience member.

The child of the remote control may indeed have a "shorter" attention span   30
as defined by the behavioral psychologists of our prechaotic culture's academic institutions (which are themselves dedicated to little more than preserving their own historical stature). But this same child also has a much *broader* attention *range*. The skill to be valued in the twenty-first century is not length of attention span but the ability to multitask—to do many things at once, well. Remote control kids can keep track of ten or more programs at once, and they instinctually switch from channel to channel just in time to catch important events on each one. If several important shows are on at the same time, the remote child does not need to tape one for later viewing. He watches both at the same time, because during that "later," there will be something else to watch or do.

The other key viewing skill that kids have developed, which may be linked to   31
the so-called shortened attention span, is the ability to process visual information very rapidly. A television image that takes an adult ten seconds to absorb might be processed by a child in a second. Certain MTV videos and Saturday morning cartoons are utterly incomprehensible to adults, who must, in a step-by-step fashion, translate each image as well as its subcomponents into a language they can understand. Kids process the visual language of television directly and are so adept at this skill that they hunger for images of greater complexity. The television imagery of MTV and kids' commercials consists of frames within frames, text mixed with pictures, multiple images, and juxtapositions of images at the frequency of a strobe.

This is a new language of visual information, and it depends as much on the   32
relationship of different images and images within images as it does on what we generally understand as content. It suspends the time constraints of linear reasoning in order to allow for a rapid dissemination of ideas and data, as well as the more active participation of the viewer to piece it together and draw conclusions for himself. If anything, this development would indicate an evolutionary leap in the ability of an attention span to maintain itself over long gaps of discontinuity, either between channel surfing cycles, or from session to session.

In the workplace of the future, a broader attention range and shorter ab-   33
sorption time will be valuable assets. The stockbroker with a broad attention range will be able to keep track of many markets at once as they flash by on his terminal. He will be able to talk on the phone to a client on one line, his boss on another, and an electronic "chat" on his computer screen, all simultaneously. His shortened attention span will keep him from getting too unconsciously engrossed in any one conversation or activity, and always ready for something new.

Meanwhile, the ability to process visual information quickly will enable the   34
worker of the future to cope with the "information overload" our data highway naysayers are busy warning us about. If we are about to enter an age of information

glut, those who can wade through it will be people with the ability to inspect, evaluate, and discard a screen of data immediately. This information skimming will need to be practiced on many different levels, and sometimes simultaneously. A person might scan his online services for the one that has a high volume of new messages. Once logged on, he will scan his list of incoming messages for the ones that might be important. Once inside a message—say, an electronic newsletter— he will scan within it for articles, then paragraphs of relevance. He will then need to file or forward it to the appropriate place for later use, if any.

35   Like a surfer who comes to understand the self-similar quality of beaches, tides, waves, and their components, the data surfer comes to recognize the qualities of different sorts of data structures. A television image directed at a sports fan or automobile purchaser will have a great deal of horizontal motion. (In the sports event this results from the camera moving back and forth across the screen; in the automobile ad it comes from panning with the car across the highway.) The quality of the image—which can be gleaned almost instantaneously—is enough for the channel surfer to decide whether to hold still. An experienced surfer keeping track of sports scores may only stop on the sports station when a graphic image of the score is onscreen. As he skims by this channel, he watches the bottom of the screen, because he knows this is where that graphic material will be superimposed. The same sort of multitiered scanning will be an essential skill in wading through electronic mail. The "subject line" of an e-mail message in a list will have certain elements if the message is important. The important paragraphs within that message will have similar qualities, drawing the experienced recipient's attention. Like Beavis and Butt-head, the executive of the future will be able to determine which e-mail is "cool" and which "sucks" in a fraction of a second.

36   This ability to recognize the quality of something from its shape and to trust one's impulses based on this recognition, may be the key skill in understanding any chaotic landscape. We all find nature so reassuring because we can recognize the self-similarity of its systems. The leaves of a tree have structures resonant with the branches, which are resonant with the other trees. Any truly chaotic system has such patterns, which, once recognized, provide a way to understand the system on an intuitive level. To recognize the pattern is the first step. To take the leap of faith that this pattern is correct or even that it exists, is the second and more dangerous step. But, as the snowboarder advised, it is usually always better to overshoot than to underestimate.

37   Understanding the modern language of visual information and coping with the culture it has spawned is an ongoing process. I was once in a crowded bar watching a basketball game on TV with the sound turned off. During a time out, most of us began drinking our beer and conversing with each other. All of a sudden, an older woman jumped up on her stool and screamed "Yes!" We all turned to her, confused, until we realized that she was watching a replay of a rather spectacular moment from last night's game. She sat back down, embarrassed. Because she did not understand the grammar of video replay in a basketball game (a small

frame expands to fill the screen before the segment is shown) she had no idea that she was not watching "live" television.

For most people, sports bar skills are not of paramount importance in achieving life success, but the inability to process and interpret visual media will soon be much more debilitating than many of us care to admit. Rather than locking up our television sets and crippling our children's ability to compete or even participate in the mediated culture ahead, it is we who should take a remedial course in postlinear, visual communication.   38

We should read comics.   39

Steps in Writing a Causal Argument

If your instructor asks for a topic proposal, use steps 1–4 to guide you in writing the proposal.

1. **Make a causal claim on a controversial trend, event, or phenomenon.** Use this formula: *X causes (or does not cause) Y* or *X causes Y, which in turn causes Z.*

   Examples:

   ■ One-parent families (or television violence, bad diet, and so on) is (or is not) the cause of emotional and behavioral problems in children.

   ■ Firearms control laws (or right-to-carry-handgun laws) reduce (or increase) violent crimes.

   ■ The trend toward home schooling (or private schools) is (or is not) improving the quality of education.

   ■ The length of U.S. presidential campaigns forces candidates to become too much influenced by big-dollar contributors (or prepares them for the constant media scrutiny that they will endure as president).

   ■ Putting grade school children into competitive sports teaches them how to succeed in later life (or puts undue emphasis on winning, subjecting them to stress and teaching many who are slower to mature to have a negative self-image).

2. **What's at stake in your claim?** If the cause is obvious to everyone, then it probably isn't worth writing about. Sex is the cause of STDs among college students, of course, but why do some students engage in unprotected sex when they know they are at risk?

3. **Make a diagram of causes.** Write as many causes as you can think of. Then make a fishbone diagram in which you show the causes.

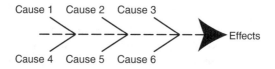

Which are the immediate causes? Which are the background causes? Which are the hidden causes? Which are the causes that most people have not recognized?

4. **Analyze your potential readers.** Who are your primary and secondary readers? How familiar will they be with the trend, event, or phenomenon that you're writing about? What are they likely to know and not know? How does it affect them? How likely are they to accept your causal explanation? What alternative explanation might they argue for?

5. **Write a draft.**

   Introduction:

   ■ Describe the controversial trend, event, or phenomenon.

   ■ Give the background necessary for your intended readers.

   Body:

   ■ For a trend, event, or phenomenon that is unfamiliar to your readers, you can explain the cause or chain of causation. Remember that providing facts is not the same thing as establishing causes, although facts can help to support your causal analysis.

   ■ Another way of organizing the body is to set out the causes that have been offered and reject them one by one. Then you can present the cause that you think is most important.

   ■ A third way is to treat a series of causes one by one, analyzing the importance of each.

   Conclusion:

   ■ Do more than simply summarize what you have said. You might consider additional effects beyond those that have been previously noted.

6. **Take your draft through the revision steps in chapter 15.**

Chapter 7

Evaluation Arguments

People make evaluations all the time. Newspapers and magazines have picked up on this love of evaluation by running "best of" polls. They ask their readers what's the best Mexican, Italian, or Chinese restaurant; the best pizza; the best local band; the best coffeehouse; the best dance club; the best neighborhood park; the best swimming hole; the best bike ride (scenic and challenging); the best volleyball court; the best place to get married; and so on. If you ask one of your friends who voted in a "best" poll why she picked a particular restaurant as the best of its kind, she might respond by saying simply, "I like it." But if you ask her why she likes it, she might start offering good reasons such as these: The food is good, the service prompt, the prices fair, and the atmosphere comfortable. It's really not a mystery why these polls are often quite predictable and why the same restaurants tend to win year after year. Many people think that evaluations are matters of personal taste, but when we begin probing the reasons, we often discover that the criteria that different people use to make evaluations have a lot in common.

If you simply want to announce that you like or don't like something, then all you have to do is say so, but if you want to convince other people that your judgment is sound, then you have to appeal to criteria that they will agree with and, if necessary, argue for the validity of additional criteria that you think your readers should also consider. Once you have established the criteria you will use for your evaluation, then you can apply those criteria to whatever you are evaluating to see how well it measures up. You make judgments of good or bad, best or worst, on the basis of the match with the criteria. For some things the criteria are relatively easy to establish and the judgment easy to make. If you accidentally knock your clock radio off your nightstand, break it, and have to replace it, you might do a little comparison shopping. Setting the alarm on your old clock was more difficult than it should have been, so you want an alarm that is easy to set. You need to see the clock at night, so you want a luminous display. You sometimes listen to the radio while you're waking up, so the radio needs to sound good enough to get your day off to a pleasant start. And you don't want to pay much. So you decide to test several brands that all cost about $20, and you buy the one that is easiest to use with the best sound and display.

Most people have a lot of practice making consumer evaluations, and when they have enough time to do their homework, they usually make an informed decision. But sometimes, criteria for evaluations are not so obvious, and evaluations are much more difficult to make. Sometimes, one set of criteria favors one choice while another set of criteria favors another. You might have encountered this problem when you chose a college. If you were able to leave home to go to school, you had a potential choice of going to over 1,400 accredited colleges and universities. Until a few years ago, there wasn't much information about choosing a college other than what colleges said about themselves. You could find out the price of tuition and what courses were offered, but it was hard to compare one college with another.

In 1983, the magazine *U.S. News and World Report* began ranking U.S. colleges and universities from a consumer's perspective. Those rankings have remained highly controversial ever since. Many college officials have attacked the criteria that *U.S. News* uses to make its evaluations. In an August 1998 *U.S. News & World Report* article, Gerhard Casper, the president of Stanford University (which is consistently near the top of the rankings), says, "Much about these rankings—particularly their specious formulas and spurious precision—is utterly misleading." Casper argues that using graduation rates as a criterion of quality rewards easy schools. Other college presidents have called for a national boycott of the *U.S. News* rankings (without much success).

U.S. News replies in its defense that colleges and universities themselves do a lot of ranking, beginning with ranking students for admissions, using their SAT or ACT scores, high school GPA, ranking in high school class, quality of high school, and other factors, and then grading the students and ranking them against each other when they are enrolled in college. Furthermore, schools also evaluate faculty members and take great interest in the national ranking of their departments. They care very much about where they stand in relation to each other. Why, then, *U.S. News* argues, shouldn't people be able to evaluate colleges and universities, since colleges and universities are so much in the business of evaluating people?

Arguing for the right to evaluate colleges and universities is one thing; actually doing comprehensive and reliable evaluations is quite another. *U.S. News* uses a formula in which 25 percent of a school's ranking is based on a survey of reputation in which the president, provost, and dean of admissions at each college rate the quality of schools in the same category, and the remaining 75 percent is based on statistical criteria of quality. These statistical criteria fall into six major categories: retention of students, faculty resources, student selectivity, financial resources, alumni giving, and (for national universities and liberal arts colleges only) "graduation rate performance," the difference between the proportion of students who are expected to graduate and the proportion that actually do. These major categories are made up of factors that are weighted for their importance. For example, the faculty resources category is determined by the size of classes (the proportion of classes with fewer than twenty students and the proportion of classes with fifty or more students), the average faculty pay weighted by the cost of living in different regions of the country, the percentage of professors with the highest degree in their field, the overall student-faculty ratio, and the percentage of faculty who are full time.

Those who have challenged the *U.S. News* rankings argue that the magazine should use different criteria or weight the criteria differently. Here is how *U.S. News* answers those charges on its Web site (http://www.usnews.com/usnews/edu/college/corank.htm):

> *Our views of the appropriate weights may differ from those of other higher education experts. The weights were chosen based on years of reporting about education, on reviews of research about education, and after consultation with experts in higher education. Over time, we have placed greater weight on the "outcome" measures of quality (such as graduation rate) and de-emphasized the "input" measures (such as entering test scores). This change is consistent with a growing emphasis by education experts on "outcomes" in assessing the performance of complex institutions such as colleges.*

If you are curious about where your school ranks, take a look at the *U.S. News* Web site.

The *U.S. News* system of evaluating schools was developed by many people working over several years. You might never be asked to make evaluations on this scale. But many occupations do require you to make formal evaluations. If you are in a supervisory position of any kind, you will likely have to evaluate the performance of those people who work under you. You might also be asked to evaluate the processes through which work gets done. In many cases, the criteria that you will use are not obvious at the beginning. Often, you will have to think carefully and examine thoroughly to identify the right criteria.

Arguments of evaluation are structured much like arguments of definition. Recall that the criteria in arguments of definition are set out in because clauses: *X is a Y because it has criteria A and B.* In arguments of evaluation, the claim takes the form *X is a good (bad, the best, the worst) Y if measured by criteria A, B, and C.*

X ←—— LINK (because) ——→ good (bad, best, worst) Y

X is ←—— LINK (because) ——→ the best clock radio for under $20

  A) it has the best display

  B) it has the best sounding radio

  C) it is easy to use

So the key move in writing most evaluative arguments is first deciding which criteria to use.

Reviews are one of the most common kinds of evaluative arguments. When you read movie reviews, concert reviews, or other reviews, notice how the writer identifies criteria. Sometimes, these criteria are not obvious, and you will notice that the writer makes an argument about what criteria make a truly excellent horror film or a superior rock concert. You might have to argue for your criteria too. For example, suppose you want to argue that the 1955 film *Rebel without a Cause,* starring James Dean, Natalie Wood, and Sal Mineo, is a classic of teen drama films. The obvious definitional criteria are that *Rebel without a Cause* is a film, is a drama, and is about teens. But if you want to argue that *Rebel without a Cause* is exemplary of the genre and has qualities that make it timeless, then you have to define qualities that make a film a classic in this genre.

You mention your idea to your roommate, and she says, "That's total nonsense. Have you seen it recently? The dialog is awful, and the plot is even worse with that sappy ending. If James Dean hadn't gotten killed in a car wreck at age twenty-four, believe me, nobody would ever watch it now." You realize that she has a point about the tragic deaths of the main characters. Not only did James Dean die in the most famous car crash in history before Princess Diana, but also Natalie Wood later drowned mysteriously in a boating accident off Catalina, and Sal Mineo was murdered near his West Hollywood apartment. And she's right that the dialog hasn't aged well and that the ending, in which the James Dean character reconciles with his father, doesn't fit with the rest of the film. But there's still something about *Rebel without a Cause* that makes it a classic, and that's what you want to convince her of.

First, you realize that even though there have been a lot of bad films about teens since *Rebel without a Cause,* there really were none before it. So you argue that *Rebel without a Cause* is a classic because it pioneered much of what was to come later. It was the first film to portray teens in a somewhat realistic fashion (though the stars did overact). The main character, Jim Stark (played by James Dean), is both vulnerable and defiant. His friend Plato (the Sal Mineo character) is about as gay as a film character could be in the 1950s, when di-

James Dean

rect portrayal of homosexuality was banned by the censors. Jim's eventual girl-friend, Judy (Natalie Wood), who snubs him at the beginning, is confused and rejected by her parents. And the parents in the film are totally ineffectual. Jim has a weak father (played by Jim Backus, the voice of Mr. Magoo) who won't stand up against his domineering wife. Judy also lacks parental support, and Plato's parents have abandoned him. So even if *Rebel without a Cause* is a little cheesy, it's honest about teen problems.

You decide to argue that another criterion that makes *Rebel without a Cause* a classic is its implicit critique of U.S. culture. It was released in 1955 at the peak of U.S. self-confidence and at the high water mark of what later came to be called family values. These were supposed to be the years of the family ideal—of *Father Knows Best, Leave It to Beaver,* and *Donna Reed*—yet the film depicted an entire generation of young men and women who were strug-gling to find an identity. The film was the first to ask why U.S. teenagers were so troubled if everything was supposed to be so good. It exposed a big flaw in the portrait of the United States as the ideal society and accused the parents of being responsible for the alienation of the teenagers.

Finally, you won't concede that the fame of the film is strictly because of James Dean's early death. It's no accident, you argue, that boys in the 1950s spent hours trying to comb their hair into pompadours to look like James Dean. He has a terrific screen presence, and he conveys many conflicting emotions. But above all, he's always lonely, always groping for love from a family and society he finds unresponsive. Dean's role is the blueprint for the alienated teen. He's still a rebel after all these years.

The argument that we've just outlined depends on **aesthetic** criteria. Nearly all reviews of movies, plays, concerts, and other performances rely on aesthetic criteria. Another kind of evaluative argument is one that argues that something is good or bad on the basis of practical criteria because of the effects it produces. These arguments are evaluative arguments of cause, and they conform to the structure of a causal argument with an evaluative term (good, bad, best, worst) inserted: *X causes (or does not cause) a good (or bad) Y.* Sometimes, the evaluation is made by contrasting the effects that something is claimed to have with the effects that it actually has. In May 1990, Shelby Steele, an English professor at San Jose State, published an essay entitled "A Negative Vote on Affirmative Action" in the *New York Times Magazine.* Steele begins the essay speaking as a parent who will shortly be sending his two children off to college:

> In a few short years, when my two children will be applying to college, the affirmative-action policies by which most universities offer black students some form of preferential treatment will present me with a dilemma. I am a middle-class black, a college professor, far from wealthy but also well removed from the kind of deprivation that would qualify my children for the label "disadvantaged." Both of them have endured racial insensitivity from whites. They have been called names, have suffered slights and have experienced first hand the peculiar malevolence that racism brings out in people. Yet they have never experienced racial discrimination, have never been stopped by their race on any path they have chosen to follow. Still, their society now tells them that if they will only designate themselves as black on their college applications, they will probably do better in the college lottery than if they conceal this fact. I think there is something of a Faustian bargain in this.

Ending the first paragraph by saying that affirmative action is a "Faustian bargain" seems a little heavy. After all, the various Faust stories involve selling one's soul to the devil. But Steele does signal early on that he believes affirmative action has serious negative consequences for African-Americans. Before he describes those effects, however, he summarizes in the next paragraph the arguments for affirmative action:

Of course many blacks and a considerable number of whites would say that I was sanctimoniously making affirmative action into a test of character. They would say that this small preference is the meagerest recompense for centuries of unrelieved oppression. And to these arguments other very obvious facts must be added. In America, many marginally competent or flatly incompetent whites are hired every day—some because their white skin suits the conscious or unconscious racial preference of their employers. The white children of alumni are often grandfathered into elite universities in what can only be seen as a residual benefit of historic white privilege. Worse, white incompetence is always an individual matter, but for blacks it is often confirmation of ugly stereotypes. Given that unfairness cuts both ways, doesn't it only balance the scales of history, doesn't this repair, in a small way, the systematic denial under which my children's grandfather lived out his days?

Here, Steele acknowledges the strongest arguments for the position he will shortly argue against. It's a risky strategy because at the end of the second paragraph, he positions his readers in agreement with the opposing point of view. Steele does not deny that African-Americans and members of other racial minorities still suffer from effects of racism, and he concedes that even if affirmative action policies are unfair, the long-term beneficiaries of unfairness are overwhelmingly white Americans. Thus, Steele would seem to have put himself at an extreme disadvantage after two paragraphs.

But Steele is well aware that he is escalating the stakes. He can concede the opposing arguments because he believes that his argument is more powerful. He argues that affirmative action is bad because it does not redress the effects of racism; rather, it reinforces some of them. Steele writes:

I think one of the most troubling effects of racial preferences for blacks is a kind of demoralization. Under affirmative action, the quality that earns us preferential treatment is an implied inferiority. However this inferiority is explained—and it is easily enough explained by the myriad deprivations that grew out of our oppression—it is still inferiority. There are explanations and then there is the fact. And the fact must be borne by the individual as a condition apart from the explanation, apart even from the fact that others like himself also bear this condition. In integrated situations in which blacks must compete with whites who may be better prepared, these explanations may quickly wear thin and expose the individual to racial as well as personal self-doubt. (Of course whites also feel doubt, but only personally, not racially.)

Steele also argues that affirmative action promotes an attitude of victimization among blacks and the expectation that they are "owed" something as a form of reparation. This point gets at a third source of evaluative criteria: morality and fairness. Here's how Steele argues the issue of fairness:

> But this logic overlooks a much harder and less digestible reality, that it is impossible to repay blacks living today for the historic suffering of the race. If all blacks were given a million dollars tomorrow it would not amount to a dime on the dollar for three centuries of oppression that we still carry today. The concept of historic reparation grows out of man's need to impose on the world a degree of justice that simply does not exist. Suffering can be endured and overcome, it cannot be repaid. To think otherwise is to prolong the suffering.

Steele's argument against affirmative action might not convince those who support it as a solution to racial inequality. But he does stimulate those who would disagree with him to think about the underlying problems in more complex ways. He would shift the focus from trying to redress historical wrongs to what is best for African-American students entering college today. Like all good arguments, Steele's invites further response.

Eric Gable and Richard Handler

In Colonial Williamsburg, the New History Meets the Old

Eric Gable is an assistant professor of sociology and anthropology at Mary Washington College. Richard Handler is a professor of anthropology at the University of Virginia. They are the authors of *The New History in an Old Museum: Creating the Past at Colonial Williamsburg* (Duke University Press, 1997).

Some evaluations are obviously evaluations from the moment you glance at them. Reviews fall into this category. But other evaluations can be more subtle. "In Colonial Williamsburg, the New History Meets the Old," originally published in the *Chronicle of Higher Education*, takes a long time giving background before the authors begin to make evaluative judgments. Notice how they define the criteria for a good museum. Do you agree with these criteria?

1   In recent years, the way in which museums and other public displays have presented history often has generated vituperative debate among scholars and the public at large. The popular media have portrayed public history as an ideological struggle—left-wing professors shattering (desecrating) popular assumptions. In the most common media treatment, "tenured radicals" view the previous generation's scholarly work as little more than ruling-class propaganda papering over the negative aspects of American history. In reaction, today's historians promul-

An interpreter explains eighteenth-century life at the reconstructed slave quarters of Colonial Williamsburg.

gate a more pessimistic version of America's past—one that destroys Americans' grounds for taking pride in their country.

We stepped into the middle of these often contentious appraisals of public   2 history a few years ago, when we conducted an ethnographic study of Colonial Williamsburg, arguably America's premier public-history site. Colonial Williamsburg is a replica of the capital of Revolutionary-era Virginia. The reconstruction of this entire town, begun in 1926, was initially underwritten by John D. Rockefeller's largesse, but it is now financed by public donations, ticket sales, hotel and restaurant revenues, the marketing of Colonial-era reproductions, and revenue from an endowment established by Rockefeller.

For much of its history, the replica was widely criticized by historians and   3 knowledgeable laypeople as little more than an airbrushed, consumer-oriented, patriotic shrine celebrating an upscale idyll loosely based on the life styles of Virginia's Colonial elite. But beginning in the 1970s, a new group of historians was hired as researchers and curators to refashion the site. They were trained in the "new social history," which emerged out of the social turmoil of the 1960s and which focused on groups and individuals neglected by older, traditional scholars.

The top administrators prompted this change in part to keep Colonial Williamsburg at the cutting edge of scholarship, and in part because historians have argued convincingly that a new version of the past will be more popular, accurate, and inclusive than the entrenched story.

4   As a result of this shift, we wanted to see how public history was being made "on the ground." We focused on the way it was managed, as historians attempted to use the materials at this particular site to create their vision of the past; as middle-level managers trained front-line staff members (dressed in reproduction costumes as craftworkers, farmers, and other residents of the town) to deliver historical stories to the public; as these front-line employees resisted or opposed new interpretations; and as visitors digested what they heard and saw.

5   We found that, during the past decade, Colonial Williamsburg has changed in significant ways the history that it presents to the public. Most notable is the greater prominence of African Americans—those the museum calls "the other half"—in its narrative of nationhood. A small but active unit devoted to African-American history has created dozens of special programs and tours to illuminate the lives of slaves and free black people in colonial Virginia. For example, you can now tour a reconstructed slave quarter and meet a costumed African-American guide who will tell you about the daily life of the enslaved. Or you can stroll Williamsburg's back alleys with such characters as the entrepreneurial Chicken Hattie, who sells eggs to the town's white inhabitants.

6   Some programs do not dodge the horror of slavery: an enactment of a slave auction, a video about a runaway slave, a tour with graphic discussions of the Middle Passage on slave ships, and discussions of the breakup of African-American families.

7   Yet the more widely disseminated story still is an upbeat one, in which slaves, like other immigrants, establish themselves in a new land and work hard to improve their lot. Moreover, black history remains secondary at Williamsburg. It is still easy for visitors to tour the entire site without hearing anything about African Americans other than how much they cost their owners, and how many lived and worked in a particular white person's residence.

8   At Colonial Williamsburg, then, the influence of social historians has apparently been less than media depictions of "tenured radicals" might lead one to expect. There has been no all-out ideological struggle, and the bulk of the history told here is not so different from that told 30 years ago. We asked ourselves why.

9   It seems to us that Colonial Williamsburg and sites like it remain stages for the retelling of such conventional American narratives as the Horatio Alger story. In this scenario, individuals or ethnic groups are depicted as pulling themselves up by their bootstraps. This narrative is applied as readily to African slaves such as Chicken Hattie as to a European-immigrant-turned-entrepreneurial-businessman such as Mr. Benjamin Powell, whose house you can visit. What this narrative does not do is challenge visitors to rethink their notions of America's past, or its present.

10   Like many other museums, Colonial Williamsburg is a tourist attraction as well as an educational institution, and the ideas of hospitality and courtesy are

deeply ingrained in its corporate culture. Management repeats ceaselessly that visitors—customers—will not return unless they enjoy their visits. The assumption is that stories depicting the harshness of slavery—and, more generally, histories critical of America's shortcomings—will pain, embarrass, and ultimately turn away tourists.

Moreover, on the front line, where employees meet visitors—and behind the   11 scenes, where managers of competing programs at the site wage institutional turf wars—facts are weapons more readily wielded than are the complicated arguments that social historians favor about the ideological underpinnings of history. Thus, for example, at one point we observed African-American guides and white guides at a particular re-created house debate how to discuss miscegenation: The general issue of the entanglement of sexual practices and racial politics was displaced by an unresolvable factual dispute: whether a particular slaveholder had fathered a particular child by a particular slave.

Time and again, we watched as seemingly productive debates deteriorated   12 into narrowly construed arguments about fact. Even staff historians were prone to lose sight of the big picture as they chased after stray details. This "just the facts, please" tendency was exacerbated because the market niche of history museums depends on their claim to possess "real" history, embodied in their buildings and objects, in contrast to what the museums see as the "fakery" of their major competitors—theme parks such as those of Disney.

Thus, despite some changes, the new social history has not transformed this   13 particular old museum and its decades-old culture of patriotic realism. The Fife and Drum Corps continues to play patriotic songs as it marches down the main street—the high point of a tourist's day. More significantly, the corps continues to be the central icon in the photographs, brochures, and commercials that the museum produces to attract visitors and convince people that donating to the site's continuing work is an act of patriotism. Other such icons are the coach and coachmen (usually black) in livery. Visitors continue to pay extra for the privilege of a short coach ride through town, perhaps to identify themselves with the masters.

Because of the efforts of historians who have worked at Williamsburg, the site   14 is now demographically more diverse than it used to be. It has more African-American employees in positions other than menial ones, and African Americans are often included in the stories that guides tell about America's Revolutionary past. But, by and large, these changes are just additional pieces in a narrative framework that continues to celebrate America while playing down inequalities.

In the end, then, Colonial Williamsburg continues to be a patriotic shrine that   15 fosters tourists' fantasies. Despite media portrayals of ideological revolutions in the nation's museums, the new social historians at this site have not subverted the old story. It is not so much that they have been muzzled—or have backed down—as that their efforts have not overcome a wider cultural tendency, in which older cultural images persist and continue to frame the site as a whole. Williamsburg thus provides a fractured puzzle of the past—and continues to play down historic and current inequalities.

Natascha Pocek

The Diet Zone: A Dangerous Place

In 1997 Natascha Pocek wrote the following essay as a response to an assignment in her first-year writing course at Penn State.

1   Diet Coke, diet Pepsi, diet Cherry Coke, diet pills, diet shakes, no-fat diet, vegetable diet, carbohydrate diet, diet, diet, diet—enough! We are assaulted by the word "diet" every time we go into a supermarket, turn on the television, listen to the radio, or read an advertisement. We are not only surrounded by the word "diet" everywhere we look and listen, but we as "Americans" are also linked with "diet" in general; Americans are automatically associated with the stereotypical image of either extreme thinness or obesity. We have so easily been lured by the promise and potential of diet products, which include everything from pills to foods, that we have stopped thinking about what diet products are doing to us. Diet products, in fact, promote the "easy way out," a most elemental form of deception. It is imperative that we realize that diet products adversely affect not only our weight, but also our values of dedication and persistence. We are paying for products that harm us, physically and psychologically. Therefore, we must stop purchasing diet products without recognizing the harm we are doing to ourselves. We must realize that in purchasing diet products we are effectively purchasing physical problems and psychological decay in a commercial package. The time has come for us to accept the fact that solutions don't come in bottles or from miracle no-calorie chemicals; solutions come from the mind, and diet products are promoting the wrong solution.

2   As a teenager, I learned the hard way that losing weight with diet products as an aid only results in a vicious cycle of failure. Statistically overweight from the age of 15 to 18, I was unhappy and sought a solution, a way to lose the extra pounds that I carried around on my frame. No bottle, pill, powder, or shake took off my excess weight; I earned the body that I now live in by watching what I ate. Period. As a typical teenager, I admit, I tried many fad diets. I attempted an advertised vegetable diet which reduced me to the meal plan of a rabbit, and a drink-as-much-water-as-you-can-so-you're-not-hungry diet. I also tried to lose weight by using diet pills and diet food products. The diet pills were, without a doubt, one of my biggest mistakes. The pills were only a temporary solution because while taking the pills my eating habits didn't change. I had not learned how to eat healthily and moderately. I had learned how to quickly lose a few pounds with no effort. The pills shifted my focus from the most important aspect, the food, and placed it on watching the clock to see when I needed to swallow the next pill. The pills circumvented the real issue of my unhealthy eating habits; I

didn't even consider my eating habits since I had not taken any foods out of my daily food intake. Consequently, as soon as I stopped popping the miracle pills, the few pounds I had lost returned, along with a few more unexpected ones. Success had obviously eluded me.

The consumption of "diet-food" products was *the* single biggest mistake that 3 I made in attempting to lose weight. I allowed myself to fall into a very relaxed mind set in which I did not really have to think about what I ate; my brain was dormant while my stomach was active. The diet foods and drinks that I consumed became my excuse for the chocolate cake at dinner, the extra helping of pasta, and the late-night cup of hot chocolate. It was acceptable to allow myself these treats because I had "saved calories" elsewhere. Needless to say, although I lost weight, it didn't stay off for long. Once again, I had not trained myself to acquire a taste for healthier foods. My eating habits stayed bad from the first Diet Coke I drank, to the last Low-Fat Granola Bar I ate. Diet foods, just like the diet pills, had been a huge failure which resulted from my lack of thought.

The mistake that I—and countless other Americans—made in using diet 4 products carries much greater significance than not losing weight for the long run: diet products significantly weaken us psychologically. On one level, we are not allowing our brains to acknowledge that our weight problems lie not in actually losing the weight, but in controlling the consumption of fatty, high-caloric, unhealthy foods. Diet products allow us to skip the thinking stage completely and instead go straight for the scale. Dr. James Ferguson, a nationally prominent clinician who specializes in treating eating disorders and teaching weight control, says that "self-observation [is the] prime method of assessing eating behaviors" (65). Precisely. Diet products only allow us to ignore the crucial issue of eating habits altogether: They bypass the real problem. In reality, we aren't the ones contributing to the loss of our pounds; the diet products are responsible for shedding the pounds from our bodies. All we have to be able to do is swallow or recognize the word "diet" in food labels. The effort we put into losing weight is zero, no effort, non-existent. Consequently, when we stop consuming diet products, our bodies lose the dictators that worked to control the unruly pounds and our eating habits fall into chaos again.

On another level, the psychological effects of diet products have much 5 greater ramifications. Every time we swallow a pill or drink a zero-calorie beverage, we are unconsciously telling ourselves that we don't have to work to get results, that we can select the "easy way out," the quick way out. I see Americans eating sweet foods endlessly because they are pacified by the low-fat label; they don't just eat the cakes and candies and cookies, they inhale them in huge amounts, and their excuse is that "they're lowfat, so it's okay." Diet products are subconsciously instilling in Americans the idea that gain comes without pain, that life can be devoid of resistance and struggle. The diet industry is not only making it easy to ignore the principle of not always getting what you want—it is, in fact, promoting its disappearance. People *can* eat whatever they want because most "bad foods" are now diet, light, or reduced fat. The diet pills and potions become important at the end of the vicious diet cycle when we say, "Oops, I ate twice as many cookies because they were low-fat and I gained weight." The diet pills become the dust pan and brush that clean up the mess we made with the diet products. The cycle of diet products is a virus that affects us psychologically and doesn't enforce any values of determination, perseverance, hard work, or self-discipline.

6   The danger of diet products lies not only in the psychological effects they have on us, but also in the immediate physical danger that they present. Death is unfortunately a possible side-effect of using diet products. In 1994, the drug Ephedrine, which is found in diet pills, was "linked to the deaths of two people and severe reactions in several others" (Rosencrans). Cellulose fiber diet pills were identified as a "cause of esophageal obstruction" (Jones) and in 1992, 26 cases were reported to the Food and Drug Administration in which diet pills were the cause of "esophageal and small bowel obstruction" (Lewis 1424). Clearly, diet pills post health threats. Diet foods become dangerous when used in place of other foods because they contain a minimal amount of nutrients. The next time you go to the supermarket and have the urge to buy a diet beverage, read the label. For example, the nutrition label of a Crystal Light bottle reads: Total Fat, 0 grams; Total Carb, 0 grams, Protein, 0 grams; Calories, 5. Wouldn't it be more appropriate to name the label the "malnutrition" label? When we drink a Crystal Light, we are swallowing a lot of precisely what, if there are 0 grams of everything in it? The answer is nothing—besides chemicals. As you continue reading the label on the bottle, you will come to the ingredient list, which includes sodium benzoate, artificial flavor, potassium sorbate, potassium citrate (controls acidity), BHA (preserves freshness) and so on. The ingredient and nutrition label illustrates the fact that diet foods can indirectly harm our bodies because consuming them instead of healthy foods means we are depriving our bodies of essential nutrients. Beyond an indirect harm, diet products can actually cause direct harm as well. Packets of Sweet n' Low and Care-Free gum carry warning labels which read, the "use of this product may be hazardous to your health. This product contains saccharin, which has been determined to cause cancer in laboratory animals." Would you like to take the chance that saccharin might give *you* cancer? The point is that diet foods and diet pills are only zero-caloric because the diet industry has created chemicals that can be manipulated to produce these miracle products. There is no insurance that a diet product is nutritional, and the chemicals that go into diet products are potentially dangerous.

7   As we walk down the aisle of the supermarket tomorrow, we will once again be bombarded by "diet" food labels that call to us from left and right. We will also see all the promising diet pills that make losing weight seem so easy. After demonstrating the harmful physical and psychological effects that diet products have on us, our instinct should be to turn and walk away. Now that we are more knowledgeable on the subject of diet products and can no longer claim ignorance about

the harms that diet products have, it is time to seriously contemplate our purchase of diet products. Losing weight lies in the power of our minds, not in the power of chemicals. Once we realize this, we will be much better able to resist diet products, and thereby resist the psychological deterioration and physical deprivation that comes from using diet products.

Works Cited

Ferguson, James M. *Habits Not Diets: The Secret to Lifetime Weight Control.* Palo Alto, CA: Bull Publishing, 1988.

Jones, K. R. "Cellulose Fiber Diet Pills, A New Cause of Esophageal Obstruction." *Archives of Otolaryngology—Head and Neck Surgery* 116 (1990): 1091.

Lewis, J. H. "Esophageal and Small Bowel Obstruction from Guar Gum-Containing 'Diet Pills.' " *American Journal of Gastroenterology* 87 (1992): 1424–28.

Rosencrans, Kendra. "Diet Pills Suspected in Deaths." *Healthy Weight Journal* 8:4 (1994): 68.

Steps in Writing an Evaluation Argument

If your instructor asks for a topic proposal, use steps 1–4 to guide you in writing the proposal.

1. **Make an evaluative claim based on criteria.** Use this formula: *X is a good (bad, the best, the worst) Y if measured by certain criteria (aesthetic, practical, or moral).*

   Examples:

   - Write a book review or a movie review.
   - Write a defense of a particular kind of music or art.
   - Evaluate a controversial aspect of sports (e.g., the current system of determining who is champion in Division I college football by a system of bowls and polls) or evaluate a sports event (e.g., this year's WNBA playoffs) or a team.
   - Evaluate a famous person from business, government, sports, entertainment, the arts, or elsewhere as a role model.
   - Evaluate the effectiveness of an educational program (such as your high school honor's program or your college's core curriculum requirement) or some other aspect of your campus.

- Evaluate a leader or an influential group (e.g., Amnesty International, PETA, Greenpeace, NOW, NAACP) on the basis of what they have or haven't accomplished.

- Evaluate the effectiveness of a social policy or law such as legislating 21 as the legal drinking age, current gun control laws, or environmental regulation.

2. **What's at stake in your claim?** If nearly everybody would agree with you, then your evaluative claim probably isn't interesting or important. If you can think of people who would disagree, then something is at stake. Who argues the opposite of your claim? Why do they make a different evaluation?

3. **Make a list of criteria (aesthetic, practical, moral).** Which criteria make something a good Y? Which are the most important? Which are fairly obvious and which will you have to argue for? Or what are all the effects of what you are evaluating? Which are the most important? Which are fairly obvious and which will you have to argue for?

4. **Analyze your potential readers.** Who are your primary and secondary readers? How familiar will they be with the person, group, institution, event, or thing that you are evaluating? What are they likely to know and not know? Which criteria are most important to them?

5. **Write a draft.**

   Introduction:

   - Introduce the person, group, institution, event, or thing that you are going to evaluate. You might want to announce your stance at this point or wait until the concluding section.

   - Give the background necessary for your intended readers.

   - If there are opposing views, briefly describe them.

   Body:

   - If you are making an evaluation by criteria, then you should describe each criterion and then analyze how well what you are evaluating meets that criterion.

   - If you are making an evaluation according to the effects someone or something produces, then describe each effect in detail.

   Conclusion:

   - If you have not announced your stance, then you can conclude that, on the basis of the criteria you set out or the effects you analyze, X is a good (bad, best, worst) Y. If you have made your stance clear from the beginning, then you can end with a compelling example or analogy.

6. **Take your draft through the revision steps in chapter 15.**

Chapter 8

Narrative Arguments

In 1980, 53,172 people were killed in traffic accidents in the United States, and over half the deaths involved alcohol. Americans had become accustomed to losing around 25,000–30,000 people every year to drunk drivers. But it was the tragic death in 1980 of Cari Lightner, a thirteen-year-old California girl who was killed by a hit-and-run drunk driver while walking along a city street, that made people start asking whether this carnage could be prevented. The driver had been out on bail only two days for another hit-and-run drunk driving crash, and he had three previous drunk driving arrests. He was allowed to plea bargain for killing Cari and avoided going to prison. Cari's mother, Candy Lightner, was outraged that so little was being done to prevent needless deaths and injuries. She and a small group of other women founded Mothers Against Drunk Driving (MADD) with the goals of getting tougher laws against drunk driving, stiffer penalties for those who kill and injure while driving drunk, and great public awareness of the seriousness of driving drunk.

Cari Lightner's story aroused to action other people who had been injured themselves or lost loved ones to drunk drivers. Chapters of MADD spread quickly across the country, and it has become one of the most effective citizen groups ever formed, succeeding in getting much new legislation against drunk driving on the books. These laws and changing attitudes about drunk driving have had a significant impact. The National Highway Traffic Safety Administration reported that in 1996, 17,126 people were killed in alcohol-related traffic accidents in the United States compared to 24,045 in 1986, a 29 percent reduction.

The success of MADD points to why arguing by narrating succeeds sometimes when other kinds of arguments have little effect. The story of

Cari Lightner appealed to shared community values in ways that statistics did not. The story vividly illustrated that something was very wrong with the criminal justice system if a repeat drunk driver was allowed to run down and kill a child on a sidewalk only two days after committing a similar crime.

Martin Luther King, Jr., was another master of using narratives to make his points. In "Letter from Birmingham Jail," he relates in one sentence the disappointment of his six-year-old daughter when he had to explain to her why, because of the color of her skin, she could not go to an amusement park in Atlanta advertised on television. This tiny story vividly illustrates the pettiness of segregation laws and their effect on children.

Using narratives for advocating change is nothing new. As far back as we have records, we find people telling stories and singing songs about their own lives that argue for change. Folk songs have always given voice to political protest and have celebrated marginalized people. When workers in the United States began to organize in the 1880s, they adapted melodies that soldiers had sung in the Civil War. In the 1930s, performers and songwriters such as Paul Robeson, Woody Guthrie, Huddie Ledbetter (Leadbelly), and Aunt Molly Jackson relied on traditions of hymns, folk songs, and African-American blues to protest social conditions. In the midst of the politically quiet 1950s, folks songs told stories that critiqued social conformity and the dangers of nuclear war. In the 1960s, the civil rights movement and the movement against the Vietnam War brought a strong resurgence of folk music. The history of folk music is a continuous recycling of old tunes, verses, and narratives to engage new political situations. What can be said for folk songs is also true for any popular narrative genre, be it the short story, novel, drama, movies, or even rap music.

Narrative arguments work in a different way from those that spell out their criteria and argue for explicit links. A narrative argument succeeds if the experience being described invokes the life experiences of the readers. Anyone who has ever been around children knows that most kids love amusement parks. Martin Luther King, Jr., did not have to explain to his readers why going to an amusement park advertised on television was such a big deal for his daughter. Likewise, the story of Cari Lightner was effective because even if you have not known someone who was killed by a drunk driver, most people have known someone who died tragically and perhaps needlessly. Furthermore, you often read about and see on television many people who die in traffic accidents. Narrative arguments allow readers to fill in the conclusion. In the cases of King's arguments against segregation laws and MADD's campaign against drunk drivers, that's exactly what happened. Public outcry led to changes in laws and public opinion.

In recent years, one of the most effective rhetoricians to use narrative arguments was President Ronald Reagan, known to some as the "Great Communicator." Reagan's critics were mystified by the success of his speeches.

They noted that even though he often got the facts wrong, contradicted himself, and offered simplistic solutions, he remained quite popular among large segments of the voting public. What those critics failed to appreciate was how Reagan relied heavily on storytelling throughout his presidency and how his stories emphasized shared values. Critics who applied a rational standard to Reagan's speeches faulted him for inconsistency and lack of realism. Those who responded favorably to Reagan credited his narratives for providing vision and inspiration.

Even when one doesn't try to argue by telling a complete story, "little narratives" are often very useful as examples. Civil rights attorney and law professor Lani Guinier uses a conversation with her four-year-old son to exemplify a much larger point in her 1994 book, *The Tyranny of the Majority:*

> Sometimes, too, we construct rules that force us to be divided into winners and losers when we might have otherwise joined together. This idea was cogently expressed by my son, Nikolas, when he was four years old. . . . While I was writing one of my law journal articles, Nikolas and I had a conversation about voting prompted by a *Sesame Street Magazine* exercise. The magazine pictured six children: four children had raised their hands because they wanted to play tag; two had their hands down because they wanted to play hide-and-seek. The magazine asked its readers to count the number of children whose hands were raised and then decide what game the children would play.
>
> Nikolas quite realistically replied, "They will play both. First they will play tag. Then they will play hide-and-seek." Despite the magazine's "rules," he was right. To children, it is natural to take turns. The winner may get to play first or more often, but even the "loser" gets something. His was a positive-sum solution that many adult rule-makers ignore.
>
> The traditional answer to the magazine's problem would have been a zero-sum solution: "The children—all the children—will play tag and only tag." As a zero-sum solution, everything is seen in terms of "I win; you lose." The conventional answer relies on winner-take-all majority rule, in which the tag players, as the majority, win the right to decide for all children what game to play. The hide-and-seek preference becomes irrelevant. The numerically more powerful majority choice simply subsumes minority preferences.

Guinier uses this story of her son to illustrate a point of constitutional law raised by James Madison at the time the United States was founded. Madison believed that "the tyranny of the majority" represented the biggest threat to the system of democracy proposed for the new nation. He believed that a majority could be just as despotic in its rule as a king. As an alternative, Guinier proposes the solution that her son offered to the *Sesame Street Magazine* exercise.

In an increasingly diverse society, Guinier argues that our concept of democratic government should include a principle of turn taking so that minority views can be represented.

Narrative arguments can be representative anecdotes, as we have seen with the examples from MADD, Martin Luther King, Jr., and Lani Guinier, or they can be longer accounts of particular events that express larger ideas. One such story is George Orwell's account of a hanging in Burma (the country that is now known as Myanmar) while he was a colonial administrator in the late 1920s. In "A Hanging," first published in 1931, Orwell narrates an execution of a nameless prisoner who was convicted of a nameless crime. Everyone quietly and dispassionately performs their jobs—the prison guards, the hangman, the superintendent, and even the prisoner, who offers no resistance when he is bound and led to the gallows. All is totally routine until a very small incident makes Orwell aware of what is happening:

> It was about forty yards to the gallows. I watched the bare brown back of the prisoner marching in front of me. He walked clumsily with his bound arms, but quite steadily, with that bobbing gait of the Indian who never straightens his knees. At each step his muscles slid neatly into place, the lock of hair on his scalp danced up and down, his feet printed themselves on the wet gravel. And once, in spite of the men who gripped him by each shoulder, he stepped lightly aside to avoid a puddle on the path.
>
> It is curious; but till that moment I had never realized what it means to destroy a healthy, conscious man. When I saw the prisoner step aside to avoid the puddle, I saw the mystery, the unspeakable wrongness, of cutting a life short when it is in full tide. This man was not dying, he was alive just as we are alive. All the organs of his body were working—bowels digesting food, skin renewing itself, nails growing, tissues forming—all toiling away in solemn foolery. His nails would still be growing when he stood on the drop, when he was falling through the air with a tenth-of-a-second to live. His eyes saw the yellow gravel and gray walls, and his brain still remembered, foresaw, reasoned—even about puddles. He and we were a party of men walking together, seeing, hearing, feeling, understanding the same world; and in two minutes, with a sudden snap, one of us would be gone—one mind less, one world less.

Orwell's narrative leads a dramatic moment of recognition, which gives this story its lasting power.

The biggest problem with narrative arguments is that anyone can tell a story. On the one hand, there are compelling stories that argue against capital punishment. For example, a mentally retarded man was executed in Arkansas who refused a piece of pie at his last meal, telling the guards that he wanted to save the pie for later. On the other hand, there are also many stories about the victims of murder and other crimes. Many families have Web sites on which they call for killing those responsible for murdering their loved ones. They too have compelling stories to tell.

Violent deaths of all kinds make for especially vivid narrative arguments. In the late 1990s, there were several incidents in which schoolchildren used guns taken from the family home to kill other students. Stories of these tragedies provided strong arguments for gun control. Gun rights organizations, including the National Rifle Association (NRA), attempted to counter these stories by claiming that they are not truly representative. The NRA claims that between sixty million and sixty-five million Americans own guns and thirty million to thirty-five million own handguns. They argue that more than 99.8 percent of all guns and 99.6 percent of handguns will not be used to commit crimes in any given year. Thus, the NRA argues that narratives of tragic gun deaths are either not representative or the result of allowing too many criminals to avoid prison or execution.

There are two keys to making effective narrative arguments: establishing credibility and establishing representativeness. It's easy enough to make up stories that suit the point you want to make. Writing from personal experience can give you a great deal of impact, but that impact vanishes if your readers doubt that you are telling the truth. Second, the story you tell may be true enough, but the question remains how representative the incident is. We don't ban bananas because someone once slipped on a banana peel. Narratives are often useful for illustrating how people are affected by particular issues or events, but narrative arguments are more effective if you have more evidence than just one incident. The death of Cari Lightner was a tragedy, but the deaths of over 25,000 people a year caused by drunk drivers made Cari Lightner's death representative of a national tragedy, a slaughter that could be prevented. Cari Lightner's tragic story had power because people understood it to be representative of a much larger problem.

 Leslie Marmon Silko

The Border Patrol State

Leslie Marmon Silko (1948–) was born in Albuquerque and graduated from the University of New Mexico. She now teaches at the University of Arizona. She has received much critical acclaim for her writings about Native Americans. Her first novel, *Ceremony* (1977), describes the struggles of a veteran returning home after World War II to civilian life on a New Mexico reservation. Her incorporation of Indian story-telling techniques in *Ceremony* drew strong praise. One critic called her "the most accomplished Indian writer of her generation." She has since published two more novels, *Almanac of the Dead* (1991) and *Gardens in the Dunes* (1999); a collection of essays, *Yellow Woman and a Beauty of the Spirit: Essays on Native American Life Today* (1996); two volumes of poems and stories; and many shorter works. Silko's talents as a storyteller are evident in this essay, which first appeared in the magazine *Nation* in 1994.

Leslie Marmon Silko

1   I used to travel the highways of New Mexico and Arizona with a wonderful sensation of absolute freedom as I cruised down the open road and across the vast desert plateaus. On the Laguna Pueblo reservation, where I was raised, the people were patriotic despite the way the U.S. government had treated Native Americans. As proud citizens, we grew up believing the freedom to travel was our inalienable right, a right that some Native Americans had been denied in the early twentieth century. Our cousin, old Bill Pratt, used to ride his horse 300 miles overland from Laguna, New Mexico, to Prescott, Arizona, every summer to work as a fire lookout.

2   In school in the 1950s, we were taught that our right to travel from state to state without special papers or threat of detainment was a right that citizens under communist and totalitarian governments did not possess. That wide open highway told us we were U.S. citizens; we were free. . . .

3   Not so long ago, my companion Gus and I were driving south from Albuquerque, returning to Tucson after a book promotion for the paperback edition of my novel *Almanac of the Dead.* I had settled back and gone to sleep while Gus drove, but I was awakened when I felt the car slowing to a stop. It was nearly midnight on New Mexico State Road 26, a dark, lonely stretch of two-lane highway between Hatch and Deming. When I sat up, I saw the headlights and emergency flashers of six vehicles—Border Patrol cars and a van were blocking both lanes of the highway. Gus stopped the car and rolled down the window to ask what was wrong. But the closest Border Patrolman and his companion did not reply; instead, the first agent ordered us to "step out of the car." Gus asked why, but his question seemed to set them off. Two more Border Patrol agents immediately approached our car, and one of them snapped, "Are you looking for trouble?" as if he would relish it.

4   I will never forget that night beside the highway. There was an awful feeling of menace and violence straining to break loose. It was clear that the uniformed men would be only too happy to drag us out of the car if we did not speedily comply with their request (asking a question is tantamount to resistance, it seems). So we

stepped out of the car and they motioned for us to stand on the shoulder of the road. The night was very dark, and no other traffic had come down the road since we had been stopped. All I could think about was a book I had read—*Nunca Mas*—the official report of a human rights commission that investigated and certified more than 12,000 "disappearances" during Argentina's "dirty war" in the late 1970s.

The weird anger of these Border Patrolmen made me think about descrip-   5
tions in the report of Argentine police and military officers who became addicted to interrogation, torture and the murder that followed. When the military and police ran out of political suspects to torture and kill, they resorted to the random abduction of citizens off the streets. I thought how easy it would be for the Border Patrol to shoot us and leave our bodies and car beside the highway, like so many bodies found in these parts and ascribed to "drug runners."

Two other Border Patrolmen stood by the white van. The one who had asked   6
if we were looking for trouble ordered his partner to "get the dog," and from the back of the van another patrolman brought a small female German shepherd on a leash. The dog apparently did not heel well enough to suit him, and the handler jerked the leash. They opened the doors of our car and pulled the dog's head into it, but I saw immediately from the expression in her eyes that the dog hated them, and that she would not serve them. When she showed no interest in the inside of the car, they brought her around back to the trunk, near where we were standing. They half-dragged her up into the trunk, but still she did not indicate any stowed-away human beings or illegal drugs.

The mood got uglier; the officers seemed outraged that the dog could not find   7
any contraband, and they dragged her over to us and commanded her to sniff our legs and feet. To my relief, the strange violence the Border Patrol agents had focused on us now seemed shifted to the dog. I no longer felt so strongly that we would be murdered. We exchanged looks—the dog and I. She was afraid of what they might do, just as I was. The dog's handler jerked the leash sharply as she sniffed us, as if to make her perform better, but the dog refused to accuse us: She had an innate dignity that did not permit her to serve the murderous impulses of those men. I can't forget the expression in the dog's eyes; it was as if she were embarrassed to be associated with them. I had a small amount of medicinal marijuana in my purse that night, but she refused to expose me. I am not partial to dogs, but I will always remember the small German shepherd that night.

Unfortunately, what happened to me is an everyday occurrence here now.   8
Since the 1980s, on top of greatly expanding border checkpoints, the Immigration and Naturalization Service and the Border Patrol have implemented policies that interfere with the rights of U.S. citizens to travel freely within our borders. I.N.S. agents now patrol all interstate highways and roads that lead to or from the U.S.-Mexico border in Texas, New Mexico, Arizona and California. Now, when you drive east from Tucson on Interstate 10 toward El Paso, you encounter an I.N.S. check station outside Las Cruces, New Mexico. When you drive north from Las Cruces up

Interstate 25, two miles north of the town of Truth or Consequences, the highway is blocked with orange emergency barriers, and all traffic is diverted into a two-lane Border Patrol checkpoint—ninety-five miles north of the U.S.-Mexico border.

9   I was detained once at Truth or Consequences, despite my and my companion's Arizona driver's licenses. Two men, both Chicanos, were detained at the same time, despite the fact that they too presented ID and spoke English without the thick Texas accents of the Border Patrol agents. While we were stopped, we watched as other vehicles—whose occupants were white—were waved through the checkpoint. White people traveling with brown people, however, can expect to be stopped on suspicion they work with the sanctuary movement, which shelters refugees. White people who appear to be clergy, those who wear ethnic clothing or jewelry and women with very long hair or very short hair (they could be nuns) are also frequently detained; white men with beards or men with long hair are likely to be detained, too, because Border Patrol agents have "profiles" of "those sorts" of white people who may help political refugees. (Most of the political refugees from Guatemala and El Salvador are Native American or mestizo because the indigenous people of the Americas have continued to resist efforts by invaders to displace them from their ancestral lands.) Alleged increases in illegal immigration by people of Asian ancestry mean that the Border Patrol now routinely detains anyone who appears to be Asian or part Asian, as well.

10   Once your car is diverted from the Interstate Highway into the checkpoint area, you are under the control of the Border Patrol, which in practical terms exercises a power that no highway patrol or city patrolman possesses: They are willing to detain anyone, for no apparent reason. Other law-enforcement officers need a shred of probable cause in order to detain someone. On the books, so does the Border Patrol; but on the road, it's another matter. They'll order you to stop your car and step out; then they'll ask you to open the trunk. If you ask why or request a search warrant, you'll be told that they'll have to have a dog sniff the car before they can request a search warrant, and the dog might not get there for two or three hours. The search warrant might require an hour or two past that. They make it clear that if you force them to obtain a search warrant for the car, they will make you submit to a strip search as well.

11   Traveling in the open, though, the sense of violation can be even worse. Never mind high-profile cases like that of former Border Patrol agent Michael Elmer, acquitted of murder by claiming self-defense, despite admitting that as an officer he shot an "illegal" immigrant in the back and then hid the body, which remained undiscovered until another Border Patrolman reported the event. (Last month, Elmer was convicted of reckless endangerment in a separate incident, for shooting at least ten rounds from his M-16 too close to a group of immigrants as they were crossing illegally into Nogales in March 1992.) Or that in El Paso a high school football coach driving a vanload of players in full uniform was pulled over on the freeway and a Border Patrol agent put a cocked revolver to his head. (The football coach was Mexican-American, as were most of the players in his van; the incident

eventually caused a federal judge to issue a restraining order against the Border Patrol.) We've a mountain of personal experiences like that which never make the newspapers. A history professor at U.C.L.A. told me she had been traveling by train from Los Angeles to Albuquerque twice a month doing research. On each of her trips, she had noticed that the Border Patrol agents were at the station in Albuquerque scrutinizing the passengers. Since she is six feet tall and of Irish and German ancestry, she was not particularly concerned. Then one day when she stepped off the train in Albuquerque, two Border Patrolmen accosted her, wanting to know what she was doing, and why she was traveling between Los Angeles and Albuquerque twice a month. She presented identification and an explanation deemed "suitable" by the agents, and was allowed to go about her business.

Just the other day, I mentioned to a friend that I was writing this article and   12
he told me about his 73-year-old father, who is half Chinese and who had set out alone by car from Tucson to Albuquerque the week before. His father had become confused by road construction and missed a turnoff from Interstate 10 to Interstate 25; when he turned around and circled back, he missed the turnoff a second time. But when he looped back for yet another try, Border Patrol agents stopped him and forced him to open his trunk. After they satisfied themselves that he was not smuggling Chinese immigrants, they sent him on his way. He was so rattled by the event that he had to be driven home by his daughter.

This is the police state that has developed in the southwestern United States   13
since the 1980s. No person, no citizen, is free to travel without the scrutiny of the Border Patrol. In the city of South Tucson, where 80 percent of the respondents were Chicano or Mexicano, a joint research project by the University of Wisconsin and the University of Arizona recently concluded that one out of every five people there had been detained, mistreated verbally or nonverbally, or questioned by I.N.S. agents in the past two years.

Manifest Destiny may lack its old grandeur of theft and blood—"lock the door" is   14
what it means now, with racism a trump card to be played again and again, shamelessly, by both major political parties. "Immigration," like "street crime" and "welfare fraud," is a political euphemism that refers to people of color. Politicians and media people talk about "illegal aliens" to dehumanize and demonize undocumented immigrants, who are for the most part people of color. Even in the days of Spanish and Mexican rule, no attempts were made to interfere with the flow of people and goods from south to north and north to south. It is the U.S. government that has continually attempted to sever contact between the tribal people north of the border and those to the south.[1]

---

[1] The Treaty of Guadalupe Hidalgo, signed in 1848, recognizes the right of Tohano O'Odom (Papago) people to move freely across the U.S.-Mexico border without documents. A treaty with Canada guarantees similar rights to those of the Iroquois nation in traversing the U.S.-Canada border. [Author's note]

15   Now that the "Iron Curtain" is gone, it is ironic that the U.S. government and its Border Patrol are constructing a steel wall ten feet high to span sections of the border with Mexico. While politicians and multinational corporations extol the virtues of NAFTA and "free trade" (in goods, not flesh), the ominous curtain is already up in a six-mile section at the border crossing at Mexicali; two miles are being erected but are not yet finished at Naco; and at Nogales, sixty miles south of Tucson, the steel wall has been all rubber-stamped and awaits construction likely to begin in March. Like the pathetic multimillion-dollar "antidrug" border surveillance balloons that were continually deflated by high winds and made only a couple of meager interceptions before they blew away, the fence along the border is a theatrical prop, a bit of pork for contractors. Border entrepreneurs have already used blowtorches to cut passageways through the fence to collect "tolls," and are doing a brisk business. Back in Washington, the I.N.S. announces a $300 million computer contract to modernize its record-keeping and Congress passes a crime bill that shunts $255 million to the I.N.S. for 1995, $181 million earmarked for border control, which is to include 700 new partners for the men who stopped Gus and me in our travels, and the history professor, and my friend's father, and as many as they could from South Tucson.

16   It is no use; borders haven't worked, and they won't work, not now, as the indigenous people of the Americas reassert their kinship and solidarity with one another. A mass migration is already under way; its roots are not simply economic. The Uto-Aztecan languages are spoken as far north as Taos Pueblo near the Colorado border, all the way south to Mexico City. Before the arrival of the Europeans, the indigenous communities throughout this region not only conducted commerce, the people shared cosmologies, and oral narratives about the Maize Mothers, the Twin Brothers and their Grandmother, Spider Woman, as well as Quetzalcoatl the benevolent snake. The great human migration within the Americas cannot be stopped; human beings are natural forces of the Earth, just as rivers and winds are natural forces.

17   Deep down the issue is simple: The so-called "Indian Wars" from the days of Sitting Bull and Red Cloud have never really ended in the Americas. The Indian people of southern Mexico, of Guatemala and those left in El Salvador, too, are still fighting for their lives and for their land against the "cavalry" patrols sent out by the governments of those lands. The Americas are Indian country, and the "Indian problem" is not about to go away.

18   One evening at sundown, we were stopped in traffic at a railroad crossing in downtown Tucson while a freight train passed us, slowly gaining speed as it headed north to Phoenix. In the twilight I saw the most amazing sight: Dozens of human beings, mostly young men, were riding the train; everywhere, on flat cars, inside open boxcars, perched on top of boxcars, hanging off ladders on tank cars and between boxcars. I couldn't count fast enough, but I saw fifty or sixty people headed north. They were dark young men, Indian and mestizo; they were smiling and a few of them waved at us in our cars. I was reminded of the ancient story of

Aztlán, told by the Aztecs but known in other Uto-Aztecan communities as well. Aztlán is the beautiful land to the north, the origin place of the Aztec people. I don't remember how or why the people left Aztlán to journey farther south, but the old story says that one day, they will return.

Steps in Writing a Narrative Argument

If your instructor asks for a topic proposal, use steps 1–4 to guide you in writing the proposal.

1. **Identify an experience that you had that makes an implicit argument.** Think about experiences that made you realize that something is wrong or that things need to be changed. The experience does not have to be one that leads to a moral lesson at the end, but it should be one that makes your readers think.

   Examples:

   ■ Being arrested and hauled to jail for carrying a glass soft drink bottle in a glass-free zone made you realize how inefficiently your police force is being used.

   ■ After going through a complicated system of getting referrals for a serious medical condition and then having the treatment your physician recommends denied by your HMO, you want to tell your story to show just how flawed the HMO system really is.

   ■ When you moved from a well-financed suburban school to a much poorer rural school, you came to realize what huge differences exist among school systems in your state.

   ■ If you have ever experienced being stereotyped in any way, narrate that experience and describe how it affected you.

2. **List all the details you can remember about the experience.** When did it happen? How old were you? Why were you there? Who else was there? Where did it happen? If the place is important, describe what it looked like. Then go through your list of details and put a check besides the ones that are important to your story.

3. **Examine the significance of the event for you.** Take a few minutes to write about how you felt about the experience at the time. How did it affect you then? What was your immediate reaction? Next, take a few

minutes to write about how you feel about the experience now. How do you see it differently now?

4. **Analyze your potential readers.** How much would your readers know about the background of the experience you are describing? Are they familiar with the place where it happened? Would anything similar ever likely have happened to them? How likely are they to agree with your feelings about the experience?

5. **Write a draft.**

   ■ You might need to give some background first, but if you have a compelling story, often it's best to launch right in.

   ■ You might want to tell the story as it happened (chronological order) or you might want to begin with a striking incident and then go back to tell how it happened (flashback).

   ■ You might want to reflect on your experience at the end, but you want your story to do most of the work. Your readers should share your feelings if you tell your story well.

6. **Take your draft through the revision steps in chapter 15.**

Chapter 9

Rebuttal Arguments

When you hear the word *rebuttal,* you might think of a debate team or the part of a trial when the attorney for the defense answers the plaintiff's accusations. Although *rebuttal* has those definitions, arguments of rebuttal can be thought of in much larger terms. Indeed, much of what people know about the world today is the result of centuries of arguments of rebuttal.

In high school and college, you no doubt have taken many courses that required the memorization of knowledge and evidence, which you demonstrated by repeating these facts on tests. You probably didn't think much about how the knowledge came about. Once in a while, though, something happens that makes people think consciously about a piece of knowledge that they have learned. For example, in elementary school, you learned that the earth rotates on its axis once a day. Maybe you didn't think about it much at the time, but once, years later, you were out on a clear night and noticed the Big Dipper in one part of the sky, and then you looked for it later and found it in another part of the sky. Perhaps you became interested enough that you watched the stars for a few hours. If you've ever spent a clear night out stargazing, you have observed that the North Star, called Polaris, stays in the same place. The stars near Polaris appear to move in a circle around Polaris, and the stars farther away move from east to west until they disappear below the horizon.

If you are lucky enough to live in a place where the night sky is often clear, you can see the same pattern repeated night after night. And if you stop to think about why you see the stars circling around Polaris, you remember what you were taught long ago—that you live on a rotating ball, so the stars appear to move across the sky, but in fact, stars are so distant from the earth that their actual movement is not visible to humans over a short term.

An alternative explanation for these facts not only is possible but is the one that people believed from ancient times until about five hundred years ago. People assumed that their position on the earth was fixed and that the entire sky rotated on an axis connecting Polaris and the earth. The big flaw in this theory for people in ancient times is the movement of the planets. If you watch the path of Mars over several nights, you will observe that it also moves across the sky from east to west, but it makes an anomalous backward movement during its journey and then goes forward again. The other planets also seem to wander back and forth as they cross the night sky. The ancient Greeks developed an explanation of the strange wanderings of the planets by theorizing that the planets move in small circles imposed on larger orbits. By graphing little circles on top of circles, the course of planets could be plotted and predicted. This theory culminated in the work of Ptolemy, who lived in Alexandria in the second century A.D. Ptolemy proposed displaced centers for the small circles called *epicycles,* which gave a better fit for predicting the path of planets.

Because Ptolemy's model of the universe was numerically accurate in its predictions, educated people for centuries assumed its validity, even though there was evidence to the contrary. For example, Aristarchus of Samos, who lived in the fourth century B.C.E., used the size of the earth's shadow cast on the moon during a lunar eclipse to compute the sizes of the moon and sun and their distances from the earth. Even though his calculations were flawed, Aristarchus recognized that the sun is much bigger than the earth, and he advanced the heliocentric hypothesis: that the earth orbits the sun.

Many centuries passed, however, before educated people believed that the sun, not the earth, was the center of the solar system. In the early sixteenth century, the Polish astronomer Nicolaus Copernicus recognized that Ptolemy's model could be greatly simplified if the sun was at the center of the solar system. He kept his theory a secret for much of his life and saw the published account of his work only a few hours before his death in 1543. Even though Copernicus made a major breakthrough, he was not able to take full advantage of the heliocentric hypothesis because he followed the tradition that orbits are perfect circles; thus, he still needed circles on top of circles to explain the motion of the planets but far fewer than did Ptolemy.

The definitive rebuttal of Ptolemy came a century later with the work of the German astronomer Johannes Kepler. Kepler performed many tedious calculations, which were complicated by the fact that he had to first assume an orbit for the earth before he could compute orbits for the planets. Finally he made a stunning discovery: All the orbits of the planets could be described as an ellipse with the sun at the center. The dominance of the Ptolemaic model of the universe was finally over.

The relationship of facts and theories lies at the heart of the scientific method. Both Ptolomy's theory and Kepler's theory explain why the stars appear to move around Polaris at night. Kepler made a convincing argument by rebuttal to the Ptolemaic model because he could give a much simpler analysis. The history of astronomy is a history of arguments of rebuttal. Modern astronomy was made possible because Copernicus challenged the established relationship of theory and evidence in astronomy. This awareness of the relationship of factual and theoretical claims in science is one definition of **critical thinking** in the sciences. What is true for the history of astronomy is true for the sciences; critical thinking in the sciences relies on arguments of rebuttal.

Similar kinds of arguments of rebuttal are presented today in the debate over global warming. One of the main sources of data for arguments of rebuttal against global warming is the twenty-year record of temperature readings from NASA weather satellites orbiting the earth at the North and South poles. These satellites use microwave sensors to measure temperature variation in the atmosphere from the surface to about six miles above the earth. Computer models predict a gradual warming in the earth's lower atmosphere along with the surface because of the buildup of carbon dioxide and other greenhouse gases, the gases produced from burning fossil fuels. But while temperatures measured on the earth's surface have gradually increased, the corresponding rises in the atmosphere as recorded by satellites haven't appeared to happen. In August 1998, however, two scientists discovered a flaw in the satellites that was making them lose altitude and therefore misreport temperature data. When adjusted, the satellite data confirm what thermometers on the ground tell us: The earth is getting warmer.

In some cases, particular disciplines have specialized training to assess the relationship of theory and evidence. But more often, people must engage in **general critical thinking** to assess the validity of claims based on evidence. Often, one has to weigh competing claims of people who have excellent qualifications. One group of nutritional experts says that people should take calcium supplements to strengthen their bones. Another group warns that people are in danger of suffering from kidney stones if they take too much calcium. Critical thinking is involved in all the kinds of arguments that are discussed in this book, but it is especially important in arguments of rebuttal.

If you think back to the basic model of how arguments work, you can see that there are two primary strategies for rebuttal arguments:

CLAIM ◄----- LINK (*because*) ◄----- REASON ◄----- EVIDENCE
⬆
CHALLENGES (So What?)

First, you can challenge the assumptions on which the claim is based. Copernicus did not question Ptolemy's data concerning how the stars and planets appear in the sky to an observer on the earth. Instead, he questioned Ptolemy's central assumption that the earth is the center of the solar system. Second, you can question the evidence. Sometimes, the evidence presented is simply wrong, as was the case for the satellites that lost altitude and reported faulty temperature data. Sometimes, the evidence is incomplete or unrepresentative, and sometimes, counterevidence can be found.

The great majority of issues that involve people cannot be decided with the certainty of the statement that the earth indeed orbits the sun. Even when the facts are generally agreed upon, there is often disagreement over the causes. Violent crime rates decreased from 1980 to 1992, and some politicians credited tougher sentencing that put more people in prison. But others pointed out that the drop could be attributed to the fact that older people, who commit fewer violent crimes, became a much larger segment of the overall population. The crime rates for the youngest age groups actually rose during this time. Those who disputed that putting more people in prison reduced violent crime argued that the drop was a reflection of the aging population of the United States.

Arguments over controversial issues lasting for many years often become primarily arguments of rebuttal. One such issue that has been debated throughout the twentieth century is drug policy in the United States. Today, almost everyone who writes about illegal drugs in the United States says that the current policy is bad. Even though U.S. jails and prisons are bursting with people who have been convicted and sentenced for drug offenses, millions of people still use illegal drugs. The social, political, and economic costs of illegal drugs are staggering, and the debate continues over what to do about these substances. On one side are those who want more police, more drug users in jail, and military forces sent to other countries to stop the drug traffic. On the other are those who compare current efforts to stop the flow of drugs to those of failed efforts under Prohibition (1919–1933) to halt the sale of alcohol. They want most illegal drugs to be legalized or decriminalized.

On September 7, 1989, Nobel Prize–winning economist Milton Friedman published in the *Wall Street Journal* an open letter to William Bennett, then the drug czar (director of the Office of National Drug Policy) under President Bush. Friedman wrote:

Dear Bill:

In Oliver Cromwell's eloquent words, "I beseech you, in the bowels of Christ, think it possible you may be mistaken" about the course you and President Bush urge us to adopt to fight drugs. The path you propose of more police, more jails, use of the military in foreign countries, harsh penalties for drug users, and a whole panoply of repressive measures can only make a bad situation worse. The drug war cannot be won by those tactics without undermining the human liberty and individual freedom that you and I cherish.

You are not mistaken in believing that drugs are a scourge that is devastating our society. You are not mistaken in believing that drugs are tearing asunder our social fabric, ruining the lives of many young people, and imposing heavy costs on some of the most disadvantaged among us. You are not mistaken in believing that the majority of the public share your concerns. In short, you are not mistaken in the end you seek to achieve.

Your mistake is failing to recognize that the very measures you favor are a major source of the evils you deplore. Of course the problem is demand, but it is not only demand, it is demand that must operate through repressed and illegal channels. Illegality creates obscene profits that finance the murderous tactics of the drug lords; illegality leads to the corruption of law enforcement officials; illegality monopolizes the efforts of honest law forces so they are starved for resources to fight the simpler crimes of robbery, theft and assault.

Drugs are a tragedy for addicts. But criminalizing their use converts that tragedy into a disaster for society, for users and non-users alike. Our experience with the prohibition of drugs is a replay of our experience with the prohibition of alcoholic beverages. . . .

Had drugs been decriminalized 17 years ago [when Friedman first made an appeal that drugs be decriminalized], "crack" would never have been invented (it was invented because the high cost of illegal drugs made it profitable to provide a cheaper version) and there would today be far fewer addicts. The lives of thousands, perhaps hundreds of thousands of innocent victims would have been saved, and not only in the U.S. The ghettos of our major cities would not be drug-and-crime-infested no-man's lands. Fewer people would be in jails, and fewer jails would have been built.

Columbia, Bolivia, and Peru would not be suffering from narco-terror, and we would not be distorting our foreign policy because of narco-terror. Hell would not, in the words with which Billy Sunday welcomed Prohibition, "be forever for rent," but it would be a lot emptier.

In the first two paragraphs, Friedman carefully identifies the common ground he shares with Bennett. Both are political conservatives, as Friedman reminds Bennett when he mentions the "human liberty and individual freedom that you and I cherish." Friedman also agrees with Bennett about the severity of the drug problem, noting that it is "tearing asunder our social fabric, ruining the lives of many young people, and imposing heavy costs on some of the most disadvantaged among us."

Where Friedman differs from Bennett is in Bennett's central assumption: If drugs are now illegal and still being used, then the solution is to make them even more illegal, increasing penalties and extending law enforcement beyond U.S. borders. Friedman calls attention to the centrality of this assumption when he quotes Oliver Cromwell's famous words: "I beseech you, in the bowels of

Christ, think it possible you may be mistaken." If, in fact, this central assumption is flawed, then the reason to spend millions of dollars, to violate civil liberties, and to antagonize other nations is suddenly taken away.

William Bennett responded to Friedman quickly. On September 19, 1989, the *Wall Street Journal* published an open letter of reply from Bennett to Friedman. Here is part of Bennett's response, which has a much more strident tone than Friedman's letter:

Dear Milton:

There was little, if anything, new in your open letter to me calling for the legalization of drugs. As your 1972 article made clear, the legalization argument is an old and familiar one, which has recently been revived by a small number of journalists and academics who insist that the only solution to the drug problem is no solution at all. What surprises me is that you would continue to advocate so unrealistic a proposal without pausing to consider seriously its consequences.

If the argument for drug legalization has one virtue it is its sheer simplicity. Eliminate laws against drugs, and street crime will disappear. Take the profit out of the black market through decriminalization and regulation, and poor neighborhoods will no longer be victimized by drug dealers. Cut back on drug enforcement, and use the money to wage a public health campaign against drugs, as we do with tobacco and alcohol.

The basic premise of all these propositions is that using our nation's laws to fight drugs is too costly. To be sure, our attempts to reduce drug use do carry with them enormous costs. But the question that must be asked—and which is totally ignored by the legalization advocates—is, what are the costs of *not* enforcing laws against drugs?

In my judgment, and in the judgment of virtually every serious scholar in this field, the potential costs of legalizing drugs would be so large as to make it a public policy disaster.

Of course, no one, including you, can say with certainty what would happen in the U.S. if drugs were suddenly to become a readily purchased product. We do know, however, that wherever drugs have become cheaper and more easily obtained, drug use—and addiction—has skyrocketed. In opium and cocaine producing countries, addiction is rampant among the peasants involved in drug production.

Professor James Q. Wilson tells us that during the years in which heroin could be legally prescribed by doctors in Britain, the number of addicts increased forty-fold. And after the repeal of Prohibition—an analogy favored but misunderstood by legalization advocates—consumption of alcohol soared by 350%.

Could we afford such dramatic increases in drug use? I doubt it. Already the toll of drug use on American society—measured in lost productivity, in rising health insurance costs, in hospitals flooded with drug overdose emergencies, in drug caused accidents, and in premature death—is surely more than we would like to bear.

You seem to believe that by spending just a little more money on treatment and rehabilitation, the costs of increased addiction can be avoided. That hope betrays a basic misunderstanding of the problems facing drug treatment. Most addicts don't suddenly decide to get help. They remain addicts either because treatment isn't available or because they don't seek it out. . . .

As for the connection between drugs and crime, your unswerving commitment to a legalization solution prevents you from appreciating the complexity of the drug market. Contrary to your claim, most addicts do not turn to crime to support their habit. Research shows that many of them were involved in criminal activity before they turned to drugs. Many former addicts who have received treatment continue to commit crimes during their recovery. And even if drugs were legal, what evidence do you have that the habitual drug user wouldn't continue to rob and steal to get money for clothes, food or shelter? Drug addicts always want more drugs than they can afford, and no legalization scheme has yet come up with a way of satisfying that appetite.

Bennett goes on to maintain that "A true friend of freedom understands that government has a responsibility to craft and uphold laws that help educate citizens about right and wrong. That, at any rate, was the Founders' view of our system of government." He ends by describing Friedman's proposal as "irresponsible and reckless public policy."

Friedman was not content to let Bennett have the last word, so he in turn wrote a reply that appeared on September 29, 1989, in the *Wall Street Journal*. At this point, Friedman drops the open letter strategy and writes instead a more conventional response, referring to Bennett as *he* instead of *you*:

William Bennett is entirely right (editorial page, Sept. 19) that "there was little, if anything, new in" my open letter to him—just as there is little, if anything, new in his proposed program to rid this nation of the scourge of drugs. That is why I am so disturbed by that program. It flies in the face of decades of experience. More police, more jails, more-stringent penalties, increased efforts at interception, increased publicity about the evils of drugs—all this has been accompanied by more, not fewer, drug addicts; more, not fewer, crimes and murders; more, not less, corruption; more, not fewer, innocent victims.

Like Mr. Bennett, his predecessors were "committed to fighting the problem on several fronts through imaginative policies and hard work over a long period of time." What evidence convinces him that the same policies on a larger scale will end the drug scourge? He offers none in his response to me, only assertion and the conjecture that legalizing drugs would produce "a public policy disaster"—as if that is not exactly what we already have.

Friedman then claims that "legalizing drugs is not equivalent to surrender" but rather the precondition for an effective fight against drug use. He allows that the number of addicts might increase, but he argues that it is certain that the number of innocent victims would drop drastically. He adds that another category of victims are foreign nations when we base our foreign policy on drug control.

Friedman's sharpest criticism of Bennett comes over Bennett's claim to represent the tradition of the Founders of the United States. Friedman completely rejects Bennett's assertion that the Founders wanted government to educate citizens about what is right and what is wrong. Friedman says "that is a totalitarian view utterly unacceptable to the Founders. I do not believe, and neither did they, that it is the responsibility of government to tell free citizens what is right and wrong."

The Faculty of the University of Washington

Open Letter to Governor Gary Locke and the 2020 Commission on the Future of Higher Education

The open letter is a frequently used genre for rebuttal arguments. Few issues in higher education today are as controversial as ambitious proposals for distance education as alternatives to traditional education. Advocates of these proposals claim that the goal is to expand access to postsecondary education. They maintain that courses offered on the Internet can be taken by anyone anywhere at anytime. These proposals have been especially popular in western states, where governors and legislators are worried about how they will meet increasing demand for higher education when the baby-boom echo generation expands the traditional college age group by 15 percent by 2008 and when more adults are returning to college. This boom has been called Tidal Wave 2, with most of the impact coming in the western states, which will see a 60 percent growth in college enrollments by 2008, in contrast to 10 percent in the Midwest, 21 percent in the Northeast, and 22 percent in the South.

The governor of the state of Washington, Gary Locke, appointed a committee, called the 2020 Commission, to develop the state's higher education plan for the next quarter-century. A member of the committee, Wallace Loh, spoke at the University of Washington in April 1998. He championed a "virtual university" that could accommodate the 70,000–80,000 additional students who are expected to want college education in Washington by the year 2020. Loh's speech and other remarks by Governor Locke greatly disturbed the faculty of the University of Washington. In June 1998, they composed an open letter to the governor that was signed by over 800 members of the faculty.

Higher education in the state of Washington is at a crossroads. Earlier this year 1
Governor Gary Locke appointed a blue ribbon commission of business and civic leaders to develop plans to meet the state's higher education needs for the next quarter century. Recommendations are due in September. The undersigned members of the faculty at the University of Washington address this letter of concern to these committees as well as to the Governor and legislature.

These are troubling times for the University of Washington and for higher ed- 2
ucation in Washington state. Our state's future depends upon providing increased access to affordable, high-quality public education. But there are signs that those charged with designing the future of our community colleges and universities are heading in disturbing directions.

Visions of education "without bricks and mortar," of education by CD-ROM 3
and internet, have dominated the initial meetings of the 2020 Commission. In a recent speech at the UW law school, Wallace Loh, ex-officio member of the Commission and Governor Locke's chief advisor on higher education, added to the impression that the planners are bent on replacing face-to-face classroom teaching with what he described as the "brave new world of digital education." Governor Locke himself, in a speech to graduating high school seniors, has anticipated the obsolescence of the University as we know it, saying that in the future there will be no need for "designer label" educations at prestigious institutions.

Hopefully these are merely exploratory remarks. But as faculty members at 4
the University of Washington (an institution we have never regarded as "designer label"), we feel called upon to respond before quixotic ideas harden into disastrous policies.

Founded as a vital public center for the exchange of ideas, the University of 5
Washington has survived periodic economic challenges to achieve its standing as an internationally renowned teaching and research institution, on a par with private universities costing more than five times as much. The University's national

reputation is crucial not only because UW is the Northwest's principal institution of higher learning, but also because the undergraduate and graduate students who avail themselves of its distinguished faculty and resources are themselves major contributors to our teaching and scholarly community.

6   Declining rankings reduce our ability to recruit and produce the finest scholars and educators in our state and, indeed, the world. Is it possible that a state that can afford to build world-class sports arenas would turn its back on the world-class university that has served it for so long and with such distinction?

7   In the last 20 years Seattle has become a major U.S. city, the state of Washington has grown, and its economy and population have expanded rapidly. What has *not* grown proportionately is our investment in public education. Despite our industry and prosperity, Washington state invests fewer dollars per capita in higher education than *any state in the nation but one.*

8   Since the 1980s, the University of Washington has faced successive budget cuts, pay freezes, and hiring freezes. Other states, notably Michigan, Illinois, Wisconsin, and North Carolina, also faced economic hardships. But their elected officials wisely saw their universities as bearing the promise of the future. Those states protected—and continue to protect—these vital assets. Meanwhile, the University of Washington has struggled to maintain its reputation. Its successes thus far testify to the loyalties and capabilities of its faculty, administration, students, and staff.

Disturbing Agendas

9   Unfortunately Washington's policy makers now seem to be considering a number of risky alternatives to the excellent system of public education we already have. Calls for "downsizing," productivity increases, and greater "accountability" carelessly echo corporate fads without taking into account the already downsized nature of the state's universities and colleges.

10   The University of Washington and its employees are "already" accountable through a range of public channels, and their achievements in providing high-quality education at what is already a uniquely low cost speaks for itself. As students know well, education is not a product, but a process, and increased "productivity" means larger classes, fewer resources, less contact with instructors and other students, and the loss of valued teachers and researchers.

11   Even riskier, some policy makers appear to have decided that higher education must undergo the rigorous reorganization endured by the health care professions. They would like to convince the public that colleges and universities should be supplanted by a profit-driven, digitalized "knowledge industry," and that teachers should be subject to the same kinds of limitations that healthcare providers have experienced under the rule of HMOs. This prospect is frightening—deeply contrary to the foundations of higher education and its role fostering a free and democratic society.

In addition there is a growing fascination with "digital education." In his April   12
27 speech Governor Locke made the surprising claim that the research university
and its national prestige are "irrelevant" to a coming "Information Age" in which
Washingtonians will simply buy their "knowledge" in "bite-sized" chunks through
private technology. A few weeks later, Wallace Loh spoke enthusiastically of a "virtual university," where education will be delivered electronically, and anony-
mously, to students seated at "the kitchen table."

Although "distance learning" presents important opportunities to specific   13
kinds of individuals, including full-time workers seeking continuing education,
for most students it imposes serious limitations. One of the problems with the
newest crop of distance-learning institutions is that they are motivated entirely
by profit. They admit students into their programs regardless of whether or not
they have suitable faculty and resources to confer degrees. The value and efficacy
of degrees attained through such unconventional means are entirely unproven.
When advanced education is turned into a business, it is the "buyer"—or student—who must beware.

While costly fantasies of this kind present a mouth-watering bonanza to soft-   14
ware manufacturers and other corporate sponsors, what they bode for education
is nothing short of disastrous. Public money diverted from "live" education into
techno-substitutes will further erode students' access to the low-cost, high-
quality education upon which their "real" futures depend. It is absurd to pretend
that the reputation or ranking of an institution of higher learning can be ignored.
The free market in education-commodities that some foresee, will, in the manner
of all markets, result in a range of products with different values and price-tags.

In reality a privileged few will continue to enjoy the personal and economic   15
benefits of face-to-face instruction at schools like Stanford, UC Berkeley, and
M.I.T. The less fortunate citizens of our state will make do with downsized and un-
derfunded campuses or settle for inferior and dehumanizing "virtual" alternatives. Chances are that neither will qualify the students of the future to compete
for the kind of jobs they want.

Education Is Not Obsolete

Far from obsolete, the University of Washington is a vibrant, living community   16
wherein diverse individuals blend an extraordinary range of skills and motiva-
tions. Its public spaces are unique: the classroom, the seminar, the student union,
the lecture hall, even the corridors. Education, moreover, is not reducible to the
downloading of information, much less to the passive and solitary activity of star-
ing at a screen. Education is an intersubjective and social process, involving
hands-on activity, spontaneity, and the communal experience of sharing in the
learning enterprise.

Education is also not the exclusive province of the young. The thousands of   17
older students demanding access to higher learning are doing so, not only to

enhance their careers and keep pace with technology, but also to be stimulated, revitalized, and rejuvenated by the one area in public life that values ideas for their own sake.

18   As University of Washington faculty we are profoundly committed to meeting these needs and fulfilling the goals of a liberal education. We seek to cultivate the active, independent, critical faculties, ethical capacities, flexible intelligences, and analytical skills without which neither democracy, nor freedom, nor creativity can thrive. *This* kind of teaching involves personal contact and sustained exchange.

19   Fortunately, it is not too late. Governor Locke and members of the 2020 Commission, we urge you to support learning as a human and social practice, an enrichment of soul and mind, the entitlement of all citizens in a democracy, and not a profit-making commodity to be offered on the cheapest terms to the highest bidder.

20   The University of Washington is a vital resource to our community, not a factory, not a corporation, and not a software package. Its excellence and integrity are not only assets that we as a community *can* afford to maintain, but also assets that we *cannot* afford to squander.

Sincerely,
[signed by over 800 members of the faculty]

Steps in Writing a Rebuttal Argument

If your instructor asks for a topic proposal, use steps 1–5 to guide you in writing the proposal.

1. **Identify an argument that you want to argue against.** Use this formula: *it is wrong (or misguided or irresponsible) to claim X.* You might consider using the open letter genre, addressing your rebuttal to a specific person but with the goal of having others read it too.

   Examples:

   ■ Requiring fine arts students to take math courses (or engineering students to take foreign language courses, or the like) is a bad idea.

   ■ Using tax dollars to pay for new stadiums for professional sports teams (or providing grants to artists and theater companies) is a misuse of public funds.

   ■ Requiring riders of bicycles and motorcycles to wear helmets is an unnecessary restriction of individual freedom.

2. **Identify the main claim(s) of the argument that you reject.** What exactly are you arguing against? If you are taking on affirmative action admissions policies for colleges and universities, then what do those policies involve and whom do they affect? Are there secondary claims attached to the main claim? A fair summary of your opponent's position might well find its way into your finished argument.

3. **Examine the facts on which the claim is based.** Are the facts accurate? Are the facts a truly representative sample? Are the facts current? Is there another body of facts that you can present as counterevidence? If the author uses statistics, is evidence for the validity of those statistics presented? Can the statistics be interpreted differently? If the author quotes from sources, how reliable are those sources? Are the sources treated fairly, or are quotes taken out of context? If the author cites outside authority, how much trust can you place in that authority?

4. **Examine the assumptions on which the claim is based.** What is the primary assumption of the claim you are rejecting? What other assumptions support that claim? How are those assumptions flawed? If you are arguing against a specific piece of writing, then how does the author fall short? Does the author resort to name calling? Use faulty reasoning? Ignore key facts?

5. **Analyze your potential readers.** To what extent do your potential readers support the claim that you are rejecting? If they strongly support that claim, then how might you appeal to them to change their minds? What common assumptions and beliefs do you share with them?

6. **Write a draft.**

   Identify the issue and the argument you are rejecting:

   - If the issue is not familiar to most of your readers, you might need to provide some background. Even if it is familiar, it might be helpful to give a quick summary of the competing positions. Remember that offering a fair and accurate summary is a good way to build credibility with your audience.

   Take on the argument that you are rejecting:

   - You might want to question the evidence that is used to support the argument. You can challenge the facts, present counterevidence and countertestimony, cast doubt on representativeness of the sample, cast doubt on the currency and relevance of the examples, challenge the credibility of any authorities cited, question the way in which statistical evidence is presented and interpreted, and argue that quotations are taken out of context.

- In most cases, you will want to question the assumptions and potential outcomes.

    Conclude with emphasis:

- You should have a strong argument in your conclusion that underscores your objections. You might wish to close with a counterargument or counterproposal.

7. **Take your draft through the revision steps in chapter 15.**

Chapter 10

Proposal Arguments

You no doubt have at least one friend who loves to argue. If you say you love a movie, your friend will trash it. If you mention that knowingly breaking the rules in a game is wrong, your friend will reply that it's fine as long as the referee doesn't catch you. These kinds of face-to-face arguments can become the basis for extended written arguments. But when someone finally gets motivated enough to write an extended argument, most often it is because she or he wants something to be changed or wants to stop something from being changed. These kinds of arguments are called **proposal arguments,** and they take the classic form: *We should (or should not) do X.*

At this moment, you might not think that you have anything you feel strong enough about to write a proposal argument. But if you make a list of things that make you mad or at least a little annoyed, then you have a start toward writing a proposal argument. Some things on your list are not going to produce proposal arguments that many people would want to read. If your roommate or partner is a slob, you might be able to write a proposal for that person to start cleaning up more, but it is hard to imagine that anyone else would be interested. Similarly, it might be annoying to you that it stays too hot for too long in the summer where you live or too cold for too long in the winter, but unless you have a direct line to God, it is hard to imagine a serious proposal to change the climate where you live. (Cutting down on air pollution, of course, is something that people can change.) Short of those extremes, however, are a lot of things that you might think, "Why hasn't someone done something about this?" If you believe that others have something to gain if this problem is solved or at least made a little better, then you might be able to develop a good proposal argument.

For instance, suppose you are living off campus, and you buy a student parking sticker when you register for courses so that you can park in the student lot. However, you quickly find out that there are too many cars and trucks for the number of available spaces, and unless you get to campus by 8:00 A.M., you aren't going to find a place to park in your assigned lot. The situation makes you angry because you believe that if you pay for a sticker, you should have a reasonable chance of finding a space to park. You see that there are unfilled lots that are reserved for faculty and staff next to the student parking lot, and you wonder why more spaces aren't allotted to students. You decide to write to the president of your college. You want her to direct parking and traffic services to give more spaces to students or else build a parking garage that will accommodate more vehicles.

But when you start talking to other students on campus, you begin to realize that the problem may be more complex than your first view of it. Your college has taken the position that the fewer students who drive to campus, the less traffic there will be on and around your campus. The administration wants more students to ride shuttle buses, form car pools, or bicycle to campus instead of driving alone. You also find out that faculty and staff members pay ten times as much as students for their parking permits, so they pay a very high premium for a guaranteed space—much too high for most students. If the president of your college is your primary audience, you first have to argue that a problem really exists. You have to convince the president that many students have no choice but to drive if they are to attend classes. You, for example, are willing to ride the shuttle buses, but they don't run often enough for you to make your classes, get back to your car that you left at home, and then drive to your job.

Next, you have to argue that your solution will solve the problem. An eight-story parking garage might be adequate to park all the cars of students who want to drive, but parking garages are very expensive to build. Even if a parking garage is the best solution, the question remains: Who is going to pay for it? Many problems in life could be solved if you had access to unlimited resources, but very few people have such resources at their command. It's not enough to have a solution that can resolve the problem. You have to be able to argue for the feasibility of your solution. If you want to argue that a parking garage is the solution to the parking problem on your campus, then you must also propose how the garage will be financed.

Proposal arguments are often complex and involve the kinds of arguments that were discussed in chapters 5–9. Successful arguments have four major components:

1. *Identifying the problem.* Sometimes, problems are evident to your intended readers. If your city is constantly tearing up the streets and then leaving them for months without doing anything to repair them, then you shouldn't

have much trouble convincing the citizens of your city that streets should be repaired more quickly. But if you raise a problem that will be unfamiliar to most of your readers, you will first have to argue that the problem exists. As we saw in chapter 1, Rachel Carson in *Silent Spring* had to use several kinds of arguments to make people aware of the dangers of pesticides, including narrative arguments, definition arguments, evaluation arguments, and arguments of comparison. Often, you will have to do similar work to establish exactly what problem you are attempting to solve. You will have to define the scope of the problem. Some of the bad roads in your city might be the responsibility of the state, not city government.

2. *Stating your proposed solution.* You need to have a clear, definite statement of exactly what you are proposing. You might want to place this statement near the beginning of your argument, or you might want to place it later, after you have considered and rejected other possible solutions.

3. *Convincing your readers with good reasons that your proposed solution is fair and will work.* When your readers agree that a problem exists and that something should be done about it, your next task is to convince them that your solution is the best one to resolve the problem. If you're writing about the problem your city has in getting streets repaired promptly, then you need to analyze carefully the process that is involved in repairing streets. Sometimes there are mandatory delays so that competing bids can be solicited and unexpected delays when tax revenue falls short of expectations. You should be able to put your finger on the problem in a detailed causal analysis. You should be able to make an evaluation argument that your solution is fair to all concerned. You should also be prepared to make arguments of rebuttal against other possible solutions.

4. *Demonstrating that your solution is feasible.* Your solution not only has to work; it must be feasible to implement. Malaysia effectively ended its drug problem by imposing mandatory death sentences for anyone caught selling even small amounts of drugs. Foreign nationals, teenagers, and grandmothers have all been hanged under this law. Malaysia came up with a good solution for its purposes, but this solution probably would not work in most countries because the punishment seems too extreme. If you want a parking garage built on your campus and you learn that no other funds can be used to construct it, then you have to be able to argue that the potential users of the garage will be willing to pay greatly increased fees for the convenience of parking on campus.

Proposal arguments don't just fall out of the sky. For any problem of major significance—gun control, poverty, teenage pregnancy, abortion, capital punishment, drug legalization—you will find long histories of debate. An issue with a much shorter history can also quickly pile up mountains of arguments if it gains wide public attention. In 1972, for example, President Richard Nixon signed into law the Education Amendments Act, including Title IX, which prohibits sex discrimination at colleges that receive federal aid. Few people at the time might have guessed that Title IX would have such far-reaching consequences. When Title IX was first passed, 31,000 women participated in intercollegiate athletics. Today, more than 120,000 women athletes participate in varsity college sports. Even more striking is the increase in girls' participation in high school sports. The number of boy athletes remains close to same as the figure for 1971 (approximately 3.6 million), while the number of girl athletes grew from 294,000 in 1971 to 2.4 million in 1995.

In spite of these impressive gains, many people believe that the pace of change has been far too slow. Spending on college athletics remains weighted toward men's sports. A 1997 National Collegiate Athletic Association (NCAA) study on gender equity found the following:

- Seventy-five percent of funds directed to athletics programs goes into men's sports.
- The ratio of those operating expenses has not budged, even though the percentage of women participating in organized sports has jumped from 31 to 37 percent since 1992.
- Women, who make up 53 percent of college and university students, receive 38 percent of scholarship dollars.
- Coaches of women's sports typically earn less than half the pay of the men's team coaches.

College officials argue that much of the reason for this imbalance is college football, which only men play. College football, they say, not only pays for itself; it is the cash cow that pays most of the bills for both men's and women's sports. The size of a football squad, with eighty-five players on scholarship at NCAA Division I schools and over a hundred players on the rosters, throws the gender statistics way out of balance. But the imbalance of revenue that is produced is even greater. Only a handful of women's basketball programs make money. All other women's sports are money losers and, like men's "minor" sports, depend on men's football and basketball revenues and student fees to pay their bills. College officials maintain that if they cut the spending for football, football will bring in less revenue, and thus all sports will be harmed.

Proponents of gender equity do not accept this answer. They have increasingly taken their battles to the courts, where they have been consistent winners. The most prominent suit to date was filed in 1992, when Brown University in Providence, Rhode Island, announced that it was dropping the women's gymnastics and volleyball teams and the men's golf and water polo teams because of a budget deficit. Amy Cohen, a gymnast, and other female athletes sued Brown, claiming that women were already underrepresented on Brown athletic teams and that dropping the two women's teams violated Title IX of the Education Amendments of 1972, which prohibits sex discrimination at colleges receiving federal aid. The *Cohen* v. *Brown* suit set off a long court battle. In December 1992, a judge issued a preliminary injunction requiring Brown to reinstate the women's gymnastics and volleyball teams. Gradually, the suit moved up through the federal courts with rulings in favor of the women plaintiffs until in April 1997, the U.S. Supreme Court announced that it would not hear Brown's appeal, giving the final victory to Amy Cohen and the women athletes who sued.

The ruling in favor of Title IX meant that Brown would have to ensure that the percentage of women athletes would have to be close to the percentage of women undergraduates. But just how close? A judge ruled in July 1998 that the percentage of women athletes would have to be within 3.5 percent of women students. Brown has about 53 percent women undergraduates, so the proportion of women athletes must be at least 49.5 percent. One of the attorneys for Brown University, Maureen E. Mahoney, made the argument for Brown's side that was published in *Sports Illustrated* in 1997, shortly after the U.S. Supreme Court chose not to review, and thus not overturn, the decision of the appeals court.

The requirement to have a certain percentage of women athletes is a definitional argument; that is, it stipulates a definition of fairness as having nearly the same balance of men and women athletes receiving scholarships as the percentages of men and women in the student body. Thus, if half the students are women, then half the scholarship athletes should be women. Here's how Mahoney took on that argument:

> Title IX should not be read to prohibit a varsity program that is 60% male at a university where half the students are women for the same reason that we do not prohibit a collegiate dance program that is 90% female or an engineering program that is 70% male. Who would advocate a rule requiring colleges that receive applications from 100 qualified dancers—75 women, 25 men—to set aside 25 spaces for men and 25 spaces for women to ensure gender balance in a program with room for 50 dancers? Is it fair to structure that dance program so that it affords qualified men a far greater chance of participating and guarantees that many more qualified women will be excluded? That's not equal opportunity; that's preferential treatment—which Title IX expressly says is not required.

So now we get to the heart of Brown's position in Cohen v. Brown: Are there substantially more men than women who have the desire and ability to compete on the varsity level? Because if there are, accomplished male athletes should not have to duke it out among themselves to get the slots that are left after all the women have been accommodated. The court didn't require that question to be answered. It said we should just presume that "women, given the opportunity, will naturally participate in athletics in numbers equal to men." That may be true someday, but is it true now? How do we square that presumption with the fact that the men in Brown's intramural program—which has no limits on participation—outnumber the women by 8 to 1, or with evidence that approximately 60% of students around the country who want to play varsity sports are men? And why do we think that it is so important to ensure that half the athletes are women when we don't seem to care that far less than half the dancers are men?

Mahoney makes a strong argument in this section against a rigid quota approach to achieving gender equity in athletics. But there are also powerful arguments on the other side. In the essay that follows, "Title IX: It's Time to Live Up to the Letter of the Law," Donna Lopiano makes the case for giving women athletes the same opportunities that men athletes enjoy. Notice how she takes on both the numbers argument that Mahoney makes and the argument that football should be exempt because it pays the bills. Notice too how she makes arguments appealing to shared values that giving equal opportunities for women to participate in athletics is the right thing to do and practical arguments that more revenue can be generated from women's athletics and that colleges can avoid costly lawsuits.

 Donna Lopiano

Title IX: It's Time to Live Up to the Letter of the Law

Donna Lopiano (1947–) is the former director of women's athletics at the University of Texas at Austin and the current executive director of the Women's Sports Foundation, founded in 1974 by the tennis star Billie Jean King. As an athlete, Lopiano participated in twenty-six national championships in four sports and was an All-American in softball in four different positions at Southern Connecticut State University. She has also coached men's and women's volleyball and women's basketball, field hockey and softball at the collegiate level. Lopiano is a member of the National Sports Hall of Fame and earned a PhD from the University of Southern California.

Lopiano has been a tireless crusader for the rights of girls and women to have equal opportunity in athletics. She is proud to point out that whereas in the early 1970s, one out of every twenty-seven high school girls participated in sports, today that figure is one in four. But because one in two boys participates in sports, Lopiano believes that one in four isn't good enough. She frequently attacks the argument that college football pays the bills for both women's and men's sports, using the NCAA's own statistics to point out that 89 percent of football programs can't support themselves and 45 percent run an average annual deficit of $638,000. Grant Teaff, former Baylor football coach and now the executive director of the American Football Coaches' Association, says of Lopiano, "She taught me at the outset, come with your facts not just what you believe." Whether you agree with her or not, Lopiano certainly knows how to make counterarguments.

The U.S. Court of Appeals for the First Circuit has upheld a district-court decision finding Brown University and its athletics program in violation of Title IX of the Education Amendments of 1972.   1

Brown argued that it should be permitted to offer fewer athletic opportunities for women because men are more interested in sports than women are. A lawsuit was filed soon after Brown eliminated varsity-level teams for women in gymnastics and volleyball.   2

To comply with Title IX, Brown has threatened to drop men's "minor" sports (such as wrestling or gymnastics) and blame it all on Title IX and women's sports. Sour grapes? Sure sounds like it. Let's not forget that the Brown lawsuit began after Brown had spent $250,000 to buy out the football coach's contract and then dropped two men's and two women's sports to balance the budget. Worse yet, Brown then spent well over half a million dollars litigating the Title IX case, a sum that could have brought the university's sports program into compliance with the statute. What is going on here? This just doesn't make any sense.   3

The Brown decision is consistent with other court decisions. In other cases in which institutions have dropped a women's sports program—despite the fact that women on campus were clearly underrepresented in athletics—the courts have sided with the female plaintiffs. Colleges and universities need to recognize that women will continue going to court to enforce the law. So isn't it time that institutions stop wasting money in legal fees and get on with the job of expanding opportunities for women athletes?   4

June 23, 1997, will mark the 25th anniversary of the passage of Title IX, the federal law prohibiting sex discrimination by educational institutions receiving federal money. Yet most colleges and universities still do not comply with the law. Has progress been made? Definitely. The glass is not as empty as it was in 1972, when women were receiving less than 1 per cent of all athletic-scholarship dollars and still buying their own uniforms and equipment. But the glass is only   5 half full. At the college level, across all divisions of the National Collegiate Athletic Association, twice as many men as women participate in sports. (The proportions are the same at the high-school level.) Women are still receiving $179-million less than men in college athletic scholarships each year. (Men receive $356-million annually.) And women's sports budgets are far short of the budgets for men's sports.

6   Let us remember that sports are not just fun and games. At the college level, athletic scholarships and admissions preferences for athletes translate into access to education. At the junior-high and high-school levels, participation in sports makes a huge impact on girls' lives: It is associated with pluses such as better grades and graduation rates, increased confidence and self-esteem, and reduced risk of breast cancer, osteoporosis, and heart disease later in life. It is no accident that 80 percent of the executive women in Fortune 500 companies identify themselves as having been "tomboys" and say that they played sports when they were young.

7   So why are so many high schools, colleges, and universities still fighting the law? In 1972, almost 100 per cent of the money in college athletics went to support athletic programs for men. The money wasn't there, and still isn't there, to give women equal athletic opportunities unless male athletes and coaches are willing to accept a smaller piece of the financial pie, and unless all athletes take a cut in traditional levels of support. Therein lies the problem. On every campus, one or two men's sports—usually football and basketball—traditionally have received a disproportionate share of the athletics budget (30 to 60 per cent) and are powerful enough to reject any effort to reduce their "standard of living." College presidents (and high-school principals) take the easy way out by cutting men's "minor" sports and blaming it on the women—pitting victims against victims.

8   Some supporters of men's teams say they are concerned that decisions like that in the Brown case will lead institutions to cut athletics opportunities for men. This issue is beside the point. The real point is that institutions need to stop hiding behind the threat of cutting men's teams and start increasing opportunities for women. Historically, institutions made progress in the 1970s in opening up athletics opportunities for women. But then they slowed down their efforts, and they got caught. When you commit a traffic violation, you can try to make excuses, but that rarely works. Or you can change your driving habits.

9   Can an institution keep sports opportunities for men intact while increasing opportunities for women? Yes, but only by avoiding easy choices and taking some less-than-popular steps.

10   Cutting the level of men's participation needs to be a last choice. Before any college or university does that, every one of its sports should cut back on excessive expenditures. Doing so may mean eliminating a spring-break trip or one or two regular-season games. Maybe uniforms should be bought every other year or every three years. The point is that all sports—including the powerhouses like

football and basketball—need to find ways to tighten their belts without cutting back on student participation.

We also need to start at the opposite end of the continuum by asking if we can generate more revenues. Colleges and universities need to put more effort into raising money for women's sports; they need to promote those sports, so that women's teams generate bigger gate receipts. They put the time and effort into raising money for men's sports; now put the same time and effort into women's sports.   11

Colleges and universities also should remember that expanding opportunities for women is not only right; over the long term, it is in their best financial interest to do so. Quite simply, colleges and universities risk further costly lawsuits if they don't "do the right thing." Even if institutions manage to avoid lawsuits, they may not be able to avoid negative publicity. As of October 1, 1996, institutions of higher education are required to publish annually their expenditures on men's and women's sports under a new federal law, the Gender Equity in Athletics Disclosure Act. Public embarrassment can be a strong force that creates change.   12

Remember, the 20-year-olds of the 1970s are the first generation of mothers and fathers who grew up fully believing that their daughters were going to have equal opportunities in sports. These 40-year-olds of the 1990s are now being asked to support their institutions of higher learning in a big way. How will they feel if their daughters are not receiving the same opportunities as their sons? Moms and dads of female athletes are paying taxes and tuition. They want equal treatment for their children.   13

The smart colleges and universities will quickly take the high ground. Institutions need to promise to achieve rates of male and female participation in athletics that are in proportion to the enrollment of male and female students. If they develop a plan that will achieve such results within five years, no one is likely to sue.   14

The bottom line is the need for strong ethical leadership by college and university presidents. They need to admit that sports are as important to our daughters as to our sons. They need to ask their alumni and alumnae to step up to the donation plate to help keep athletic opportunities for men while, at the same time, adding opportunities for women. They need to require Title IX self-evaluation studies that would show them just what their athletic directors are—or are not—doing to increase opportunities for women. They need to require their athletics directors to submit written plans with reasonable timetables to insure compliance with Title IX. Finally, they need to monitor those plans to see that progress is being made. Otherwise, they—like Brown—may end up in court.   15

While the Brown University decision can be viewed as a victory for women's sports, that victory will be hollow if other college presidents and educational institutions fail to do the right thing for our daughters who play sports.   16

Steps in Writing
a Proposal Argument

If your instructor asks for a topic proposal, use steps 1–6 to guide you in writing the proposal.

1. **Make a proposal claim advocating a specific change or course of action.** Use this formula: *We should (or should not) do X.* In an essay of five or fewer pages, it's difficult to propose solutions to big problems such as continuing poverty. Proposals that address local problems are not only more manageable; sometimes, they get actual results.

   Examples:

   - The process of registering for courses (getting appointments at the health center, getting e-mail accounts) should be made more efficient.

   - Your community should create bicycle lanes to make bicycling safer and to reduce traffic (build a pedestrian overpass over a dangerous street; make it easier to recycle newspapers, bottles, and cans).

2. **Identify the problem.** What exactly is the problem? Who is most affected by the problem? What causes the problem? Has anyone tried to do anything about it? If so, why haven't they succeeded? What is likely to happen in the future if the problem isn't solved?

3. **Propose your solution.** State your solution as specifically as you can. What exactly do you want to achieve? How exactly will your solution work? Can it be accomplished quickly, or will it have to be phased in over a few years? Has anything like it been tried elsewhere? Who will be involved? Can you think of any reasons why your solution might not work? How will you address those arguments? Can you think of any ways of strengthening your proposed solution in light of those possible criticisms?

4. **Consider other solutions.** What other solutions have been or might be proposed for this problem, including doing nothing? What are the advantages and disadvantages of those solutions? Why is your solution better?

5. **Examine the feasibility of your solution.** How easy is your solution to implement? Will the people who will be most affected be willing to go along with it? (For example, lots of things can be accomplished if enough people volunteer, but groups often have difficulty getting enough

volunteers to work without pay.) If it costs money, how do you propose paying for it? Who is most likely to reject your proposal because it is not practical enough? How can you convince your readers that your proposal can be achieved?

6. **Analyze your potential readers.** Who are you writing for? You might be writing a letter addressed to a specific person. You might be writing a guest editorial to appear in your campus newspaper or in your club's or organization's newsletter. You might be creating a Web site. How interested will your readers be in this problem? How much does this problem affect them? How would your solution benefit them directly and indirectly?

7. **Write a draft.**

Define the problem:

■ Set out the issue or problem. You might begin by telling about your experience or the experience of someone you know. You might need to argue for the seriousness of the problem, and you might have to give some background on how it came about.

Present your solution:

■ You might want to set out your solution first and explain how it will work, then consider other possible solutions and argue that yours is better; or you might want to set out other possible solutions first, argue that they don't solve the problem or are not feasible, and then present your solution.

■ Make clear the goals of your solution. Many solutions cannot solve problems completely. If you are proposing a solution for juvenile crime in your neighborhood, for example, you cannot expect to eliminate all juvenile crime.

■ Describe in detail the steps in implementing your solution and how they will solve the problem you have identified. You can impress your readers by the care with which you have thought through this problem.

■ Explain the positive consequences that will follow from your proposal. What good things will happen and what bad things will be avoided if your advice is taken?

Argue that your proposal is feasible:

■ Your proposal for solving the problem is a truly good idea only if it can be put into practice. If people have to change the ways they are doing things now, explain why they would want to change. If your proposal costs money, you need to identify exactly where the money would come from.

Conclude with a call for action:

- Your conclusion should be a call for action. You should put your readers in a position such that if they agree with you, they will take action. You might restate and emphasize what exactly they need to do.

8. **Take your draft through the revision steps in chapter 15.**

Part III

Effective Arguments

Designing, Documenting, and Revising Arguments

It seems hard to believe today that, except for a few hobbyists who assembled computers from kits, personal computers didn't exist until 1977 when the Apple II was introduced. Most computers in the late 1970s and early 1980s were still behemoths housed in secure, air-conditioned rooms behind thick plate glass. Most users punched cards, submitted a deck of such cards on a batch basis, then waited hours for the output. (The computers were fast; their attendants weren't.) If you made an error in punching the cards or arranging the deck, you had to resubmit the batch and wait more hours for the job to be repeated. Only the lucky few who had access to a terminal connected to the mainframe computer could avoid the step of punching and submitting the cards. Modem access from dumb terminals was available twenty years ago, and primitive word processing was even possible, but to work from home on a 300-baud modem meant that a full-screen text editor took more than a minute to record each change, so text editing had to be done "blind," using a programming language with commands that said the equivalent of "in line 17, character 21, substitute 'p' for 'j.' " This tedious process required a physical printed text on which you did your best to keep up with the changes you had made. Sooner or later, you lost track of what was actually in line 17; therefore, revising a text from home meant frequent trips to the computation center to get printouts of the latest version.

The IBM PC, introduced in 1981 with ten times as much memory as its competitors, made word processing at home possible. Another big breakthrough came in 1984 with the first Macintoshes, which displayed on the screen what was printed on the page. With WYSIWYG ("what you see is what you get") text editors, desktop publishing became a reality for many amateurs. The printing of a club, church, or neighborhood newsletter that formerly required a laborious process of typing and formatting was suddenly a cinch using a template on a word-processing program. Now a newsletter can be published on the World Wide Web, eliminating the need to print address labels and the costs of postage. Furthermore, because the process of scanning and publishing images has become increasingly simpler, that newsletter can contain many photographs and illustrations.

The World Wide Web not only enables you to publish your work easily, it also allows you to do a great deal of research from wherever you have a connection to the Internet. Large libraries have effectively put the entire reference room online. There are now hundreds of online newspaper services, and thousands of magazines and other journals are also available via the Web. Major museum collections can be accessed by the Web, as can massive collections of government documents.

Computers also have made the process of revising a great deal easier. Before computers were available for writing, major revisions often required rewriting or retyping an entire document. Needless to say, the labor involved in retyping discouraged large-scale revising. Now you can keep revising what you write until you are ready to submit it or call it finished.

But if new technologies for writing have given us a great deal of potential power, they have also presented us with a variety of challenges. Design of a piece of writing isn't much of an issue with a typewriter. You can either single or double space, and you can increase or decrease the margins. But with computers, you can change the type style and/or the type size, insert illustrations, create and insert tables and other graphics, print in color, and, with the World Wide Web, even introduce sound and animation. Sometimes, it seems that there are too many choices.

Likewise, when you do research on the Web, you often find too much rather than too little. Much of what you find is of little value for a serious argument. And if the physical act of making changes to what you write is easier with a computer, the mental part is still hard work. Even experienced writers struggle with getting what they write into the shape they want. In the chapters in part III, you will find some strategies for using both new and old technologies for creating effective arguments.

Chapter 11

Effective Visual Design

Understanding Visual Arguments

The average American is exposed to over 3,000 arguments each day, the great majority of which come in the form of advertisements. The arguments of many of these ads cannot be analyzed completely by the methods we used in chapters 1–5 because they rely on images in addition to text. A typical example is a magazine ad for a leading department store that includes only a picture of a handsome professional woman dressed in a black suit looking at herself in a mirror, the name of the store, and the caption "Somehow you just know." Because the effects of such ads are difficult to explain, some people have called them irrational and even deceptive. But they are anything but irrational. We don't need to be told that being well dressed is important for a professional image.

Products such as clothing, detergent, deodorant, cigarettes, and soft drinks rely heavily on images to sell their products. Nonetheless, as was discussed in the previous chapters, writers also offer images of themselves in order to be convincing. The key difference, of course, is that we are presented with visual images when we encounter advertising while we have to construct our image of a writer from the voice in the text. Yet it isn't quite that simple. Some ads include a fair amount of text, and increasingly, writers incorporate graphics in what they write.

Let's take a look at an ad that has both text and images. The text of the ad for Harrison K-9 Security Services in Figure 11.1 is framed by a header across the top: the word "VIGILANCE" imposed over an image of a woman, a child, and a dog and a proportionally much larger image of a German shepherd positioned in the left third of the frame. We can describe three main elements of this ad: the text, the images, and the graphic design.

Figure 11.1   Advertisement for Harrison K-9 Security Services

Text

The text fills the center right of the frame. The first paragraph gives the argument of the ad:

> *When you're away from home, you need to know that your family is safe. There is no substitute for the vigilant eyes and ears of Harrison K-9 Security Services European German Shepherd protectors.*

The second paragraph describes the training the dogs receive and who has bought them: "families, business executives, entertainers, and professional athletes." The third paragraph describes training for the purchasers of the dogs, and finally, the logo of the company is followed by its address and phone number.

Images

The image of the German shepherd on the left of the frame is shot from a low angle, making the dog appear quite large. Its coat is thick, and its ears point up toward the word "VIGILANCE" at the top. The smaller second image shows a woman seated on a carpet, a young child kneeling beside her, and a dog resting nearby. The woman and child are looking at something in the child's hand. They are dressed casually in jeans, and the viewer assumes that they are a mother and daughter at home. The dog looks both relaxed and alert, its gaze fixed on the viewer.

This small image is consistent with the text in several ways. First, since there is no man in the frame, the father is presumably absent. The text says that people who have bought dogs include "families, business executives, entertainers, and professional athletes." The image thus suggests that the buyer of the dog will likely be a man who travels, leaving his wife and children at home, rather than a woman who is employed as a business executive, entertainer, or professional athlete. But the image can also be viewed from the perspective of the "intruder" mentioned in the text. The dog is between the intruder and the woman and child. To get to them requires getting past the dog.

Graphic Design

Graphic designers consider the relationship of the elements when they design an ad. The images and text support each other in this ad, but through good graphic design, these relationships can be enhanced. When you page through the magazine where the ad appeared, your eyes are first drawn to the image of the dog. The background color of the ad is maroon, which enhances the rich, light brown tones of the dog's coat. The dog's ears direct attention to the word "VIGILANCE," printed in a color very similar to that of the dog's coat. "VIGILANCE" is superimposed over the image of the woman, child, and dog; thus, even a quick glance at the ad takes in the two images and the word. If you continue looking at the ad, you next move clockwise to the text, which is set in a sans serif typeface (we'll explain typefaces shortly) in white letters against the dark maroon background. The typeface and background color set the text of the ad apart from the text of the magazine, which uses black serif type against a white background.

This ad demonstrates how a graphic designer coordinates images with the message of an ad. A designer organizes words and images to achieve a desired effect for a particular audience and purpose. These principles of graphic design are not so very different from the rhetorical principles that were discussed in the previous chapters. It all has to do with understanding how particular effects can be achieved for particular readers in particular situations. Best of all, if you use a computer for writing, you too can use graphic design to your own advantage.

Print Is a Visual Medium

Throughout most of the twentieth century, writers with few exceptions were limited to what they could produce using a pencil, pen, or typewriter. Typewriters offer few graphic options. On a conventional typewriter, you can change the margins or choose single or double spacing, but that's about it. Visual effects such as selecting typefaces (called fonts) and type sizes, inserting illustrations and graphics, and using color were achievable only by people who had access to a graphic design staff. In the early 1980s, the introduction of PCs began to provide many more options to writers. Early Macintosh computers offered a choice of fonts. Most writers had never thought much about fonts, and now they could choose among fonts with strange-sounding names such as Helvetica, Lucida, and Palatino. That was only the beginning.

People became accustomed to seeing more graphics in newspapers and magazines because computers made these graphics much easier to produce. Traditionalists sneered at the *USA Today* when it first appeared with its many color photos and graphics. But it wasn't long before other newspapers also included more graphics, and even the conservative look of the *New York Times* changed with the appearance of many charts, illustrations, and color photographs. It also wasn't long before PCs became more powerful and word-processing programs more sophisticated. By the late 1980s, someone using desktop publishing programs could do what had formerly required a team of graphic designers. Most people, however, didn't have the hard drives to hold big image files, their software allowed them to do only elementary design, their printers were crude, and the World Wide Web had not been invented. Furthermore, most people wouldn't have known how to use these tools if they had been available because they lacked the principles of design necessary for making good design decisions.

During the past ten years, image technologies have become available to everyone using a newer PC. PCs now come equipped with big hard drives and fast processors that can handle software programs with powerful graphics capabilities. Furthermore, you can move graphics from one application to another. Publishing for individuals has also taken a great leap ahead as laser and color printers are now affordable, and the World Wide Web allows anyone to publish images and graphics. People who once barely knew how to design a letter are now cranking out newsletters, printing brochures, and putting up Web sites (which we'll talk about in the next chapter).

If you use a computer for writing, it's no longer difficult to include graphics in your writing. The question that you face is not whether you can put in graphics but how best to incorporate graphics for what effects? This chapter will help you to think about those choices. Perhaps the most important thing to know about design is that there are very few hard-and-fast rules. As for all arguments, everything depends on the rhetorical situation. All your decisions hinge on your purpose(s) for writing, your subject matter and the type of document you are writing, your intended audience(s), and how you want your reader(s) to perceive you. Sometimes, you succeed by breaking the rules.

Let's start with how your readers perceive you. You see an ad for a part-time position designing brochures and newsletters for a copy shop that pays good money, and since you have the necessary skills, you decide to apply. You write your letter of application:

Jennifer Barnes

308 Bruffee Street
Minneapolis, MN 55423

January 5, 1999

Andrew J. Johnson, Vice President
Copy Mart
742 Church Street S.E.
Minneapolis, MN 55454

Dear Mr. Johnson:

I wish to apply for the Web design position that you advertised in the *Minneapolis Tribune* on June 5, 1998.

I am a communications major at the University of Minnesota, and I have three years experience designing brochures, newsletters, and Web pages for businesses and nonprofit organizations in the Twin Cities. I am skilled in using JavaScript, QuickTime, Adobe Pagemill, Photoshop, and Illustrator, Fractal Painter, and Macromedia Director, Dreamweaver, and Shockwave. My résumé is enclosed, complete with a list of Web sites that I have designed and the names, addresses, and phone numbers of people who have employed me.

You may reach me by email or at my home phone, (612) 634-5789, on most afternoons. I look forward to hearing from you.

Sincerely,

Jennifer Barnes

The letter is fine, but it looks a little bland. You are, after all, applying for a design position. So you decide to change your letterhead using the WordArt feature of your word-processing program and use a different font for the body to make it more snappy. After a little while, you come up with this:

Jennifer Barnes

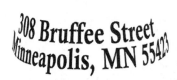

January 5, 1999

Andrew J. Johnson, Vice President
Copy Mart
742 Church Street S.E.
Minneapolis, MN 55454

Dear Mr. Johnson:

I wish to apply for the Web design position that you advertised in the *Minneapolis Tribune* on June 5, 1998.

I am a communications major at the University of Minnesota, and I have three years experience designing brochures, newsletters, and Web pages for businesses and nonprofit organizations in the Twin Cities. I am skilled in using JavaScript, QuickTime, Adobe Pagemill, Photoshop, and Illustrator, Fractal Painter, and Macromedia Director, Dreamweaver, and Shockwave. My résumé is enclosed, complete with a list of Web sites that I have designed and the names, addresses, and phone numbers of people who have employed me.

You may reach me by email or at my home phone, (612) 634-5789, on most afternoons. I look forward to hearing from you.

Sincerely,

Jennifer Barnes

This is better, you think, but maybe still not professional enough. You try one more time, simply using shading and a different font for the letterhead:

jennifer barnes

308 bruffee street, minneapolis, mn 55423

January 5, 1999

Andrew J. Johnson, Vice President
Copy Mart
742 Church Street S.E.
Minneapolis, MN 55454

Dear Mr. Johnson:

I wish to apply for the Web design position that you advertised in the *Minneapolis Tribune* on June 5, 1998.

I am a communications major at the University of Minnesota, and I have three years experience designing brochures, newsletters, and Web pages for businesses and nonprofit organizations in the Twin Cities. I am skilled in using JavaScript, QuickTime, Adobe Pagemill, Photoshop, and Illustrator, Fractal Painter, and Macromedia Director, Dreamweaver, and Shockwave. My résumé is enclosed, complete with a list of Web sites that I have designed and the names, addresses, and phone numbers of people who have employed me.

You may reach me by email or at my home phone, (612) 634-5789, on most afternoons. I look forward to hearing from you.

Sincerely,

Jennifer Barnes

That's the professional look you want. You send the letter, and you get the job.

Your first newsletter assignment comes from a local group, Stop Stadium Welfare (SSW), which is opposed to using taxpayer dollars to pay for a new stadium. Like most people, the members of SSW want their newsletter in a hurry, and what they bring you is a visual mess. They hand you several short articles and no model to follow, since this is the group's first newsletter.

You start reading what they hand you. The first article has the title "Do Stadiums Really Bring in Jobs and New Businesses?" It begins:

Stadium boosters like to claim fabulous economic impacts from building new stadiums with taxpayers' dollars. But the record suggests just the opposite. Most sports stadiums lose money. Stadiums built in the 1970s and 1980s, including the Superdome in New Orleans, the Silverdome in suburban Detroit, the Kingdome in Seattle, and the Meadowlands in New Jersey, are now considered obsolete, and each loses over a million government dollars a year. They are drains on the local economy, not economic multipliers.

Before the Metrodome, we had Metropolitan Stadium, south of Minneapolis in the suburb of Bloomington. It was built with local business support in an open field. The old Met virtually made the Hwy 494 "strip," a belt of restaurants, clubs, hotels and stores. It was an outdoor stadium, like the ones the owners want built now. The controversial government-built successor, the Metrodome, has not had the same impact on downtown Minneapolis. Downtown Minneapolis has continued to decline.

What is most amazing is that the same arguments used to justify the Metrodome are being made for a new stadium. If the Metrodome failed to revive downtown,

```
why would another stadium be different? The

Metrodome's primary economic spinoffs appear to

be a few $5 parking lots.
```

There are four other, shorter articles, so there's plenty of material for a four-page newsletter. But how will you put it together?

You start out by making a header and then type in the stories one after the other (see Figure 11.2). You quickly realize that putting the stories in 1, 2, 3 order is not the solution. Your newsletter looks like a term paper with long

Stop Stadium Welfare

Volume 1, Issue 1   1998

Do Stadiums Really Bring in Jobs and New Businesses?
By Reginald Alexander

Stadium boosters like to claim fabulous economic impacts from building new stadiums with taxpayers' dollars. But the record suggests just the opposite. Most sports stadiums lose money. Stadiums built in the 1970s and 1980s, including the Superdome in New Orleans, the Silverdome in suburban Detroit, the Kingdome in Seattle, and the Meadowlands in New Jersey, are now obsolete, and each lose over a million government dollars a year. They are drains on the local economy, not multipliers.

Before the Metrodome, we had Metropolitan Stadium, south of Minneapolis in the suburb of Bloomington. It was built with local business support in an open field. The old Met virtually made the Hwy 494 "strip," a belt of restaurants, clubs, hotels and stores. It was an outdoor stadium, like the ones the owners want built now. The controversial government-built successor, the Metrodome, has not had the same impact on downtown Minneapolis. Downtown Minneapolis has continued to decline.

What is most amazing is that the same arguments used to justify the Metrodome are being made for a new stadium. If the Metrodome failed to revive downtown, why would another stadium be different? The Metrodome's primary economic spinoffs appear to be a few $5 parking lots.

A study by the Brookings Institution published in 1997 examined sports facilities from a variety of economic perspectives. The authors conclude that the economic impact of a new sports facility is very small at best and often negative. In no case do the effects justify the enormous investment in a new stadium. Probably the most successful new stadium has been Oriole Park in Baltimore, which brings in many people from outside the area. Nevertheless, the net gain for Baltimore's economy in terms of tax revenues and jobs created is only $3 million a year—a minimal return on a $200 million investment.

Meanwhile, local politicians talk about giving the Twins an even bigger subsidy to help reduce their losses. These losses are not documented, or at least the figures not shown to the public. And the owner of the Twins, Carl Pohlad, is a billionaire. Even if the Twins are losing money, why would Mr. Pohlad expect taxpayers to cover his baseball losses any more than they would bail out another venture?

North Carolina Voters Just Say No to Stadium Tax
By Arlene Smith

North Carolina voters rejected the use of taxes to help build a new stadium so theTwins could move to North Carolina. Referendum results show Forsythe County 41-59% against, Guilford County 33-67% against. Commisioner of Baseball Bud Selig made the following statement: "There's no other way to say it: The people in the Twin Cities have to deal with it. They still have to deal with the stadium issue."

Figure 11.2   **Version 1 of Stop Stadium Welfare Newsletter**

stretches of unbroken text. It has little visual interest, and it's not easy to read. You remember that a professor once said that lines with more than twelve to fourteen words become hard to read. So the first thing you do is to divide the page into two columns. That's simple to do using the columns command in your word-processing program. But you still haven't solved the problem of the long article that you started out with. You then decide to make the columns into text boxes so that you can carry over some text to later pages. That allows you to get three stories on the first page.

Next you change the font from Times Roman to Arial, which allows you to use smaller type to get more on the page and gives your newsletter a clean, simple look. You decide that a photo would be nice, and you quickly find a shot of the Metrodome in your office's photo file. Since the Metrodome has become a symbol of Minneapolis, it works well to point out that people want to tear it down less than twenty years after it was built. You add some headings and subheadings to break up the text and give emphasis. Finally, you put in a table of contents so that people will know what else is in the newsletter besides what is on the front page. You're pleased with the result (see Figure 11.3), and it took nothing more than using the commands on your word-processing program. Good design doesn't necessarily require fancy tools.

Design Basics

Before a discussion of principles of graphic design, it is important to know, in the most basic terms, how language and visual design work. Language is extremely well adapted for describing things that fall into a linear order. Because humans perceive time as linear, language allows them from a very young age to tell stories. It's also possible to tell stories with images; indeed, images have become the preferred medium with the invention of movies and later television in the twentieth century. But it's not so easy to put together a video story, say of your last vacation, no matter how easy the editing features are on your camcorder. Telling someone the story of your vacation, however, is easy. You just have to remember where you went and what you did.

Even if you are describing a place, you still have to decide what to tell about first. Suppose someone asks you how your house is laid out. You might begin by saying that inside the front door, there is an entryway that goes to the living room. The dining room is on the right, and the kitchen is adjacent. On the left is a hallway, which connects to two bedrooms on the right, one on the left, and a bathroom at the end. But if you draw a floor plan, you can show at once how the house is arranged. That's the basic difference between describing with spoken language and describing with visual images. Spoken language forces you to put things in a *sequence;* visual design forces you to arrange

Stop Stadium Welfare

Volume 1, Issue 1 · 1998

North Carolina Voters Just Say No to Stadium Tax

Arlene Smith

North Carolina voters rejected the use of taxes to help build a new stadium so the Twins could move to North Carolina. Referendum results show Forsythe County 41-59% against, Guilford County 33-67% against. Commissioner of Baseball Bud Selig made the following statement: "There's no other way to say it: The people in the Twin Cities have to deal with it. They still have to deal with the stadium issue."

Deal with what, Bud? Do you think we are too stupid to know what is in our best interest? We're tired of paying for sweetheart deals that benefit only the rich owners and overpaid players. We're tired of giving welfare payments to rich owners who then complain they need even more money out of our pockets.

Entertainment for the Elite

Sports stadiums used to bring people together. The rich people had the best seats, but they were only a few rows in front of where ordinary people sat. Now the wealthy want to sit in luxury boxes, separated from the crowd. What's wrong with most older stadiums is not that they are obsolete but that they lack dozens of luxury boxes.

continued on page 2

INSIDE THIS ISSUE

Do Stadiums Really Bring in Jobs and New Businesses?

Reginald Alexander

Stadium boosters like to claim fabulous economic impacts from building new stadiums with taxpayers' dollars. But the record suggests just the opposite. Most sports stadiums lose money. Stadiums built in the 1970s and 1980s, including the Superdome in New Orleans, the Silverdome in suburban Detroit, the Kingdome in Seattle, and the Meadowlands in New Jersey, are now obsolete, and each lose over a million government dollars a year. They are drains on the local economy, not multipliers.

The Metrodome Hasn't Delivered on the Promise to Revive Downtown

Before the Metrodome, we had Metropolitan Stadium, south of Minneapolis in the suburb of Bloomington. It was built with local business support in an open field. The old Met virtually made the Hwy 494 "strip," a belt of restaurants, clubs, hotels and stores. It was an outdoor stadium, like the ones the owners want built now. The controversial government-built successor, the Metrodome, has not had the same impact on downtown Minneapolis. Downtown Minneapolis has continued to decline.

The Metrodome was opened in 1982 and remains one of the newer baseball stadiums.

What is most amazing is that the same arguments used to justify the Metrodome are being made for a new stadium. If the Metrodome failed to revive downtown, why would another stadium be different? The Metrodome's primary economic spinoffs appear to be a few $5 parking lots.

continued on page 3

Figure 11.3   **Version 2 of Stop Stadium Welfare Newsletter**

things in *space.* Written language—especially writing on a computer—permits you to do both: to use sequence and space simultaneously. Some of the same principles apply for both language and design when you write. Three of the most important groups of design principles are arrangement, consistency, and contrast.

Arrangement

Many people get through high school by mastering the five-paragraph theme. When they get the assignment, they first have to figure out exactly three points about the topic. Then they write an introduction announcing that they have three points, write a paragraph on each of the three points, and conclude with a paragraph that repeats the three points. It is amazing how far that formula can carry one. The basic structure of announcing the subject, developing it sequentially, and concluding with a summary works well enough in a great many circumstances—from business letters to short reports. Even many PhD dissertations are five-paragraph themes on a larger scale.

But if you translate the five-paragraph formula to space, it's not so simple. Think about putting it on a business card. How would you do it?

Introduction		Point 1
	My Topic	
Conclusion	Point 3	Point 2

Your eyes naturally go to the center, where the topic is boldfaced. But where do they go after that? It's not a given that a reader will start in the upper left-hand corner and go clockwise around the card.

Let's switch to an example of an actual business card.

(919) 684-2741		23 Maple Street Durham, NC 27703
	Todd Smith	
Westin Associates		Management Consulting

Again, the name in the middle is where you go first, but where do your eyes go after that? The problem is that nothing on the card has any obvious visual relationship with anything else.

The way beginning designers often solve this problem is to put everything in the center. This strategy forces you to think about what is most important, and you usually put that at the top. On the card below, the information is grouped so that the relationship of the elements is clear. One of the most important design tools—white space—separates the main elements.

Todd Smith

Westin Associates

Management Consulting

23 Maple Street
Durham, NC 27703
(919) 684-2741

But centering everything isn't the only solution for showing the relationship of elements. Another way is by **alignment.** In the next example, the elements are aligned on the right margin and connected by an invisible line. This alignment is often called **flush right.**

Todd Smith

Westin Associates

Management Consulting

23 Maple Street
Durham, NC 27703
(919) 684-2741

If you are in the habit of centering title pages and other elements, try using the flush left and flush right commands along with grouping similar elements. You'll be surprised what a difference it makes and how much more professional and persuasive your work will appear. Turn back to the revised Stop

Stadium Welfare newsletter on page 219 to see how the strong flush left alignment of text, headings, and the picture produces a professional look.

Consistency

> **Make what is similar look similar.**

You learned the principle of consistency in elementary school when your teacher told you to write on the lines, make the margins even, and indent your paragraphs. When you write using a computer, these things are done for you by your word-processing program. However, too many people stop there when they use a computer to write. You can do a whole lot more.

Sometime during your college years, you likely will write a report or paper that uses headings. Readers increasingly expect you to divide what you write into chunks and label those chunks with headings. It's easy enough to simply center every heading so that your report looks like this:

Title

Xxxxxxxx xxxxxxxx xxxxxxx xxxxxxx xxxxxxxx xxxxxxxx
xxxxxxx xxxxxxx xxxxxxxx xxxxxxx xxxxxxx xxxxxxxx
xxxxxxx xxxxxxx xxxxxxx xxxxxxx xxxxxxx xxxxxxx xxxxx
xxxxxxx xxxxxxx xxxxxxx xxxxxxx xxxxxxx xxxxxxx xxxxxxx
xxxxxxx

Heading 1

Xxxxxxxx xxxxxxxx xxxxxxx xxxxxxx xxxxxxxx xxxxxxxx
xxxxxxx xxxxxxx xxxxxxxx xxxxxxx xxxxxxx xxxxxxxx
xxxxxxx xxxxxxx xxxxxxx xxxxxxx xxxxxxx xxxxxxx xxxxx
xxxxxxx xxxxxxx xxxxxxx xxxxxxx xxxxxxx xxxxxxx xxxxxxx
xxxxxxx xxxxxxx xxxxxxxx xxxxxxxx xxxxxxxxx xxxxxxx xxxxxxxx
xxxxxxx

Heading 2

Xxxxxxxx xxxxxxxx xxxxxxx xxxxxxx xxxxxxxx xxxxxxxx
xxxxxxx xxxxxxx xxxxxxxx xxxxxxx xxxxxxx xxxxxxxx
xxxxxxx xxxxxxx xxxxxxx xxxxxxx xxxxxxx xxxxxxx xxxxx
xxxxxxx xxxxxxx xxxxxxx xxxxxxx xxxxxxx xxxxxxx xxxxxxx
xxxxxxx

If you write a report that looks like this one, you can make it much more visually appealing by devising a system of consistent headings that indicate the overall organization. You first have to determine the level of importance of each heading by making an outline to see what fits under what. Then you make the headings conform to the different levels so that what is equal in importance will have the same level of heading.

Title

Xxxxxxxx xxxxxxxx xxxxxxx xxxxxxx xxxxxxxx xxxxxxxx
xxxxxxx xxxxxxx xxxxxxxx xxxxxxx xxxxxxx xxxxxxxx
xxxxxxx xxxxxxx xxxxxxx xxxxxxx xxxxxxx xxxxxxx xxxxx
xxxxxxx xxxxxxx xxxxxxx xxxxxxx xxxxxxx xxxxxxx xxxxxxx
xxxxxxx

Major Heading

Xxxxxxxx xxxxxxxx xxxxxxx xxxxxxx xxxxxxxx xxxxxxxx
xxxxxxx xxxxxxx xxxxxxxx xxxxxxx xxxxxxx xxxxxxxx
xxxxxxx xxxxxxx xxxxxxx xxxxxxx xxxxxxx xxxxxxx xxxxx
xxxxxxx xxxxxxx xxxxxxx xxxxxxx xxxxxxx xxxxxxx xxxxxxx
xxxxxxx

Level 2 Heading Xxxxxxxx xxxxxxxx xxxxxxx xxxxxxx
xxxxxxxx xxxxxxxx xxxxxxx xxxxxxx xxxxxxxx xxxxxxx
xxxxxxx xxxxx xxxxxxx xxxxxxx xxxxxxx xxxxxxx xxxxxxx
xxxxxxx xxxxxxx xxxxxxxx xxxxxxx xxxxxxx xxxxxxx xxxxx
xxxxxxx xxxxx xxxxxxx

Other useful tools that word-processing programs offer are ways of making lists. Bullet lists are used frequently to present good reasons for claims and proposals. For example:

The proposed new major in Technology, Literacy, and Culture will:

- Prepare our students for the changing demands of the professions and public citizenship.
- Help students to move beyond technical skills and strategies to understand the historical, economic, political, and scientific impacts of new technologies.
- Allow students to practice new literacies that mix text, graphics, sound, video, animation, hypermedia, and real-time communication.
- Help to ensure that wise decisions are made about the collection, organization, storage, and distribution of and access to information via new technologies.
- Provide students with a deeper, richer, and more profound understanding of the dynamic relationships among technology, culture, and the individual.

A bullet list is an effective way of presenting a series of items or giving an overview of what is to come. However, bullet lists can be ineffective if the items in the list are not similar.

Contrast

Make what is different look different.

We tend to follow the principle of consistency because that's what we've been taught and that's what writing technologies—from typewriters to computers—do for us. But the principle of contrast takes some conscious effort on our part to implement. Take a simple résumé as an example:

Roberto Salazar

Address: 3819 East Jefferson Avenue, Escondido, CA 92027

Send email to: salazar@capaccess.org

Job Title: Financial Consulting, Credit Reviewer, Financial Analyst

Relocation: Yes—particular interest in Latin America.

Experience

1997-present. Credit Services Group, Carpenter & Tokaz LLP, 3000 Wilshire Boulevard, Los Angeles, California 90017, 213 677-2440

CONSULTING: Presented Directorate with report findings, conclusions, and recommendations for operation improvements. Coordinated a process improvement engagement for a large finance company, which resulted in the consolidation of credit operations.

SUPERVISION: Supervised, trained, and assessed the work of staff (1–4) involved in audit assists. Reviewed real estate investments, other real estate owned, and loan portfolios for documentation, structure, credit analysis, risk identification, and credit scoring.

Education

1997 San Diego State University, San Diego, California, Bachelor of Business Administration

Languages

Fluent in English and Spanish. Experience in tutoring students with Spanish lessons at San Diego State University, San Diego, California

Computers

Proficient with Microsoft Word and Excel, Lotus Notes, AmiPro, Lotus 1-2-3, WordPerfect, and Sendero SV simulation modeling software. Familiarity with several on-line information retrieval methods.

References Available On Request.

The résumé has consistency but there is no contrast between what is more important and what is less important. The overall impression is that the person is dull, dull, dull.

Your résumé, along with your letter of application, might be the most important piece of persuasive writing you'll do in your life. It's worth taking some extra time to distinguish yourself. Your ability to write a convincing letter and produce a handsome résumé is a good reason for an employer to hire you. Remember why you are paying attention to graphic design. You want your readers to focus on certain elements, and you want to create the right ethos. Use of contrast can emphasize the key features of the résumé and contribute to a much more forceful and dynamic image.

Roberto Salazar

3819 East Jefferson Avenue
Escondido, CA 92027
salazar@capaccess.org

Position Titles Sought

Financial Consulting
Credit Reviewer
Financial Analyst
(Willing to relocate, especially to Latin America)

Education

1997	**Bachelor of Business Administration.** San Diego State University.

Experience

1997-present · **Credit Services Group, Carpenter & Tokaz, LLP.**
3000 Wilshire Boulevard
Los Angeles, California 90017
(213) 677-2440

Consulting: Presented Directorate with report findings, conclusions, and recommendations for operation improvements. Coordinated a process improvement engagement for a large finance company, which resulted in the consolidation of credit operations.

Supervision: Supervised, trained, and assessed the work of four staff involved in audit assists. Reviewed real estate investments, other real estate owned, and loan portfolios for documentation, structure, credit analysis, risk identification, and credit scoring.

Languages

Fluent in English and Spanish. Experience as a Spanish Tutor at SDSU.

Computer Skills

Proficient with Microsoft Word & Excel, Lotus Notes, AmiPro, Lotus 1-2-3, WordPerfect, and Sendero SV simulation modeling software. Familiarity with several online information retrieval methods.

References

Available on request.

Notice that arrangement and consistency are also important to the revised résumé. Good design requires that all elements be brought into play to produce the desired results.

The Rhetoric of Type

Until computers and word-processing software came along, most writers had little or no control over the type style they used. If they typed, they likely used Courier, a fact that many typists didn't even know. Furthermore, the typewriter gave no choice about type size. Writers worked with either 10-point type or 12-point type. (A point is a printer's measure. One inch equals 72 points.) You had no way to include italics. The convention was to underline the word so that the printer would later set the word in italics. Bold-facing could be accomplished only by typing the word over again, making it darker.

Even if the general public knew little about type styles and other aspects of printing before computers came along, printers had five hundred years' experience learning about which type styles were easiest to read and what effects different styles produced. Type styles are called **fonts.** When you open the pull-down font menu of your word-processing program, you see a small part of that five hundred year tradition of developing type styles. At first, many of the fonts will look about the same to you, but after you get some practice with using various fonts, you will begin to notice how they differ.

Fonts are described according to families, and the two most important families are **serif** and **sans serif** fonts. Serif (rhymes with "sheriff") fonts were developed first, imitating the stokes of an ink pen. *Serifs* are the little wedge-shaped ends on letter forms, which scribes produced with wedge-tipped pens. Serif fonts also have thick and thin transitions on the curved strokes. Five of the most common serif fonts are the following:

Times

Palatino

Bookman

Garamond

New Century Schoolbook

If these fonts look almost alike to you, it's not an accident. Serif fonts were designed to be easy to read. They don't call attention to themselves. Therefore, they are well suited for long stretches of text and are used frequently.

Sans serif fonts (*sans* is French for "without") don't have the little wedge-shape ends on letters, and the thickness of the letters is the same. Popular sans serif fonts include the following:

Helvetica

Avant Garde

Arial

Sans serif fonts work well for headings and short stretches of text. They give a crisp, modern look. And some sans serif fonts are easy to read on a computer screen.

Finally, there are many script and decorative fonts. These fonts tend to draw attention to themselves. They are harder to read, but sometimes they can be used for good effects. Some script and decorative fonts include the following:

Zapf Chancery

STENCIL

Mistral

Braggadocio

Tekton

Changing fonts will draw attention. It is usually better to be consistent in using fonts within a text unless you want to signal something.

It's easy to change the size of type when you compose on a computer. The font size displays on the menu bar. For long stretches of text, you probably should use at least 10-point or 12-point type. For headings, you can use larger type.

type	8 point
type	10 point
type	12 point
type	14 point
type	18 point
type	24 point
type	36 point
type	48 point
type	72 point

Fonts also have different weights. **Weight** refers to the thickness of the strokes. Take a look at the fonts on your font menu. You probably have some fonts that offer options ranging from light to bold, such as Arial Condensed Light, Arial, Arial Rounded MT Bold, and Arial Black. Here's what each of these looks like as a heading:

1. *Arial Condensed Light*

Position Titles Sought
_____

Financial Consulting
Credit Reviewer
Financial Analyst
(Willing to relocate, especially to Latin America)

2. *Arial*

Position Titles Sought

Financial Consulting
Credit Reviewer
Financial Analyst
(Willing to relocate, especially to Latin America)

3. *Arial Rounded MT Bold*

Position Titles Sought

Financial Consulting
Credit Reviewer
Financial Analyst
(Willing to relocate, especially to Latin America)

4. *Arial Black*

Position Titles Sought

Financial Consulting
Credit Reviewer
Financial Analyst
(Willing to relocate, especially to Latin America)

You can get strong contrasts by using heavier weights of black type for headings and using white space to accent what is different.

Finally, most word-processing programs have some special effects that you can employ. The three most common are **boldface,** *italics,* and underlining. All three are used for emphasis, but underlining should be avoided because it makes text harder to read.

Graphic Presentation of Information

Tables and Charts

Word-processing software gives you the capability of creating tables, graphs, and charts in one software program and then importing those graphics into a text file. For example, tables and charts created with Microsoft Excel can easily be imported into Microsoft Word files. Many arguments can be made more effective with the visual presentation of important information. If you have statistical information to support your argument, you should consider whether to present that information in words, as a table, or as a graphic—or in some combination of these.

Let's take as an example the ongoing debate between gun rights advocates and gun control advocates. Gun rights advocates typically rely on definitional arguments. Their foremost argument is based on their interpretation of the Second Amendment to the U.S. Constitution, which reads "A well regulated Militia, being necessary to the security of a free State, the right of the people to keep and bear Arms, shall not be infringed." What exactly the Second Amendment means today is much disputed. Gun control advocates interpret the Second Amendment in its historical context, in which the newly formed states of the United States required local armies to battle against American Indians. The Supreme Court reached the same conclusion in a 1939 case (*U.S.* v. *Miller,* 307 U.S. 174), finding that possession of a firearm is not protected by the Second Amendment unless it has some reasonable relationship to the preservation or efficiency of a well-regulated militia. No gun control law ever brought before the Supreme Court or other federal courts has ever been overturned on Second Amendment grounds. Nevertheless, the National Rifle Association and other gun rights advocates continue to argue that ownership of guns is protected by the Bill of Rights.

Those who wish to regulate firearms, however, often bypass the constitutional argument in favor of arguments of consequence. Gun control advocates point to comparisons between the United States and other advanced nations of the world, all of which have much stricter gun laws than the United States and much lower rates of deaths by firearms. The rate of firearm deaths in the United States is three times higher than Canada's, four times higher than Australia's, nine times higher than Germany's, twenty-four times higher than the United Kingdom's (even including Northern Ireland), and almost two hundred times higher than Japan's.

The problem when you start giving a lot of statistics in words is that your readers shortly lose track of your numbers. If you want to argue effectively using statistics, you have to put the numbers in formats that permit your readers to take them in. Tables are quite useful for presenting a lot of numerical data at one glance. If you have the numbers, you can make the table quickly and easily with a program like Microsoft Excel.

Figure 11.4 shows a tabular comparison of the death rates due to firearms in the United States and other advanced nations:

	Total Firearm Deaths		Firearm Homicides		Firearm Suicides		Fatal Firearm Accidents	
	Rate	Number	Rate	Number	Rate	Number	Rate	Number
United States (1995)	13.7	35,957	6	15,835	7	18,503	0.5	1,225
Australia (1994)	3.05	536	0.56	96	2.38	420	0.11	20
Canada (1994)	4.08	1,189	0.6	176	3.35	975	0.13	38
Germany (1995)	1.47	1,197	0.21	168	1.23	1,004	0.03	20
Japan (1995)	0.07	93	0.03	34	0.04	49	0.01	10
Sweden (1992)	2.31	200	0.31	27	1.95	169	0.05	4
Spain (1994)	1.01	396	0.19	76	0.55	219	0.26	101
United Kingdom (1994)	0.57	277	0.13	72	0.33	193	0.02	12

(rates are per 100,000 people)

Source: United Nations, *United Nations International Study on Firearms Regulation* (Vienna, Austria: United Nations Crime Prevention and Criminal Justice Division, 1997) 109.

Figure 11.4   Column Chart of Firearm Deaths by Country

Although tables can present an array of numbers at once, they lack the dramatic impact of charts. Charts visually represent the magnitude and proportion of data. The differences in death rates due to firearms is striking when presented as a chart. One of the easiest charts to make is a simple bar chart (Figure 11.5).

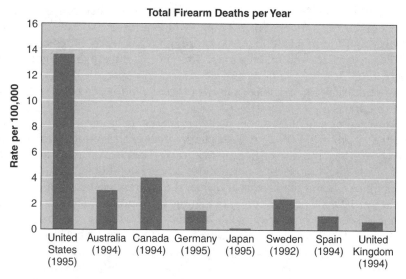

Figure 11.5   Bar Chart of Firearm Deaths by Country

231

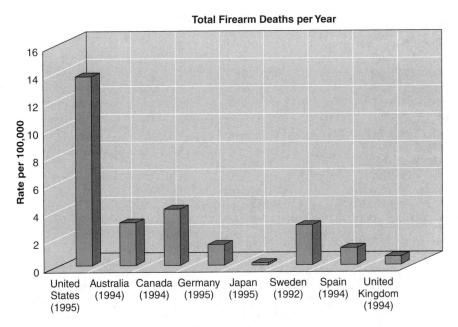

Figure 11.6 3-D Bar Chart of Firearm Deaths by Country

The tools available in a software program such as Microsoft Excel allow you a number of options. For example, you can represent the bars in three dimensions (Figure 11.6). Be aware, though, that three-dimensional bars can distort the data and make it more difficult to compare the heights of the columns.

Alternatively, you can make a horizontal bar chart instead of a vertical bar chart (Figure 11.7).

The options available to you involve rhetorical decisions. You can manipulate the length of the axes on a bar chart, either exaggerating or minimizing differences. Or in the case of firearm deaths, you can use the total numbers instead of the rate. Notice how much more exaggerated the number of firearm deaths in the United States appears when the total number is used instead of the rate per 100,000 people (compare Figures 11.8 and 11.9). As always it's important to keep your rhetorical goals in mind when you make a chart.

Another family of charts that are very easy to create are pie charts. As the name suggests, **pie charts** illustrate how the pie is divided. They are especially useful for representing percentages, but they work only if the percentages of the parts add up to 100%. Gun control advocates frequently cite a study done in Seattle that identified all gunshot deaths over a six-year period (A. L. Kellermann and D. L. Reay, "Protection or Peril: An Analysis of Firearm-Related Deaths in the Home," *New England Journal of Medicine* 314 (1986): 1557–1560).

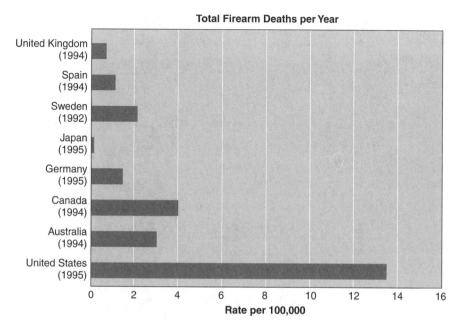

Figure 11.7   Horizontal Bar Chart of Firearm Deaths by Country

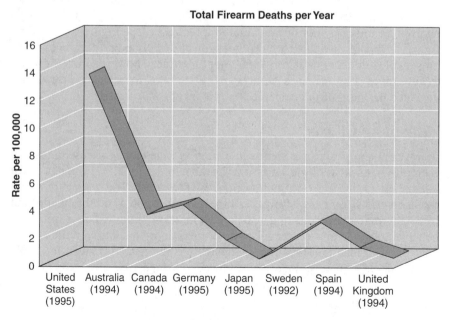

Figure 11.8   3-D Line Chart of Firearm Deaths by Rate per 100,000

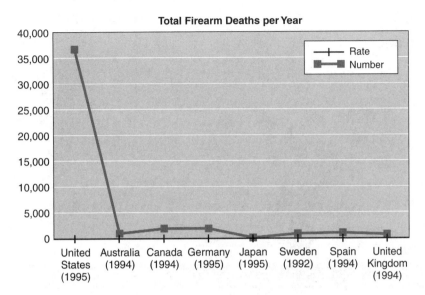

Figure 11.9   Line Chart of Firearm Deaths by Number

Of the 733 deaths by firearms, a majority (398) occurred in the home in which the firearm involved was kept. Of those 398 deaths, 333 (83.6 percent) were suicides, 41 (10.3 percent) were criminal homicides, 12 (3.0 percent) were accidental, 7 (1.7 percent) were justifiable self-defense, and only 2 (0.5 percent) involved an intruder shot during an attempted entry (see Figure 11.10). Gun control advocates use this study to question the advisability of keeping firearms in the home for protection. Gun rights advocates, however, fault the study because there is no evidence on how many attempts to enter the home were prevented because intruders feared that the owner was armed.

Misleading Charts

Charts can be misleading as well as informative. Line graphs are useful for representing changes over time, and from the table in Figure 11.11, you can make a line chart of energy consumption from 1970 to 1995. The line chart would appear to rise significantly from 1970 to 1995, from 66.4 to 90.6 quadrillion British thermal units, indicating a 36 percent increase. If plotted on a line chart, the increase would appear steep. But if the growth in population in the United States is taken into consideration, the increase is not nearly as great, from 327 to 345, only a 5.5 percent increase. A line chart would appear relatively flat.

Other Graphics

Other graphics, such as maps and pictures, can also be useful in arguments. If you want to argue for the preservation of old-growth forests, for example,

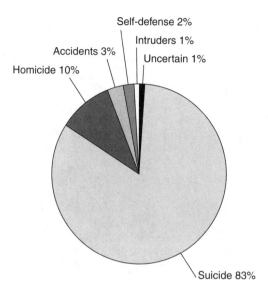

Figure 11.10   Pie Chart of Firearm Deaths in the Home

including maps of the surviving old-growth forests are a good tactic because so little of the this type of forest survives. The problem is that good maps and images take a long time to create. You can find maps and images on the World Wide Web that may be useful. For example, if you are writing about the depletion of the ozone layer over the earth, you can find this composite image of the antarctic ozone hole in 1995 on the Environmental Protection Agency's Web site (Figure 11.12).

Year	Energy Consumption in Quadrillion British Thermal Units	Energy Consumption per Capita in BTUs
1970	66.4	327
1975	70.6	327
1980	76	334
1985	74	311
1990	84.2	337
1995	90.6	345

Source: Bureau of the Census. *Statistical Abstract of the United States, 1997* (Washington, DC: U.S. Department of Commerce, 1997) 592.

Figure 11.11   Table of Energy Consumption in the United States, 1970–1995

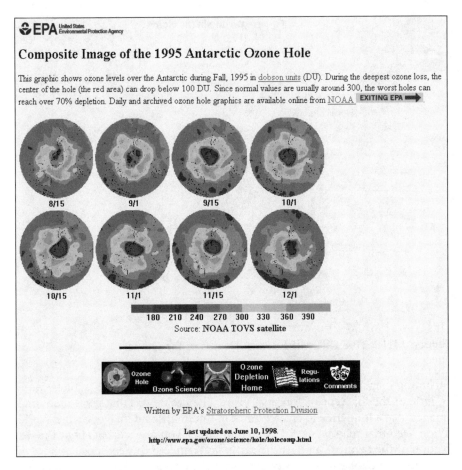

Figure 11.12 Composite Image of the Antarctic Ozone Hole in 1995
(http://www.epa.gov/docs/ozone/science/hole/
holecomp.html)

If you download maps and images from the Web, you might have to change their format. Images on the Web are usually in JPEG or GIF format, which we'll describe in the next chapter, and if your word-processing program does not do the conversion for you, you might have to convert the file yourself with a program such as Graphic Converter or Adobe Photoshop.

The main thing you want to avoid is using images strictly for decoration. Readers quickly get tired of pictures and other graphics that don't contribute to the content. Think of pictures, charts, and graphics as alternative means of presenting information. Good use of graphics contributes to your overall argument.

Chapter 12

Effective Web Design

The Basics of the Web

It's hard to believe that the World Wide Web barely existed before 1993. At the beginning of 1993, there were only fifty Web servers, and only a handful of people knew of its existence. Today, there are more Web pages than people on the planet. In less than a decade, the Web became the most powerful publishing technology ever, surpassing not only the number of words that are printed every day but even the volume of spoken words on telephone traffic. When you put up a Web site, you have the potential to reach millions of people around the world. Although it is highly unlikely that most people who have access to the Web will visit your site, many students have put up sites that are visited by hundreds and, in a few cases, even thousands of people each week—sites whose content ranges from international politics, such as recognition of Taiwan as a nation, to issues of local interest, such as making lacrosse a varsity sport.

You've likely done at least a little browsing on the Web, and you might have wondered how it works. The answer is fairly simple. The Web is a vast collection of documents stored on millions of computers around the world connected by the Internet. Computers that are set up as Web **servers** store computer files organized as Web sites that you can access with a software program called a **browser.** The two most popular browsers are the great rivals: Netscape Navigator (or the more recent Netscape Communicator) and Microsoft's Internet Explorer. The browser allows you to request and see Web sites on servers around the world. Most of the time, you make these connections through links—by clicking on an underlined or highlighted word or graphic on a Web site. Clicking on a link activates an electronic address, called a **URL** (Uniform

Resource Locator). When you first use the Web, you might not pay much attention to the URLs, but later you realize that they are just as important as knowing phone numbers and street addresses. For example, the URL for the Quick Reference page for the libraries at the University of Texas at Austin is *http://www.lib.utexas.edu/Libs/PCL/Reference.html.* These long addresses have three parts. First, they begin with *http://,* which tells Netscape or Internet Explorer that the file is a Web page (*http* is an acronym for *Hypertext Transfer Protocol*). Some URLs begin with *gopher://, ftp://,* or other abbreviations. These links go to files that are not Web pages.

Next, URLs include a **domain name**—the address of the server where the page is located. The server address contains important clues about who owns the Web site. Some names are obvious, like pepsi.com or toyota.com. The end tag tells you what kind of organization sponsors the site: **.com** (commercial), **.edu** (education), **.gov** (goverment), **.mil** (military), **.net** (commercial), and **.org** (nonprofit organization). For Web sites outside the United States, you will find codes for countries such as **.au** (Australia), **.ca** (Canada), **.de** (Germany), **.jp** (Japan), **.mx** (Mexico), and **.uk** (United Kingdom). Thus, for *www.lib. utexas.edu,* you know immediately that the site belongs to an educational institution. The rest of the address—*lib.utexas*—often identifies the sponsor: in this case, the General Libraries at the University of Texas at Austin.

Finally, URLs give a **path** on the server to the particular Web page: *Libs/PCL/Reference.html.* Files on a Web server are placed in directories (also called *folders*) just like files on personal computers. So when the browser connects with the server for the General Libraries at the University of Texas, it looks inside the directory *Libs* for the directory *PCL*. Then it looks inside *PCL* for the file named *Reference.html.* One reason it is important to know how a URL address works is that search tools on the Web often take you deep into a Web site. Sometimes you have no idea who put up the page other than what you can figure out from the URL. Another thing to remember about the path segment of a URL address is that often it is **case sensitive,** meaning that the browser distinguishes between uppercase and lowercase. Therefore, a browser will not find *Reference.html* if you type *reference.html.*

Now you know a little bit about the Web and how it works. But why in five years did it become the most popular communications technology, in terms of volume, ever invented? When you first saw a Web site, you might have wondered what the big deal was. It is more pleasant to read a long text on paper than to read it on a screen; indeed, most people who visit Web sites never scroll down to read long blocks of texts. The pictures and images are good on the Web, but they are not yet up to the quality of illustrations in slick magazines. Sound files are not up to the standard of FM radio. And video clips, unless you have access to the very best technology, are clunky and slow on the Web. So if other media are better, why the rush to the Web?

Even though the Web still lacks the high quality found in other media, it combines the features of all of them. Much more important, Web sites are extremely cheap to produce and receive, and the variety is staggering. Your cable TV provider offers you maybe 75–150 channels, and even satellite television gives you only a few hundred. Web sites now number in the hundreds of millions. With an account from your college or university or an Internet provider such as AOL, you can spend every waking hour on the Web and not run out of interesting material to read and look at. And with an inexpensive computer, you too can have a Web server and produce thousands of Web pages (though most students use their school's server for their own Web sites). The Web has overcome major barriers of time and space. Unlike television or radio, people do not have to be watching or listening at a particular time to see a particular Web site. Visitors to a Web site can be located anywhere on the earth as long as they have an Internet connection. Furthermore, the Web offers many more opportunities for participation than other mass media do. You can download articles, forms, pictures, sounds, and video from a Web site. You can find links to other Web sites that are of interest to you. You can do searches for all sorts of information. You can also contact people by email and leave messages.

A Very Brief History of the Internet and the World Wide Web

The Web is part of the Internet, which has been around only since the late 1960s. The Internet has its origins in a Cold War project to solve the problem of how the military would maintain communications in the aftermath of a nuclear war, when presumably many, if not most, lines of communication and most major communications centers would be destroyed. The ingenious solution was to flatten the communications hierarchy, making every node equivalent so that the loss of any one node would not collapse the system. Each node would have the capability to originate, pass, and receive individually addresses messages bundled in packets. The routing of messages became relatively unimportant. Messages would bounce from host to host like a beach ball batted around in the crowd at a concert until they finally reached their destination.

In 1969, the Pentagon began connecting researchers at military and university sites, enabling them to transmit data at high speeds and access each other's computers. This network grew rapidly in the 1970s because its usefulness was obvious and its structure accommodated different kinds of machines, overcoming the problem of incompatibility. Soon

(continued)

researchers who had personal accounts began to exploit the Internet for person-to-person communication that ranged from project collaboration to chitchat to the first hobby bulletin boards. The Internet soon grew beyond the community of scientists as corporations and individuals began to take advantage of the Internet's speed and low cost.

In 1990, Tim Berners-Lee and Robert Cailliau, two scientists working at CERN, the European Laboratory for Particle Physics, invented the World Wide Web. Their goal was to make possible the sharing of scientific papers, so at first, the Web was a no-frills medium. In 1993, the first browser, named Mosaic, was developed at the University of Illinois, Urbana-Champaign. Browsers extended the potential of the Web to the many people who had learned to use the Web for email. Browsers also made possible the slick magazine look of many Web sites with sophisticated graphic design. The growth of the Internet and of the number of Web sites continues at a high rate. With much faster connections now available, we will likely see much more audio and video on the Web. There has never been anything quite like it, and we have seen only a glimpse of what the Web will soon become.

Arguments on the Web

Because the Web is a grass-roots medium with millions of people putting up Web sites, it's no surprise that it has turned out to be a vast forum for arguments. Many organizations and individuals have taken advantage of the low cost of the Web to publicize their stands on issues. To get a sense of the range of interest groups that use the Web to publicize their views, go to Yahoo! (www.yahoo.com), where you'll find, under the "Society and Culture" heading, the subheading "Issues and Causes" (see Figure 12.1). As you can see from the list, the issues extend from abortion, affirmative action, and animal rights to weight and nutrition, welfare reform, and xenotransplantation. It seems that if anyone has an opinion about anything, there is a Web site representing that position. If you have strong feelings about any broad issue, you can find on the Web people who think as you do.

Most of the argument sites listed by Yahoo! have been posted by organizations. One of the most frequently visited issue sites is the Electronic Frontier Foundation (EFF), an organization devoted to protecting privacy of individuals and the free flow of information on the Internet. The EFF was one of the leading opponents of the Communications Decency Amendment to the Telecommunications Act of 1996, which was aimed at censoring pornography on the Internet. The Communications Decency Amendment (CDA) sailed through

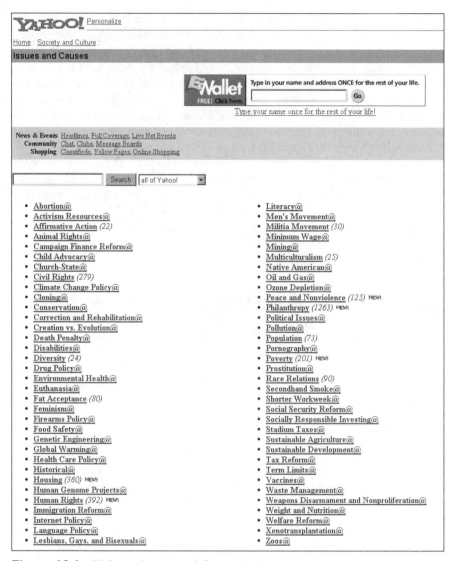

Figure 12.1   Yahoo's Issues and Causes Index
(http://www.yahoo.com/Society_and_Culture/
Issues_and_Causes/)

Congress with almost unanimous support from both Republicans and Democrats. But members of the EFF, alarmed at the potential abuse of massive censorship, launched the Blue Ribbon Campaign against the CDA. Soon the blue ribbon icon supporting the right of free speech appeared all over the Web.

The EFF mobilized Internet users against censorship of the Internet and demonstrated the power of grass-roots political action against the major political parties in the United States. The resulting outcry supporting freedom of speech caused both parties to back away from their initial position, and in 1997, the courts ruled the CDA unconstitutional. The EFF site is one of the most important on the Web for those who don't want the government to censor the Internet. Let's take a look at how it is organized. The first page of the site provides a menu of EFF activities and services and a list of press releases and news items (see Figure 12.2).

If you visited the site in August 1999 and clicked on the link "More headlines & information," you would find the item "Internet 'decency' bill (aka CDA II) to be signed into law: EFF joins other civil liberties groups in preparing legal challenge." This item would take you to another screen that gave the text of a press release on October 15, 1998 (see Figure 12.3). Even though this link is not found on the home page, the press release could have been found by using the site's search function or its browse feature.

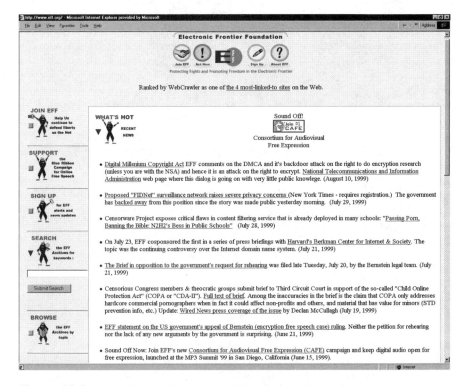

**Figure 12.2   The Electronic Frontier Foundation Home Page
(http://www.eff.org)**

Electronic Frontier Foundation

Join EFF   Act Now   Sign Up   About EFF

See also other recent press releases:
Congress about to pass two draconian Internet Censorship bills today: Joint ACLU/EFF/EPIC press release - (October 7, 1998)
EFF and other members of Internet Free Expression Alliance testify against Net censorship bills in Congress - (September 11, 1998)

FOR IMMEDIATE RELEASE
October 15, 1998

Rights Groups Prepare Legal Challenge as President Prepares to Sign Internet "Indecency" Bill

WASHINGTON--With a second Congressional attempt to censor the Internet all but certain, the American Civil Liberties Union, Electronic Privacy Information Center and Electronic Frontier Foundation today vowed yet another legal challenge if the measure includes criminal penalties and fines for communicating protected speech.

During last-minute budget negotiations, the Clinton Administration reportedly objected to provisions of the bill pushed by Rep. Michael Oxley, R-OH, citing a Justice Department analysis that it was probably unconstitutional and would likely draw resources away from more important law enforcement efforts. But negotiators apparently failed to strike the Oxley language from the $500 billion Omnibus Appropriations measure due to be voted on in both the House and Senate and signed by the President tomorrow.

The ACLU, with EPIC and EFF acting as co-plaintiffs and co-counsel, led the successful challenge to the Communications Decency Act, which the Supreme Court struck down last year. The groups said today that they anticipate filing a legal challenge as early as next week, on behalf of a diverse range of online speakers representing news organizations, gay and lesbian groups, artists, musicians, booksellers and any websites that distributed the Starr report.

"It's deja vu all over again," said Ann Beeson, Staff Attorney for the ACLU and a member of the Reno v. ACLU legal team that led the fight against a 1996 federal Internet law. "Just like the CDA, this bill will once again criminalize socially valuable adult speech and reduce the Internet to what is considered suitable for a six-year-old."

"Following a landmark Supreme Court ruling and constitutional objections from the Justice Department," Beeson added, "Congress can plead politics, but it can't plead ignorance."

Barry Steinhardt, President of the Electronic Frontier Foundation, agreed. "It is the height of irony that the same Congress that plastered the salacious Starr Report all over the Internet now passes a plainly unconstitutional law to suppress a vaguely defined category of 'harmful' material. You would think Congress would have learned that 'harmfulness' is in the eye of the beholder."

David Sobel, EPIC's General Counsel, said, "This law violates both the free speech rights and the privacy of Internet users. It requires, in effect, that any adult wishing to receive constitutionally protected material must register with a website before receiving information."

"The Supreme Court has, on several occasions, said that such procedures violate the First Amendment," Sobel added. "We are confident that the courts will continue to protect the right of all Americans to receive information without sacrificing their privacy."

+++++

The Electronic Frontier Foundation is one of the leading civil liberties organizations devoted to ensuring that the Internet remains the world's first truly global vehicle for free speech, and that the privacy and security of all on-line communication is preserved. Founded in 1990 as a nonprofit, public interest organization, EFF is based in San Francisco, California. EFF maintains an extensive archive of information on free speech, privacy, and encryption policy at http://www.eff.org.

**Figure 12.3   EFF Press Release, October 15, 1998
(http://www.eff.org/pub/Censorship/
Internet_censorship_bills/1998_bills/HTML/
19981015_cda2_release.html)**

The EFF press release is a print argument that has been converted to a Web page. Many arguments on the Web are like the EFF press release. For example, many newspaper editorials and opinion columns are available on the Web. The major difference between arguments on the Web and arguments in print is the potential to link to other pages. The EFF press release offers links to two other press releases on the same subject. If you go back to the home page, however, and click on BROWSE, you can find a large collection of documents related to the Communications Decency Amendment, including the text of the amendment, EFF's critical analysis of the amendment, and the full text of the U.S. Supreme Court decision that ruled the amendment unconstitutional. The designer of a Web site can layer information on the site, giving both an overview and opportunities to explore in depth.

The problem with many argument sites on the Web is that they don't provide much depth. If they have any links, they are to similar sites with no context for making the link. It's up to the reader to figure out the relevance of the link. This strategy works for people who are already convinced of the position being advocated, but it does not work well for people who haven't made up their minds. When you create a Web site that advocates a position, the ease of linking on the Web doesn't make your work any easier. Good arguments still require much thinking on your part and careful planning. You can't expect your readers to do your work for you. You still have to supply good reasons.

Intranets

Many companies, organizations, colleges, and universities have developed intranets, which are similar to the larger Internet and World Wide Web except that they restrict access to employees or students. The advantage of an intranet is privacy. Web sites can be shared by those involved without making them available to everyone.

Putting Text on Your Web Site

Creating a Web site used to be a chore because the files for the site had to be hand coded in Hypertext Markup Language (HTML). HTML works in the same way early word-processing programs worked. If you wanted boldface type, you had to insert a switch to turn on the boldfacing and another to turn off the boldfacing. Similarly, HTML uses switches called *tags*. To boldface a word, you insert <b> before the word and </b> after the word so that it looks like this:

<b>**boldface**</b>

As word-processing programs improved and computer memory expanded, soon it was no longer necessary to insert tags in the text. Word-processing programs display on the screen what gets printed on the page—known among computer users by the acronym WYSIWYG ("what you see is what you get").

Today, **web authoring software** programs write the HTML code in much the same way that word-processing programs do. The user doesn't have to know about HTML to make a Web page. Nonetheless, it's still good to know how HTML works because you might want to change something in a file or do something other than what your Web editing program allows you to do. A lot of free tutorials on HTML are available on the Web; we've listed a few at the end of the chapter. The best way to learn how HTML works is to look at the files that produce the pages you see on the Web. You can see these files under the pulldown menu under "View" on your browser. Click on "Source" or "Document Source" to see the HTML file.

Web Authoring Software

Until recently, you had to know how to write HTML code to make Web pages. Now, you don't have to know any HTML to make Web pages. Web authoring software makes composing Web pages very easy. Most of these programs work much like word-processing programs. When you want to make a heading or a link, you simply highlight that text with your mouse and then click to get what you want—bigger or smaller text, bold-face, italics, centering, links, and so on. Almost all Web authoring programs come in Macintosh and Windows versions. The most popular Web authoring programs are the following:

Adobe PageMill
Claris Home Page
Macromedia Dreamweaver
Microsoft FrontPage
Netscape Composer (free with Netscape)
Symantec Visual Page

Check for educational discounts through your college or university if you want to purchase one of these programs.

This section focuses on what the HTML guides don't tell you. They show you how to put text on the Web, but they don't tell you how reading is different on the Web. In most printed books, magazines, and newspapers, the text is continuous. Printed text isn't necessarily linear—witness the boxes and side-bars in almost any magazine. Although it's possible to go back and forth in print, the basic movement in print is linear, and the basic unit is the paragraph. By contrast, the basic movement on the Web is nonlinear, and the basic unit is the screen. Perhaps the most important fact to remember is that fewer than 10 percent of people who click on a Web site ever scroll down the page. Their eyes stop at the bottom of the screen. And those who do scroll down usually don't scroll down very far.

The First Screen Is the Most Important

People who browse Web sites don't hang around long if they aren't interested or if it takes too long to find out what's on the Web site. That's why your first screen is critical. If you have something to tell your visitors, tell them right away. They probably aren't going to click through a bunch of screens or scroll though long stretches to find out where you stand on an issue. You have to let your readers know on the first screen what your site is about.

The first screen is also the front door to your site, and when visitors enter your front door, they need to know where to go next. Supplying navigation tools on the first page is critical. These can take the form of menu bars, buttons, or clickable images. Whatever form they take, the labels should indicate what the visitor will find on the next screen.

The Web site in Figure 12.4 is the home page of Californians for Population Stabilization (CAPS), an organization that is seeking to limit the population growth of California. The CAPS home page features a prominent image of a

Figure 12.4   Californians for Population Stabilization Home Page
(http://www.calweb.com/~caps/)

stopwatch placed over an outline of the state, filled in with a photograph of a crowd. The main areas of the site are listed by buttons connected to the watch. The space on the home page of an advocacy group like CAPS is precious. The graphic of the watch superimposed over the state is effective, but it takes up a lot of screen real estate. CAPS is left with only a few inches of space at the bottom of the home page to convey some sense of the problem the organization seeks to address. CAPS elected to use a short quote that begins "In the 6 seconds it takes you to read this sentence, 17 people will be added to the earth's population. Of those, one will be from California." CAPS evidently believes that the facts of growth alone make the most compelling statement of its position.

Divide Your Text into Chunks

Long stretches of text on the Web tend not to get read. Part of the problem is that most people don't have large-screen monitors. For those people, reading text on the Web is like trying to read a newspaper through a three-inch square hole. It's possible to do, but it isn't much fun. Newspapers grew to their present size because our eyes can take in a large expanse of information when we scan the page. Perhaps in the next few years, large-screen monitors will give us a similar experience, but for now, most of us are still using small-screen monitors, and you have to design your page with your audience in mind.

Given the limitations of most monitors, many Web designers try to divide text into chunks whenever possible. For example, when they present a list of facts, they often put space between items rather than putting the facts together in a big paragraph. On the CAPS Web site are pages that describe how California's soaring population affects the state. One page (Figure 12.5) deals with the effects of population growth on agricultural land.

The CAPS page on Agriculture and Population Growth is typical of many informative pages on the Web. It provides a short statement of the problem: Population growth requires more land, and because "agricultural land is usually level, stable, and well-drained, it is often the first land lost to 'development.'" That statement is followed by facts in a bullet list. Bullet lists are popular on Web sites because they are easy to make. Bullet lists themselves require a mental linking between the claim and the evidence. They typically do not use any transitional rhetoric. On the CAPS agriculture page, the reader has to understand that the points in the bullets are supporting the major claim—that too-rapid population growth is harming California in many ways.

There are certain advantages and disadvantages to putting text on the Web. You can put a great deal of background information on a Web site connected by links to the main argument. Thus, you can offer a short summary on the main page with links to other pages that give background and evidence. One advantage of this strategy is that you design a single site both for people who know a great deal about the subject and will skip the background information and for those who know little and need the background. You can include additional evidence that would be hard to work into a paper otherwise. Furthermore, the act

Agriculture and Population Growth

California's explosive population growth causes the need for more housing and industrial buildings. Since agricultural land is usually level, stable, and well-drained, it is often the first land lost to "development."

The Problem:

- Over 100,000 acres of arable land are lost to "development" and erosion in California every year. The U.S. loses over one million acres annually

- In the fertile Central Valley, where the population growth rate is three times that of the state as a whole, thousands of residences are being built over prime agricultural land

- "Development" takes land out of production, eliminating the jobs associated with it. Including related industries such as canning and transportation, the land is often the only employer in rural areas.

- As population growth forces more people into rural areas, inadvertent and purposeful vandalization to agriculture occurs, raising operational costs such as insurance costs and management costs (like building fire breaks).

- Farmland that disappears under parking lots and houses can never be used again to produce food. As our own and the world's population grows, and political and economic instability continue to exist, providing food security will become increasingly important. We must avoid destroying agriculture at home and relying on external sources for food

- In 1964 there were 25,000 miles of divided highways. By 1977 that # had doubled. Since 1977 another 50,000 miles of divided highway has been added (1986). Airports occupied 1.76 million acres of rural land in 1968 and over 2.5 million in 1986.

- Besides the irreplaceable loss of some of the most fertile land in the world, economically the agricultural land which gains more revenue than causes expenditures is being replaced by residential land which studies show generate more expenditures than revenues.

Urban Sprawl

Because most of our cities were originally established as agricultural communities, good farmland surrounds them. As urban areas expand, they cover farmland with houses, office buildings, shopping malls, and parking lots.

Water Competition

In California, half of the farms are totally dependent on off-farm water supplies. As urban areas grow, they compete with agriculture for finite water supplies.

[WHO IS CAPS][JUST THE FACTS][CAPS IN THE CAPITOL][POPULATION NEWS][JUST FOR ACTIVISTS][JUST FOR MEDIA][WHATS NEW][E-MAIL CAPS] [BACK TO HOME PAGE]

Figure 12.5   CAPS Page on Agriculture and Population Growth (http://www.calweb.com/~caps/factag.html)

of clicking on particular words can make readers aware of the links in an argument. The design of the CAPS site indicates to readers that the CAPS agriculture page is evidence for the main argument.

But because text on the Web is usually truncated and readers skim quickly and jump from one page to another, it's more difficult to place a detailed, sustained argument on a Web site. Some people don't even try. They simply place a long text on the Web and assume that the people who are really interested will download that text, print it, and read it. However, that assumption risks losing all but the most interested readers. Readers increasingly expect arguments on the Web to be designed for the Web.

Format So That the Text Is Readable

One of the goals of CAPS is to limit the numbers of legal and illegal immigrants moving into California. An organization that takes the opposite position is the Center for Equal Opportunity (CEO). Below a heading, CEO lists three primary issues on its home page: racial preferences, immigration and assimilation, and multicultural education. For each of the major issues, CEO gives a short description and offers a quotation from a prominent public figure. Part of the CEO home page is reproduced in Figure 12.6.

● RACIAL PREFERENCES.

Racial preferences are now a well established part of employment, education, and voting rights practices. The federal government runs 19 programs for "disadvantaged" bankers. Even adoption agencies are required to consider race when finding homes for parent-less children.

CEO supports colorblind public policies and seeks to block the expansion of racial preferences and to prevent their use in employment, education, and voting.

"We ought to construct a society and set of laws that focus on an individual's character, not color of skin."

Randall Kennedy, Harvard Law School.

● IMMIGRATION AND ASSIMILATION.

With the United States admitting high numbers of immigrants, America's ability to accept newcomers will increasingly depend upon finding a pro-assimilation middle-ground between nativists who say that today's immigrants cannot assimilate and multiculturalist who say that they should not.

CEO promotes the assimilation of immigrants into our society and research on their economic and social impact on the United States.

"Teaching English to children who speak another language is a key to individual opportunity in America."

William J. Bennett, Former Secretary of Education.

● MULTICULTURAL EDUCATION.

Multiculturalists have a firm grip on both elementary and secondary schools and the universities. Their ideology of racial and ethnic difference risks balkanizing our multiracial society. Students who don't speak English are locked away in special programs that try to maintain native languages rather than teach English, often without their parents' consent. In many urban schools, African American students are fed a racialist "Afrocentric" curriculum of dubious merit.

CEO seeks to promote educational policies grounded in America's motto: e pluribus unum, "out of many, one."

"The menace to America today is the emphasis on what separates us rather than what brings us together."

Daniel J. Boorstin, Librarian of Congress Emeritus.

About CEO. | Join CEO. | Publications. | Staff. | Racial Preferences. | Immigration and Assimilation. | Multicultural Education. | Links. | CEO Bookstore. | What's New. | E-Mail.

Figure 12.6 **Center for Equal Opportunity Home Page**
(http://www.ceousa.org/)

The CEO page, like the CAPS page, uses short blocks of text effectively to outline its major issues and its stance on those issues. The CEO summaries are accompanied by quotes on these issues from well-known public figures.

Above all, make your text readable. Remember that other people's monitors may be smaller than yours; what appears as small type on your monitor may require a magnifying glass for others. Also, dark backgrounds make for tough reading. If you use a dark background and want people to read what you write, be sure to increase the font size, make sure the contrast between font and background is adequate, and avoid using all caps and italics.

> TEXT IN ALL CAPS IS HARD TO READ ON A BLACK BACKGROUND, *ESPECIALLY IF THE TEXT IS IN ITALICS.*

Anticipate Readers' Questions and Objections

Arguments on the Web have the same responsibility of addressing readers' questions and objections that print arguments have. Just like print arguments, arguments on the Web that ignore readers' questions and objections generally reach only people who are already convinced of the writer's position. To convince those who have not made up their mind or whose positions are not set in stone requires thinking about the questions and objections they might have.

Many Web arguments include a Questions and Answers page or a FAQ (Frequently Asked Question) where they address possible objections. These pages allow the writer to go into more depth because if the readers do not have questions or objections, they can quickly move back to the main argument. The American Council on Education maintains the Web site for the Alliance to Save Student Aid, a coalition made up of more than sixty organizations representing college students, administrators, and faculty members and aimed at preserving federal student aid. The main page has a link to a Question and Answers page (Figure 12.7). The first question they raise on their Question and Answers page is "Why should the federal government help students go to college?" This question is the most basic one for this organization because readers must believe that the federal government should provide aid for all qualified students if they are to support the goals of the organization. They may come to the issue with an assumption that the responsibility for higher education lies

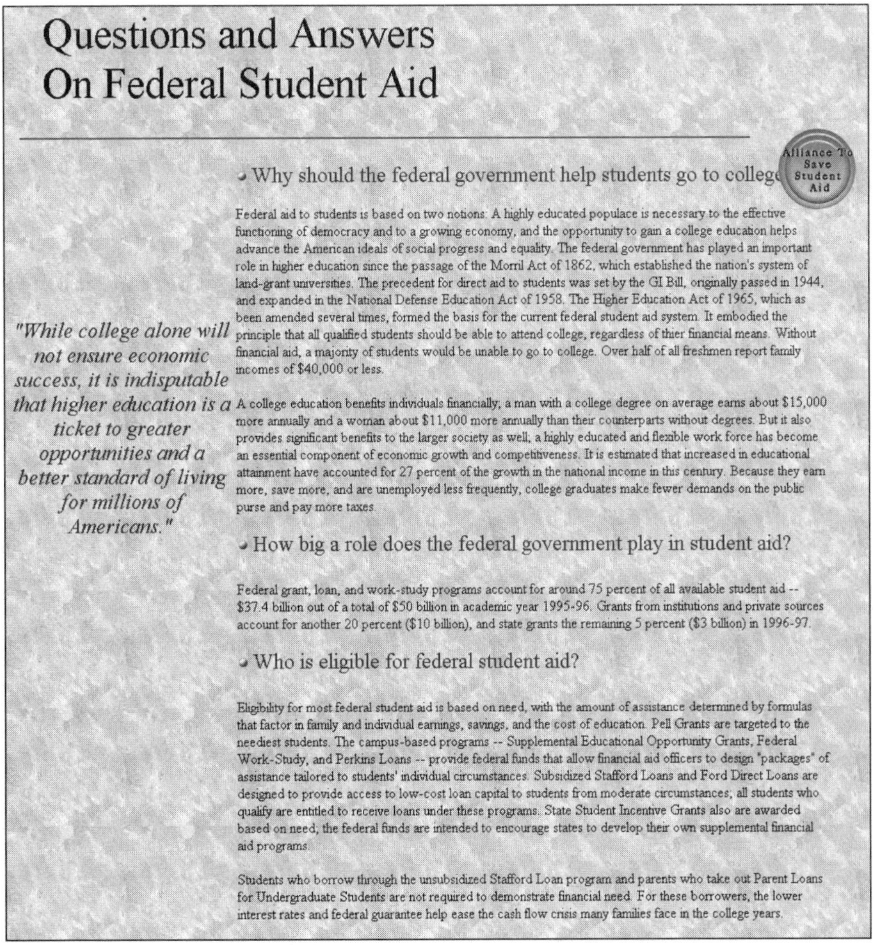

Questions and Answers
On Federal Student Aid

→ Why should the federal government help students go to college

Federal aid to students is based on two notions. A highly educated populace is necessary to the effective functioning of democracy and to a growing economy, and the opportunity to gain a college education helps advance the American ideals of social progress and equality. The federal government has played an important role in higher education since the passage of the Morril Act of 1862, which established the nation's system of land-grant universities. The precedent for direct aid to students was set by the GI Bill, originally passed in 1944, and expanded in the National Defense Education Act of 1958. The Higher Education Act of 1965, which as been amended several times, formed the basis for the current federal student aid system. It embodied the principle that all qualified students should be able to attend college, regardless of thier financial means. Without financial aid, a majority of students would be unable to go to college. Over half of all freshmen report family incomes of $40,000 or less.

"While college alone will not ensure economic success, it is indisputable that higher education is a ticket to greater opportunities and a better standard of living for millions of Americans."

A college education benefits individuals financially; a man with a college degree on average earns about $15,000 more annually and a woman about $11,000 more annually than their counterparts without degrees. But it also provides significant benefits to the larger society as well; a highly educated and flexible work force has become an essential component of economic growth and competitiveness. It is estimated that increased in educational attainment have accounted for 27 percent of the growth in the national income in this century. Because they earn more, save more, and are unemployed less frequently, college graduates make fewer demands on the public purse and pay more taxes.

→ How big a role does the federal government play in student aid?

Federal grant, loan, and work-study programs account for around 75 percent of all available student aid -- $37.4 billion out of a total of $50 billion in academic year 1995-96. Grants from institutions and private sources account for another 20 percent ($10 billion), and state grants the remaining 5 percent ($3 billion) in 1996-97.

→ Who is eligible for federal student aid?

Eligibility for most federal student aid is based on need, with the amount of assistance determined by formulas that factor in family and individual earnings, savings, and the cost of education. Pell Grants are targeted to the neediest students. The campus-based programs -- Supplemental Educational Opportunity Grants, Federal Work-Study, and Perkins Loans -- provide federal funds that allow financial aid officers to design "packages" of assistance tailored to students' individual circumstances. Subsidized Stafford Loans and Ford Direct Loans are designed to provide access to low-cost loan capital to students from moderate circumstances; all students who qualify are entitled to receive loans under these programs. State Student Incentive Grants also are awarded based on need; the federal funds are intended to encourage states to develop their own supplemental financial aid programs.

Students who borrow through the unsubsidized Stafford Loan program and parents who take out Parent Loans for Undergraduate Students are not required to demonstrate financial need. For these borrowers, the lower interest rates and federal guarantee help ease the cash flow crisis many families face in the college years.

Figure 12.7   American Council on Education's Alliance to Save Student Aid Site, Question and Answer Page (http://student-aid.nche.edu/qanda.HTML)

with state or local governments or that no government aid should be provided for college students.

The Question and Answer page has the additional advantage of allowing the writer to phrase the question for the reader. Often, the way a question is phrased determines the kind of answer. Thus, writers can address readers' possible objections in a way that facilitates their position rather than undermining it.

Stay Organized

When you decide to put up a Web site, it's critical that you do some planning in advance.

1. **Make an outline of your site.** Draw on paper how you want your site organized.

2. **Collect all the source materials for your site.** These materials include text and images. Keep the paper together in a manila folder. When you have this material in digital form, put it in a folder labeled *Sources* or the name of your project on your hard drive and on a disk backup.

3. **Figure out your system for naming files.** Use only lowercase letters; you will eventually get confused if you use capitals. Don't put in any odd characters such as semicolons; they will cause you problems down the road. All Web pages have to end in **.htm** or **.html.** Label image files by their type, either **.gif** (for GIF files) or **.jpg** (for JPEG files).

4. **Put your files in a folder.** You're going to put the files on your Web site's server in a folder just as you do on your computer. The simplest way is to put the whole folder on the server when you are ready. You will probably need only one folder. But if you are designing a site that might become bigger down the road, you might think about using more than one folder.

5. **Save, save, save.** It is always a good idea to make backup copies of all your files. Make copies on a floppy or a zip disk, which can store a lot of big files.

Principles of Web Design

When you design your Web site, many tools are available that you don't have with ordinary text. You can add graphics and create links to your own pages and pages made by others. When your skills become more advanced, you can even add animations and audio and video clips. Pictures and graphics can make your Web site appealing and can give it emotional impact. But pictures can also be confusing and turn people off, distracting them from the substance of your argument. You have to think about the Web in ways that are different from thinking about ordinary printed texts.

The design principles that were discussed in chapter 11—arrangement, consistency, and contrast—are extremely important when you design Web pages. There are also other design principles that you need to keep in mind. Pictures and graphics help people to understand the structure of your site and how to navigate from page to page. Pictures and graphics also have a lot to do with the performance of your site—how long it takes for pages to load on the screen. Thus, the effectiveness of a Web site depends a great deal on its pictures and graphics.

Determine the Visual Theme of Your Site

Most Web sites contain more than one page, and because it is so easy to move from one page to another on the Web, it's important to make your site as unified as possible. In addition to having links to the major parts of the site on every page, using a common design also contributes to the unity of the site. Americans for Medical Progress Educational Foundation (AMPEF) is an organization that justifies the use of animals in medical research. In their words, their goal is "to assure that scientists and doctors have the freedom and resources necessary to pursue their lifesaving and life-enhancing research." In practice, AMPEF's primary mission is to counter the efforts of animal rights activists who oppose the use of animals for medical research.

AMPEF's home page (Figure 12.8) has a simple but effective design that is repeated on other pages. The primary icon is a star imposed over a capital

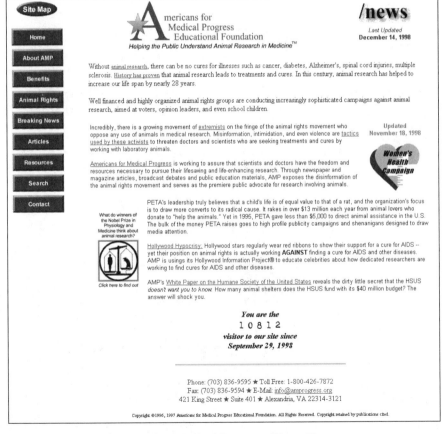

Figure 12.8   Americans for Medical Progress Home Page
(http://www.amprogress.org/)

A. The color scheme (not reproduced here) is simple, with the major headings in blue. A blue border on the left aids in identifying the site and in reducing the width of the screen. When the screen is too wide, the text becomes hard to read. The AMPEF site also uses stars for its bullet points to maintain a consistent design.

For its primary evidence, AMPEF relies on a series of facts about how animal research is beneficial in fighting human diseases. The site lists major diseases and the number of people who might have died without cures developed through animal research (see Figure 12.9).

Figure 12.9 **Americans for Medical Progress Research Page (http://www.amprogress.org/research.htm)**

Know the Messages Your Images Convey

There are relatively few images on the Americans for Medical Progress Web site. The home page (Figure 12.8) has a small graphic of a human and a rat on a balance scale that makes the visual argument against what it claims to be the position of People for the Ethical Treatment of Animals (PETA). In the sentence beside the graphic, AMPEF alleges that "PETA's leadership truly believes that a child's life is equal to that of a rat." But it's no surprise that photographic images of animals are absent on the AMPEF site, since it defends the killing of animals for research purposes.

The chief opponent of AMPEF is PETA, the largest animal rights organization in the world. PETA is opposed to eating animals, wearing their skins, or using them for entertainment or medical experiments. PETA enjoys the support of several major Hollywood stars, including Kim Basinger and Alec Baldwin, and major rock stars including Paul McCartney and his late wife Linda. PETA places images of animals on nearly all of its pages (see Figure 12.10). In its stories on the abuse of animals, there are often images of sad-looking animals in cages and animals in poor condition. The images provide strong emotional content in support of PETA's claim that it is wrong to harm animals.

PETA's Web site is frequently updated. The main page of its December 10, 1998, issue features a color photo (reproduced here in black and white) of a sumptuous holiday feast. The central place that the turkey usually occupies is replaced by a large mound of casserole. Beside the image of the holiday feast are smaller ones of a mother and baby elephant running under the headline "African Elephant Babies Need Your Help" and an image of the cover of the PETA catalog with Paul and the late Linda McCartney, long-time animal rights activists. Down the side of the page are even smaller images accompanying stories of dog abuse in Taiwan and Arkansas. The primary icon repeated on other pages (not shown) is a silhouette image of a rabbit running. Like the star icon on the AMPEF site, the repeated rabbit icon provides visual continuity. The PETA site has the additional advantage of using a visual theme that is associated with the overall message of the site.

Direct the Viewer's Eyes

The design principles that we discuss in chapter 11 also hold true for the Web with one important addition. The top of a Web page is even more critical than the top of a printed page because many people have monitors that do not display an entire Web page. Web pages are smaller than printed pages. Editors make it easy to save a text page in HTML, but remember that text does not look the same on the Web as it does in print. The bottom-line advice about creating a Web page is that many people never scroll down to the bottom line.

Figure 12.10   People for the Ethical Treatment of Animals Home Page
(http://www.peta-online.org/)

You have to pay special attention to the top of the page and let your visitors know what your page is about.

Many Web pages use jarring colors for striking effects, such as hot pinks and fluorescent greens on black backgrounds. Many others have visually intense backgrounds that distract from the text or make it hard to read because of the low contrast. If you want people to read your text, use lighter tones for backgrounds and supporting images. Bright colors should be reserved for what you most wish to emphasize, and even there, you risk overwhelming the rest of the text on your site.

The AMPEF site and the PETA site are both effective in directing the eyes of viewers to the important content. However, many Web sites neglect this important aspect of design. A site that fails to direct the viewer's eyes is the AAMA Network site on travel to Nepal (Figure 12.11). The site displays a

Figure 12.11   AMAA Network Consultant Home Page
(http://www.catmando.com/travel.htm)

jumbled collection of logos from various hotels, guide services, and retailers. The only useful part of this site is the menu bar. Professional designers refer to pages like the AAMA page as "clown's pants." Besides the poor design, the logos on the AAMA page take a long time to load. When visitors who access the Web on a slow modem wait five minutes to see what's on the page and get nothing more than randomly pasted logos, they are likely to become frustrated and angry—exactly the opposite of what the company wants them to feel.

Just as a report filled with errors gives an impression of carelessness and even ignorance, a poorly designed Web site suggests that the creator is incompetent and, if it is a business site, that the business is not a professional operation. A bad Web site can be worse than no Web site.

Keep the Visuals Simple

The successful examples of Web design that we show in this chapter are the work of graphics professionals who enjoy ample resources. They could include many large pictures if they chose to. But they have deliberately kept the visual design simple. Not only is a less complicated site friendlier, because it loads faster, but if it is well designed, it can be elegant. Simple elements are also easier to repeat, such as the starred bullet points on the AMPEF site (Figures 12.8 and 12.9). Too many icons, bullets, horizontal rules, and other embellishments make a cluttered page. A simple, consistent design is always effective for pages that contain text.

Even though graphic design provides visual impact and motivates the visitor to explore a Web site, this interest value fades quickly if the visuals are not supported by substance. People still expect to come away from a Web site that makes an argument with substantial information. Good visual design makes your Web site more appealing, but it does not do the work of argument for you.

Navigational Design

People don't read a Web site the way they read a book. They scan quickly and move around a lot. They don't necessarily read from top to bottom. If you are trying to make an argument on the Web, you have to think differently about how the reader is going to encounter your argument. If you put the argument on more than one page, then you have to plan the site so that readers can get back to the beginning. You don't want to leave visitors to your site lost in cyberspace.

Designing navigational tools for your Web site is a three-step process. First, you should decide on the overall layout of your Web site if you use more than one page. Web sites have a main page, which may be linked to other pages on the same site or on other sites. For example, the course Web site in Figure 12.12 has four attached pages. The layout of this site is quite simple.

The navigational tools on the course Web site reflect this organization. They make it easy to get to any of the subordinate pages. The main page (Figure 12.13) includes buttons in the left margin and a menu bar at the bottom.

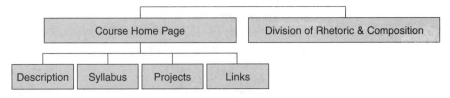

Figure 12.12 Layout of Class Web Site Example

They offer visitors to the site two ways of moving through it. The buttons are actually image files, and they add to the visual design of the site in addition to their navigational function. But some people who access the Web by modems turn off the images, so its important to have either ALT tags on the

Figure 12.13 Class Web Site Example

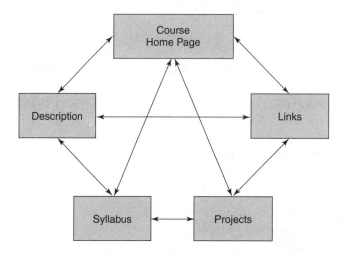

Figure 12.14   Navigation Map of Class Web Site Example

images, which give text instead of the images, or a text menu bar like the one at the bottom.

Even a simply organized Web site can quickly become complicated. Let's say that the design of the main page is repeated on the Description, Syllabus, Projects and Links pages, complete with the buttons and the text bar at the bottom. The map of the site would then connect each page with every other page (see Figure 12.14).

But if other pages are added, say, to the Projects page, the site designer is faced with another decision. Should these pages link back only to the Projects page, or should they link to all the major pages? If the designer chooses the latter, then every page would have to include buttons, menu bars, or both. What you want to avoid is having a link to a page on your site that has no links back. You should have no dead ends on your site.

Audience Considerations on the Web

The Web gives you the potential to reach millions of people, which is its greatest asset but at the same time a major difficulty in planning your site. The concept of audience becomes more complicated on the Web. HTML was written as a *display* language rather than a *design* language; that is, it is intended to work on any computer platform—Macintosh, Windows, or UNIX workstation. Users can select how they want the HTML file to look, down to selecting font and type size. (You too can control the display by looking on the "Preferences" menu of your browser and choosing how you want Web pages to appear.)

The display aspect of HTML drives graphic designers nuts. Designers are accustomed to deciding how things will look down to the smallest details. The ability of users to change the display creates many headaches for designers. Bigger headaches are the problems of different computers, different connections, and different browsers. Not only do you not know who will click on your Web site, but you also don't know exactly how they will see or hear what you put up. Some people will have the latest Web browsers, powerful computers, big-screen monitors, and very fast Ethernet, ADSL, or cable modem connections. Others may be connecting to your Web site by slower dial-up modem connections and may have older, less-powerful computers that cannot run the latest versions of Web browsers. The Web allows you the opportunity to include sound, image, and even movie files, but not everyone can download these files. If you want such people to see everything on your Web site without waiting minutes for your pages to load, you have to think about them when you are designing your site.

A famous architect, Ludwig Mies van der Rohe, is best known for his three-word aphorism, "less is more." He was talking about a general principle for the design of buildings, in which simple is better. His ideas about architecture are controversial, since some of his less-talented followers created many ugly buildings. In Web design, however, his principle is a good one to keep in mind. On the Web, less size means more speed. So we might change van der Rohe's aphorism to "less is faster." Pay attention to size when you put images on the Web. Smaller images not only load faster but also look better. You can make your images smaller by using the cropping tool in Photoshop or whatever graphics editor you use. Trimming a little off the edges can save seconds in the time it takes an image to load.

If you are designing a site you hope many people will visit, you should read and use the guidelines developed by the World Wide Web Consortium (w3c), which is responsible for the development and propagation of Web standards (http://www.w3.org/TR/WD-WAI-PAGEAUTH). These guidelines contain important advice about making Web sites accessible for people who have disabilities.

Online Guides for Publishing on the Web

Introductory HTML Guides

Computer Writing and Research Lab's HTML Tutorial

http://www.cwrl.utexas.edu/studentresources/tutorial/index.html
See the background and color links for making snazzy Web pages.

(continued)

NCSA Beginner's Guide to HTML

http://www.ncsa.uiuc.edu/General/Internet/WWW/
HTMLPrimer.html
A basic guide.

Professional Web Design

http://junior.apk.net/~jbarta/
Excellent step-by-step tutorials on basic design, tables, forms, and frames, plus a great resources collection.

More Advanced HTML Resources

HTML 4.0—the latest version of HTML

http://www.w3.org/MarkUp/

Links for learning CSS—Cascading Style Sheets

http://www.w3.org/Style/css/

Yale C/AIM Web Style Guide

http://info.med.yale.edu/caim/manual/index.html

Sun Microsystems Guide to Web Style

http://www.sun.com/styleguide/tables/Welcome.html

Chapter 13

Effective Research

Research: Knowing Information You Need

The writing that you do in school sometimes seems isolated from the real world. After all, when you write for a class, your real audience is usually the teacher. For the same reason, the research associated with writing for school tends to get isolated from real-world problems. Instead of asking questions such as how compounds that mimic estrogen might be causing reproductive abnormalities in certain animal species (as in chapter 2), students ask questions such as "What do I need to know to write this paper?" This approach tends to separate research from writing. If you've ever said to yourself, "I'll go to the library to do the research tonight, and then tomorrow afternoon I'll start writing the paper," you might be making some assumptions about the nature of research and writing that will actually make your task harder instead of easier. So for now, set aside what you already know about how to do research and think instead in terms of gathering information to solve problems and answer questions.

Effective research depends on two things: knowing what kind of information you are looking for and knowing where to get it. What you already know about writing arguments will help you to make some decisions about what kind of information you should be looking for. For instance, if you have decided to write a proposal for solving the problem of HMOs limiting subscribers' health care options, you already know that you will need to find statistics (to help your readers understand the urgency and scope of the problem) and several different analyses of the situation by writers from different camps (to help you make sure your own understanding of the situation is accurate, complete, and fair to all participants). But if you keep thinking about the demands of the proposal as a type of argument, you might also decide that you need to look at how this problem has been solved in the British or Canadian health system or how programs like Medicare and Medicaid are dealing with it.

Even if you don't yet know enough about your subject to know what type of argument you will want to write, there are still some basic questions you can use to plan your research. To make a thoughtful and mature contribution to any debate in the realm of public discourse, you will need to know the background of the issue. As you begin your research, then, you can use the following questions as a guide:

1. *Who are the speakers on this issue and what are they saying?* Subdividing the group of everyone who has something to say on this issue and everything that is being said into narrower categories will help you to gain a better understanding of what the debate looks like. For example, you might divide it like this:
   - Who are the experts on this issue? What do the experts say?
   - Who else is talking about it? What do they say?
   - Are the people whose interests are most at stake participating in the debate? What are they saying?

   In addition to the categories of experts, nonexpert speakers, and those whose interests are at stake, there are other general categories you can begin from, such as supporters and opponents of a position, liberals and conservatives, and so on.

   Also remember that any given debate will have its own specific set of opponents. In a debate about constructing a storage facility for nuclear waste in Nevada, for instance, conservationists and proponents of growth in the state of Nevada are lining up against the federal government. On another significant issue—water usage—proponents of growth stand in opposition to conservationists, who object to the demands Las Vegas makes on the waters of the Colorado River. On yet other issues, conservationists depend on the federal government to use its power to protect land, water, and other resources that are vulnerable to the activities of businesses and individuals.

2. *What is at stake?* Political debates often boil down to arguments about control of, or access to, resources or power. Therefore, resources and power are good places to start looking for what is at stake in any given debate. Depending on the nature of the debate, you might also look at what is at stake in terms of ethical and moral issues. For example, as a country and as a human community, what does this nation stand to lose if a whole generation of African-American urban young people grows up alienated from other people in the United States? To help narrow down your search, you might rephrase this question in several different ways:
   - How or why does this issue matter: to the world, to the citizens of this country, to the people whose interests are at stake, to me?

■ What stands to be gained or lost for any of these stakeholders?

■ Who is likely to be helped and hurt the most?

3. ***What kinds of arguments are being made about this issue?*** Just as it is help-ful to subdivide the whole field of speakers on your issue into narrower groups that line up according to sides, it is also helpful to subdivide the whole field of what is being said according to types or categories of argu-ments. It might help to set up a chart of speakers and their primary argu-ments to see how they line up.

■ What are the main claims being offered?

■ What reasons are offered in support of these claims?

■ What are the primary sources of evidence?

■ Is some significant aspect of this issue being ignored or displaced in favor of others?

■ If so, why?

4. ***Who are the audiences for this debate?*** Sometimes, the audience for a de-bate is every responsible member of society, everyone living in a certain region, or everyone who cares about the fate of the human species on this planet. More often, however, arguments are made to specific types of au-diences, and knowing something about those audiences can help you to understand the choices that the writers make. Even more important, know-ing who is already part of the audience for a debate can help you to plan your own strategies.

■ Do you want to write to one of the existing audiences to try to change its mind or make it take action?

■ Or do you want to try to persuade a new, as-yet-uninvolved audience to get involved in the debate?

■ How much do they know about the issues involved?

■ Where do they likely stand on these issues?

■ Will they define the issues the same way you do?

5. ***What is your role?*** At some point, as you continue to research the issue and plan your writing strategies, you will need to decide what your role should be in this debate. Ask yourself:

■ What do I think about it?

■ What do I think should be done about it?

■ What kind of argument should I write, and to whom?

Use these questions to take inventory of how much you already know about the issue and what you need to find out more about. When you have worked through these questions, then you are ready to make a claim that will guide your research efforts. See the Steps in Writing exercises at the end of chapters 5–10 to get started.

What Makes a Good Subject for Research

- **Find a subject that you are interested in.** Research can be enjoyable if you are finding out new things rather than just confirming what you already know. The most exciting part of doing research is making small discoveries.

- **Make sure that you can do a thorough job of research.** If you select a topic that is too broad, such as proposing how to end poverty, you will not be able to do an adequate job.

- **Develop a strategy for your research early on.** If you are researching a campus issue such as a parking problem, then you probably will rely most on interviews, observations, and possibly a survey. But if you find out that one of the earliest baseball stadiums, Lakefront Park in Chicago (built in 1883), had the equivalent of today's luxury boxes and you want to make an argument that the trend toward building stadiums with luxury boxes is not a new development, then you will have to do library research.

- **Give yourself enough time to do a thorough job.** You should expect to find a few dead ends, and you should expect to better focus your subject as you proceed. If you are going to do research in the field, by survey, or in the library, remember the first principle of doing research: *Things take longer than you think they do.*

Planning Your Research

Once you have a general idea about the kind of information you need to make your argument, the next step is to decide where to look for it. People who write on the job—lawyers preparing briefs, journalists covering news stories, policy analysts preparing reports, engineers describing a manufacturing process, members of Congress reporting to committees, and a host of others—have general research strategies available to them. The first is to gather the information themselves, which is called **primary** or **first-hand evidence.** We can distinguish two basic kinds of primary research.

Experiential research involves all the information you gather just through observing and taking note of events as they occur in the real world. You meet with clients, interview a candidate, go to a committee meeting, talk to coworkers, read a report from a colleague, observe a manufacturing process, witness an event, or examine a patient. In all these ways, you are adding to your store of knowledge about a problem or issue. In many cases, however, the knowledge that is gained through experience is not enough to answer all the questions or solve all the problems. In that case, writers supplement experiential research with empirical research and research in the library.

Empirical research is a way of gathering specific and narrowly defined data by developing a test situation and then observing and recording events as they occur in the test situation. Analysis of tissue samples and cell cultures in a laboratory, for instance, can add important information to what a doctor can learn by examining a patient. Crash tests of cars help automakers and materials engineers to understand why crumpling is an important part of a car's ability to protect its passengers in a crash. Surveys of adult children of divorced parents make it possible for psychologists to identify the long-term effects of divorce on family members. Many people believe that this kind of research is what adds new information to the store of human knowledge; so for many audiences, reporting the results of empirical research is an important part of making a strong argument. (Therefore, writers often use statistics and reports of research done by experts in the field to support their claims.)

For the most part, however, debates about public issues occur outside the fairly narrow intellectual spaces occupied by the true experts in any given field. Experts do, of course, participate in public debates, but so do all other interested citizens and policymakers. The majority of speakers on an issue rely on the work of others as sources of information—what is known as **secondary** or **second-hand evidence.** Many people think of library research as secondary research—the process of gathering information by reading what other people have written on a subject. In the past, library research was based almost exclusively on collections of print materials housed in libraries; in addition to public and university libraries, organizations of all kinds had their own collections of reference materials specific to their work. As is discussed in chapter 12, however, the Internet has brought significant changes in the way people record, store, view, distribute, and gain access to documents. For most issues, searching the Internet will be an important part of your library research.

Interviews, Observations, and Surveys

Interviews

- Decide first why one or more interviews could be important for your argument. Knowing the goals of your interview will help you to determine whom you need to interview and to structure the questions in the interview. You might, for example, learn more about the history of a campus issue than you were able to find out in the campus newspaper archives.

(continued)

- Schedule each interview in advance, preferably by email or letter. Let the person know why you are conducting the interview. Then follow up with a phone call to find out whether the person is willing and what he or she might be able to tell you.

- Plan your questions. You should have a few questions in mind as well as written down. Listen carefully so that you can follow up on key points.

- Come prepared with at least a notebook and pencil. If you use a tape recorder, be sure to get the person's permission in advance and be sure that the equipment is working.

Observations

- Detailed observations can be an important source of evidence if you can link them to your claim. For example, if you believe that the long lines in your student services building are caused by inefficient use of staff, you could observe how many staff members are on duty at peak and slack times.

- Choose a place where you can observe without intrusion. Public places work best because you can sit for a long time without people wondering what you are doing.

- Carry a notebook and write extensive notes whenever you can. Write down as much as you can. Be sure to record where you were, the date, exactly when you arrived and left, and important details such as the number of people present.

Surveys

- Like interview questions, questions on surveys should relate directly to the issue of your argument. Take some time to decide what exactly you want to know first.

- Write a few specific, unambiguous questions. The people you contact should be able to fill out your survey quickly, and they should not have to guess about what a question means. It's always a good idea to test the questions on a few people to find out whether they are clear before you conduct the survey.

- You might include one or two open-ended questions, such as "What do you like about X?" or "What don't you like about X?" Answers to these questions can be difficult to interpret, but sometimes they provide insights.

- Decide who you want to participate in your survey and how you will contact them. If you are going to use your survey results to claim that they represent the views of undergraduates at your school, then you should pay attention to matching the gender, ethnic, and racial balance to the proportions at your school.

- If you are going to mail or email your survey, include a statement about what the survey is for and how the results will be used.

- Interpreting your results should be straightforward if your questions require definite responses. Multiple-choice formats make data easy to tabulate, but they often miss key information. If you included one or more open-ended questions, you need to figure out a way to group responses.

Finding What You Are Looking for in Print Sources

Large libraries can be intimidating, even to experienced researchers when they begin working on a new subject. You can save time and frustration if you have some idea of how you want to proceed when you enter the library. Libraries have two major kinds of sources: books and periodicals. Periodicals include a range of items from daily newspapers to scholarly journals that are bound and put on the shelves like books.

Most books are shelved according to the Library of Congress Classification System, which uses a combination of letters and numbers to give you the book's unique location in the library. The Library of Congress call number begins with a letter or letters that represent the broad subject area into which the book is classified. The Library of Congress system has the advantage of shelving books on the same subject together, so you can sometimes find additional books by browsing in the stacks. You can use the *Library of Congress Subject Headings,* available in print in your library's reference area or on the Web (http://lcweb. loc.gov), to help you find out how your subject might be indexed.

If you want to do research on cloning, you might type "cloning" in the subject index of your online card catalog, which would yield something like the following results:

1 Cloning—23 item(s)

2 Cloning—Bibliography.—1 item(s)

3 Cloning—Congresses.—2 item(s)

4 Cloning—Fiction.—6 item(s)

5 Cloning—Government policy—United States.—2 item(s)
6 Cloning—History.—1 item(s)
7 Cloning, Molecular—36 item(s) Indexed as: MOLECULAR CLONING
8 Cloning—Moral and ethical aspects.—13 item(s)
9 Cloning—Moral and ethical aspects—Government policy—United States.—1 item(s)
10 Cloning—Moral and ethical aspects—United States.—2 item(s)
11 Cloning—Religious aspects—Christianity.—2 item(s)
12 Cloning—Research—History—1 item(s)
13 Cloning—Research—Law and legislation—United States.—1 item(s)
14 Cloning—Research—United States—Finance.—1 item(s)
15 Cloning—Social aspects.—1 item(s)
16 Cloning—United States—Religious aspects.—1 item(s)

This initial search helps you to identify more precisely what you are looking for. If you are most interested in the ethical aspects of cloning, then the books listed under number 8 would be most useful to you.

Finding articles in periodicals works much the same way. To find relevant newspaper and magazine articles, use a periodical index. These indexes are located in the reference area of your library. They may be in print form, on CD-ROM, or sometimes available on your library's Web site. General indexes that list citations to articles on popular and current topics include:

ArticleFirst (electronic)
CARL Uncover (electronic)
Expanded Academic ASAP (electronic)
InfoTrac (electronic)
Lexis/Nexis (electronic)
Readers' Guide to Periodical Literature (print)
Periodical Abstracts (electronic)
ProQuest (electronic)

Some of these indexes contain the full text of articles, which you can print out. Others will give you a reference, which you then have to find in your library. In addition to these general periodical indexes, there are many specialized indexes that list citations to journal articles in various fields. Deciding which kind of articles you want to look for—scholarly, trade, or popular—will help you to select the right index.

Follow these steps to find articles:

1. Select an index that is appropriate to your subject.
2. Search the index using relevant subject headings(s).
3. Print or copy the complete citation to the articles(s).
4. Check the periodicals holdings to see whether your library has the journal.

Scholarly, Trade, and Popular Journals

Some indexes give citations for only one kind of journal. Others include more than one type. Although the difference between types of journals is not always obvious, you should be able to judge whether a journal is scholarly, trade, or popular by its characteristics.

Characteristics of Scholarly Journals

- Articles are long with few illustrations.
- Articles are written by scholars in the field, usually affiliated with a university or research center.
- Articles have footnotes or a works cited list at the end.
- Articles usually report original research.
- Authors write in the language of their discipline, and readers are assumed to know a great deal about the field.
- Scholarly journals contain relatively few advertisements.
  Examples: *American Journal of Mathematics, College English, JAMA: Journal of the American Medical Association, Plasma Physics*

Characteristics of Trade Journals

- Articles are frequently related to practical job concerns.
- Articles usually do not report original research.
- Articles usually don't have footnotes or relatively few footnotes.
- Items of interest to people in particular professions and job listings are typical features.
- Advertisements are aimed at people in the specific field.
  Examples: *Advertising Age, Industry Week, Macworld, Teacher Magazine*

Characteristics of Popular Journals

- Articles are short and often illustrated with color photographs.
- Articles seldom have footnotes or acknowledge where their information came from.
- Authors are usually staff writers for the magazine or freelance writers.
- Advertisements are aimed at the general public.
- Copies can be bought at newsstands.
  Examples: *Cosmopolitan, Newsweek, Sports Illustrated, GQ, People*

Finding What You Are Looking for in Electronic Sources

If you are familiar with searchable electronic databases like your library's catalog, you might want to think of the Internet as just another database. However, there are two significant differences between the Internet and your library's catalog and other indexes you might have used in the library. The first difference, obviously, is that while catalogs and indexes of print material give you information *about* books, articles, and other resources, they don't usually contain the documents themselves. An Internet search, on the other hand, can give you direct access to sources that are available all over the world. In the early days of public access to the Internet, when Internet resources were very limited and not as useful as readily available print resources, that kind of access was not very helpful in most areas of research. But as the Internet grows up, it is becoming accepted as a legitimate—and even essential—part of our ability to record and share knowledge.

The other significant difference between the Internet and other research databases is that while only "authorized personnel" can add entries to or delete them from a traditional database, anyone who has access to a server can create a Web site (add an entry), and anyone who has a Web site can shut it down (delete an entry) or move it to a different location. There are literally millions of Web sites (entries) in the Internet's giant database, and sites are being added, moved, and deleted every day. To navigate this global library, we have search engines, programs that are so fast and sophisticated that they can sort through the wealth of available material and return a list of sites that match your search request (called *hits*) within seconds if you have a fast connection.

Using Search Engines

A search engine is a set of programs that use the incredible power of a computer to construct indexes to information found on the Internet. A search engine uses both a **robot,** which moves through the Web capturing information about Web sites, and an **indexer,** which organizes the information found by the robot. Search engines give different results because they assign different weights to the information they find. They often use words in the title of a Web site or words in a meta tag (which you don't see when you click on a Web site) to order the results they report. If you don't have much experience with search engines, try out a few different ones until you find one or two favorites, and then learn how to use them well.

Using Search Engines

- To start your search, enter your Web browser (such as Netscape Navigator or Communicator or Microsoft Explorer) and click on "Search." This will take you to a screen offering a selection of Web navigators and search engines. The Netscape search screen offers links (clickable text or screen buttons that will take you directly to another location) to the most commonly used search tools: Excite, Infoseek, Lycos, Alta Vista, LookSmart, HotBot, WebCrawler, and Yahoo, among others.

- A key word can be a single word, a name, or a phrase. Most search engines allow you to use quotation marks to indicate a phrase, such as "tax deductions" or "student loans." Using the key words *student* and *loans* without quotation marks would lead you to sites about home mortgages, business financing, and many other types of loans in addition to the student loans you were actually looking for, as well as to student sites totally unrelated to loans.

- To narrow your search, combine search terms. Most search engines allow you to use AND to retrieve only sites that include both terms (as in "student loans" AND "tax deductions") and OR to retrieve sites that include either term. Note that replacing AND with OR in the previous search would yield very different results, since using OR would make the search retrieve all sites about student loans and all sites about tax deductions, not just sites related to tax deductions for student loans.

- Some search engines use + to indicate that a term is required (as in "student loans" +subsidized) and – to indicate that sites containing that term should not be included ("student loans" –legislation).

- When you want the search to retrieve any form of a word, such as both *loan* and *loans* or *child, children,* and *children's,* you can use * to replace the part of the word that you want the search to ignore (as in *loan** or *child**).

- Most search engines will retrieve only exact matches to the terms you use in your search request. A key word search for "snake bite," for example, will not pick up the phrase "the adder's sting." To find this possibly relevant item using a key word search, you would need

(continued)

to do another search using either *adder* or *sting*. For that reason, the thoroughness of your search will depend on your patience and persistence in trying all the obvious variations of your initial search term.

■ Be sure to follow the format guidelines for the search engine you are using. There is usually a text link labeled "search tips" or "help" that will take you to advice about formatting your search request.

Searching by Key Word

A *key word* is a word or phrase that identifies the subject's central concepts. Most key words are so obvious that even people who are completely new to a topic would recognize them intuitively. For example, if you are looking for information about tax deductions for student loan payments, you would probably use "tax deductions" or "student loans" as your starting point. In fact, either search term will get you to information about a 1997 tax law that phases in tax deductions for the interest paid on student loans. Using the two terms together will get you there even faster.

In some cases, however, an obvious key word will be too general to get you the kind of information you need in a usable form. An everyday kind of problem will serve as an example. You move into your apartment or dormitory and find a major problem with cockroaches. You want to get rid of them, but you wonder whether spraying a pesticide would put your health at risk. So you turn on your computer, go to the search engine Excite, and start with what seem to be the obvious key words: cockroaches, "health hazards," and pesticides. However, the Excite search (on January 8, 1999) turns up 5,129 hits for cockroaches, 11,780 hits for "health hazards," and 40,640 for pesticides. Clearly, these key words are too general to be effective search terms. Combining them to create the search term +pesticides +"health hazards" reduces the number of hits to 581—much better but still an unmanageably large body of information.

Refining the search using the form +cockroach* +pesticide* +"health hazard*" brings the number of hits down to 5, a manageable number (see Figure 13.1). You can survey the results and decide what you want to view.

Item 1 mentions insecticides that are useful in home cockroach control. So you click on it and find a Web site for the University of Minnesota Extension Service (Figure 13.2). The page starts off by giving information about the life cycle of cockroaches and the kinds of cockroaches. But you're not interested

Figure 13.1   Excite Search: +cockroach* +pesticide* +"heath hazard*"
(http://search.excite.com)

in identifying them; you just want to get rid of them. So you scroll down the page and find what you are looking for: the kinds of insecticides that can be used safely for preventing cockroaches (Figure 13.3).

Often, you're not so lucky to be able to narrow a search to five items, but anytime you can get the number below a hundred, you can scroll through and find the Web sites that are most relevant to what you're looking for.

FO-1003-GO
Revised 1991
To Order
College of Agricultural, Food,
and Environmental Sciences

UNIVERSITY OF MINNESOTA

Cockroaches

Jeffrey D. Hahn and Mark E. Ascerno

NOTE: *At this time,* figure labels and cutlines indicate location of photos and graphics available only in publication form. Click here for ordering information.

Cockroaches are probably the most persistent household pests in Minnesota. Cockroaches are scavengers and will eat almost any food as well as backing glue, leather, bookbindings, and even television and microwave wiring. They are nocturnal, hiding during the day and becoming active at night. The number of cockroaches seen running for cover when the lights are turned on represents a small portion of the total population. Therefore, the visible presence of only a few cockroaches at night can signal a much larger population that should be controlled. Cockroaches generally breed in warm, moist and narrow locations.

Correct identification of suspected cockroaches is important, as there are insects, e.g. long-horned beetles, crickets, and ground beetles, that may be confused with cockroaches. Cockroaches are identified by their flattened, oval shape, long antennae (about the length of their body), and their head, which is hidden from view (underneath the pronotum). They have six stout, conspicuous legs covered with spines. Cockroaches are usually not seen during the day, or if they are, they usually run for cover. If there is any doubt about the identification of an insect, submit a sample to an expert. There are three stages during a cockroach's life cycle: egg, nymph, and adult. This is known as simple metamorphosis, or gradual development. The nymph looks similar to the adult, but is smaller, and either lacks wings or has wing pads. Nymphs are sexually immature. Normally, nymphs are more numerous than adults when infesting a building.

Cockroaches have long been thought to carry diseases. Although they have been shown experimentally to carry human pathogens, they rarely transmit diseases and are not considered a public health hazard. Four kinds of cockroaches can become established in Minnesota homes. A fifth kind, the woods roach, may also enter and become a temporary nuisance. Additionally, there are several subtropical species that may be transported accidentally to Minnesota. These cockroaches differ in their habits. Therefore, a general understanding of each insect is basic to effective control.

Figure 13.2   **University of Minnesota Extension Service: "Cockroaches"**
                    (http://www.extension.umn.edu/Documents/D/K/
                    DK1003.html)

Searching by Subject

For researchers with a specific goal, a key word search is usually the most efficient way to get to sites that match an exact topic. When you don't yet know enough about a topic to know what the key words are, though, or when you want to get a broad, general sense of what's available, you can browse the Web using the subject listings offered by Web indexes such as Yahoo! To use the subject search, just ignore the key word search box and click on one of the sub-

---

Insecticides

Choose one of the following insecticides: chlorpyrifos, permethrin, propoxur (e.g. Baygon) [may be listed as *o* Isopropoxyphenyl methylcarbamate], cyfluthrin, fenvalerate [may be listed as cyano (3- phenoxyphenyl) methyl 4-chloro alpha-(l-methylethyl) benzeneacetate, tetramethrin, resmethrin [may be listed as (5-Benzyl-3-furyl) methyl 2,2-dimethyl-3-(2-methylpropenyl) cyclopropanecarboxylate], d-trans allethrin, hydroprene (e.g. Gencor), or fenoxycarb. These insecticides are purchased in ready-to-use aerosol or liquid forms from hardware stores, variety retail stores and similar places.

CAUTION: *Read all label directions carefully before buying insecticides and again before applying them.*

Hydroprene and fenoxycarb are known as insect growth regulators (IGRs). IGRs are very effective against cockroach nymphs and are virtually nontoxic to people and animals. IGRs control cockroaches by mimicking insect hormones that prevent them from maturing into adults. However, IGRs have little effect on adult cockroaches. IGR formulations available to the public usually contain a residual insecticide, such as permethrin, to control adult cockroaches.

Insecticidal bait stations can be used to supplement residual insecticide sprays. They are purchased in ready-to-use containers. Place them according to package directions.

Household aerosol bombs and foggers are most effective for controlling insects that are out in the open. Because cockroaches hide in cracks and crevices, they are not greatly affected by insecticides delivered by bombs and foggers. Aerosols containing pyrethrins help flush cockroaches out of their hiding places and can increase the effectiveness of residual insecticides. However, pyrethrins should not be used solely, as they have no residual activity and only affect those insects they immediately come in contact with.

Ultrasonic pest control devices have been repeatedly tested and found to be ineffective in controlling cockroaches, and their use is not suggested.

Remember to use insecticides in combination with sanitation efforts. Also, dust boric acid (available as a powder from drug stores) in isolated places, such as behind and under refrigerators, stoves, and sinks.

When using insecticides, do not contaminate food, dishes, or utensils. Store all chemicals in a safe place where children can not reach them.

Do not allow children or pets near treated surfaces until spray has dried.

Read the pesticide label and follow the instructions as a final authority on pesticide use.

Jeffrey D. Hahn   Mark E. Ascerno
Entomology   Entomology

Figure 13.3   University of Minnesota Extension Service: "Cockroaches"
(http://www.extension.umn.edu/Documents/D/K/
DK1003.html)

ject fields listed below it. This will take you to a list of narrower topics within the field. Clicking on one of these will take you to a still more specific list of items within the topic. If you continue to click on one of the available choices, you will eventually arrive at a reasonably comprehensive list of sites on a fairly narrow topic. However, a subject search, even more than a key word search, is limited by what each index has already indexed. That means that subject searches using different index sites will yield very different results. It also means that most of the time, the results produced by a subject search will be less comprehensive than the results of a key word search.

Doing the Research for an Argument about Cloning

To get the big picture about the cloning debate, Joann started with a subject search using Yahoo! (to start a Yahoo! search, go to http://www.yahoo.com). She chose "Science" from the first subject list and then "Biology" from the list of subcategories indexed under "Science." From the "Issues and Causes" menu, she chose "Cloning," which took her to the page shown in Figure 13.4.

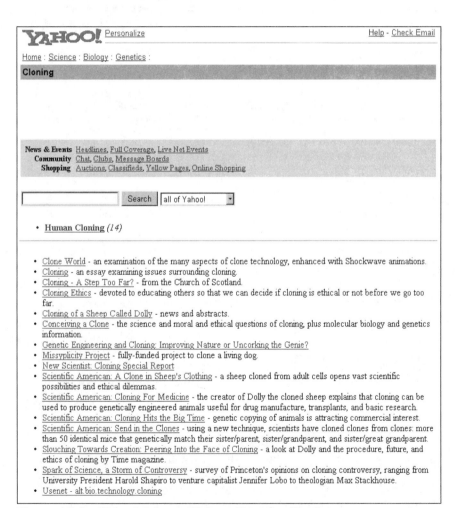

Figure 13.4   Yahoo! Science:Biology:Genetics:Cloning
(http://yahoo.com/Science/Biology/Genetics/)

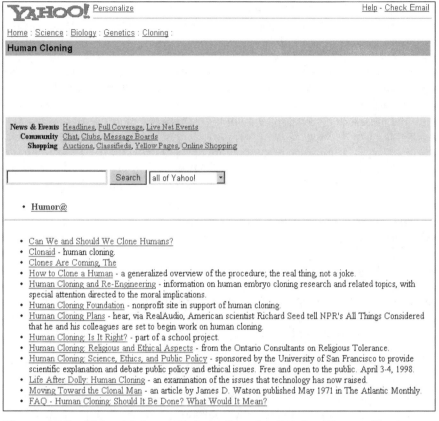

Figure 13.5   Yahoo! Science:Biology:Genetics:Cloning:Human Cloning (http://yahoo.com/Science/Biology/Genetics/ Human_Cloning)

Her interest was primarily in human cloning, so she clicked on the link at the top (see Figure 13.5). Moving through these items gave Joann a good overview of the issues in current debates over human cloning. If she wanted more information, she could go back to the key word searches, picking out key terms from the sites that she had identified.

Evaluating Sources

The examples that we have offered so far point to a problem that is common to all types of electronic search tools: They often give you far too many sources. Doing research on the Web has been compared to drinking from a fire-hose. For people who are new to the Web, it is like a vast library with the card catalog scattered on the floor. You can spend hours wandering serendipitously on the Web just as you can spend hours browsing in a large library. But when you want to make a sustained inquiry, you need assistance. Search engines help a great deal, but you still will pull up much that isn't useful. Not only is the volume often overwhelming, but the quality varies a great deal too. No one polices the Web; therefore a great deal of misinformation is posted.

The reliability and relevance of sources, however, are not new problems with the Web. Print sources also contain their share of biased, inaccurate, and misleading information. Other print sources may be accurate but not suited to the purpose of your project. A critical review can help you to sort through the sources you have gathered. Even though print and Internet sources differ in many ways, some basic principles of evaluation can be applied to both.

Traditional Criteria for Evaluating Print Sources

Over the years librarians have developed criteria for evaluating print sources.

1. *Source.* Who printed the book or article? Scholarly books that are published by university presses and articles in scholarly journals are assessed by experts in the field before they are published. Because of this strict review process, they contain generally reliable information. But since the review process takes time, scholarly books and articles are not the most current sources. For people outside the field, they also have the disadvantage of being written for other experts. Serious trade books and journals are also generally reliable, though magazines devoted to politics often have an obvious bias. Popular magazines and books vary in quality. Often, they are purchased for their entertainment value, and they tend to emphasize what is sensational or entertaining at the expense of accuracy and comprehensiveness. Many magazines and books are published to represent the viewpoint of a particular group or company, so that bias should be taken into account. Newspapers also vary in quality. National newspapers, such as the *New York Times, Washington Post,* and *Los Angeles Times,* employ fact checkers and thorough editorial review for what they print and tend to be more reliable than newspapers that lack such resources.

2. *Author.* Who wrote the book or article? Is the author's name mentioned? Are the author's qualifications listed?

3. *Timeliness.* How current is the source? Obviously, if you are researching a fast-developing subject such as cloning, then currency is very important. But if your are interested in an issue that happened years ago, then currency might not be as important.

4. **Evidence.** How adequate is the evidence to support the author's claims? Where does the evidence come from—facts, interviews, observations, surveys, experiments, expert testimony, or counterarguments? Does the author acknowledge any other ways in which the evidence might be interpreted?

5. **Biases.** Can you detect particular biases of the author? Is the author forthright about his or her biases? How do the author's biases affect the interpretation that is offered?

6. **Advertising.** Is the advertising prominent in the journal or newspaper? Is there any way that ads might affect what gets printed? For example, some magazines that ran many tobacco ads refused to run stories about the dangers of smoking.

Traditional print criteria can be helpful in evaluating some Internet sources. For example, if you evaluate messages sent to a Usenet newsgroup, most do not list the qualifications of the author or offer any support for the validity of evidence. Sources on the World Wide Web, however, present other difficulties. Some of these are inherent in the structure of the Web, with its capability for linking to other pages. When you are at a site that contains many links, you often find that some links go to pages on the same site but others take you off the site. You have to pay attention to the URLs to know where you are in relation to where you started. Furthermore, when you find a Web page using a search engine, often you go deep into a complex site without having any sense of the context of that page. You might have to spend thirty minutes or more just to get some idea of what is on the overall site. Another difficulty of doing research on the Web is that you are limited by the equipment you are using and the speed of your connection.

Additional Criteria for Evaluating Web Sources

Traditional criteria for evaluating print sources remain useful for evaluating sources on the Web, but you should keep in mind how the Web can be different.

1. **Source.** If a Web site indicates what organization or individual is responsible for the information found on it, then you can apply the traditional criteria for evaluating print sources. For example, most major newspapers maintain Web sites where you can read some of the articles that appear in print. If a Web site doesn't indicate ownership, then you have to make judgments about who put it up and why. Documents are easy to copy and put up on the Web, but they are also very easily quoted out of context or

altered. For example, you might find something that is represented as an "official" government document that is in fact a fabrication.

2. ***Author.*** Often, it is difficult to know who put up a particular Web site. Even when an author's name is present, in most cases the author's qualifications are not listed.

3. ***Timeliness.*** Many Web pages do not list when they were last updated; therefore, you do not know how current they are. Furthermore, there are thousands of ghost sites on the Web—sites that the owners have abandoned but have not bothered to remove. You can stumble onto these old sites and not realize that the organization might have a more current site elsewhere. Also, many Web site maintainers do not update their links, and when you start clicking, you get many error messages.

4. ***Evidence.*** The accuracy of any evidence found on the Web is often hard to verify. There are no editors or fact checkers guarding against mistakes or misinformation. The most reliable information on the Web stands up to the tests of print evaluation, with clear indication of an edited source, credentials of the author, references for works cited, and dates of publication.

5. ***Biases.*** Many Web sites are little more than virtual soapboxes. Someone who has an ax to grind can potentially tell millions of people why he or she is angry. Other sites are equally biased but conceal their attitude with a reasonable tone and seemingly factual evidence such as statistics.

6. ***Advertising.*** Many Web sites are "infomercials" of one sort or another. While they can provide useful information about specific products or services, the reason the information was placed on the Web is to get you to buy the product or service. Advertising on the Web costs a fraction of broadcast ads, so it's no wonder that advertisers have flocked to the Web.

Taking Notes

Before personal computers became widely available, most library research projects involved taking notes on notecards. This method was cumbersome, but it had some big advantages. You could spread out the notecards on a table or pin them to a bulletin board and get an overview of how the information that you gathered might be connected. Today, many people make notes in computer files. If you make notes in a computer file, then you don't have to retype when you write your paper. For example, if you copy a direct quote and decide to use it, you can cut and paste it. It is, of course, possible to print out all your notes from your computer and then spread them out, or you can even paste your notes on cards, having the best of both systems. Whatever way works best for you, there are a few things to keep in mind.

Make sure you get the full bibliographic information when you make notes. For books, you should get the author's name, title of the book, place of publication, publisher, and date of publication. This information is on the front and back of the title page. For journals, you need the author's name, title of the article, title of the journal, issue of the journal, date of the issue, and page numbers. For Web sites, you need the name of the page, the author if listed, the sponsoring organization if listed, the date the site was posted, the date you visited, and the complete URL.

Make photocopies of sources you plan to use in your paper. Photocopies save you the time of copying and remove a source of mistakes. If you do take notes, be sure to indicate which words are the author's and which words are yours. It's easy to forget later. If you're using electronic sources, then print the sources you plan to use. Attach the bibliographic information to photocopies and printouts so that you won't get mixed up about where the source came from.

Finally, know when to say you have enough information. Many topics can be researched for a lifetime. It's not just the quantity of sources that count. You should have enough diversity that you are confident you know the major points of view on a particular issue. When you reach a possible stopping point, group your notes and see whether a tentative organization for your paper becomes evident. People who like to work with notecards sometimes write comment cards to attach to each card, indicating how that piece of information fits. People who work with computer files sometimes type in caps how they see their notes fitting together. The method doesn't matter as much as the result. You should have a sketch outline by the time you finish the information-gathering stage.

# Chapter 14

Effective Documentation

Intellectual Property and Scholastic Honesty

Hasbro had the hit toy of the holidays in 1998 with Furby, but if Furby reminded you of Gizmo, the cuddly creature in the Warner Bros. movies *Gremlins* and *Gremlins 2: The New Batch,* you weren't alone. The executives at Warner Bros. also noticed the similarities, and reportedly, Hasbro paid Warner Bros. a large out-of-court settlement for recasting the image of Gizmo. The flap over Furby is but one of many instances of the complex issues surrounding the concept of intellectual property. Copyright laws were established in the 1700s to protect the financial interests of publishers and authors, but over the last century, the domain of intellectual property has spread to music scores and lyrics, recordings, photographs, films, radio and television broadcasts, computer software, and, as the Furby example illustrates, all sorts of other likenesses. During the past decade, the legal battles over intellectual property rights have involved the Internet, which eventually will have major consequences for how much information will be freely available on the World Wide Web.

However, intellectual property rights are not the main reason that college writing requires strict standards of documentation. Writing at the college level follows a long tradition of scholarly writing that insists on accuracy in referencing other work so that a reader can consult a writer's sources. Often, scholarly arguments build on the work of others, and experiments almost always identify an area that other researchers have addressed. Sometimes, other pieces of writing are the primary data, as when a historian uses letters and public documents to construct what happened in the past. It is important for other historians to be able to review the same documents to confirm or reject a particular interpretation.

There is also a basic issue of fairness in recognizing the work of others. If you find an idea in someone else's work that you want to use, it seems only fair to give that person proper credit. In chapter 6, we talked about Robert H. Frank and Phillip J. Cook's controversial argument that changes in attitudes help to account for the increasing divide between rich and poor people since 1973, a shift that they summarize as the winner-take-all society. The phrase "winner-take-all society" has become common enough that you might hear it in news features describing the contemporary United States, but certainly any extended treatment of the concept should acknowledge Frank and Cook for coming up with the idea. Many students now acknowledge the work of other students if they feel that their classmates have made an important contribution to their work. And why not? It's only fair.

In our culture in general and in the professions in particular, work that people claim is their own is expected to be their own. Imagine that you are the director of marketing at a company that paid a consulting firm to conduct a survey, only to find out that the work the firm presented to you had been copied from another survey. Wouldn't you be on the phone right away to your company's attorneys? Even though the unethical copying of the survey might have been the failure of only one employee, surely the reputation of the consulting firm would be damaged, if not ruined. Many noteworthy people in political and public life have been greatly embarrassed by instances of plagiarism; in some cases, people have lost their positions as a result. Short of committing a felony, plagiarism is one of the few things that can get you expelled from your college or university if the case is serious enough. So it's worth it to you to know what plagiarism is and isn't.

What Plagiarism Is

Stated most simply, you plagiarize when you use the words or ideas of someone else as your own without acknowledging the source. That definition seems easy enough, but when you think about it, how many new ideas are there? And how could you possibly acknowledge where all your ideas came from? In practical terms, you are not expected to acknowledge everything. You do not have to acknowledge what is considered general knowledge, such as facts that you could find in a variety of reference books. For example, if you wanted to assert that Lyndon Johnson's victory over Barry Goldwater in the 1964 presidential election remains the largest popular vote percentage (61 percent) in presidential election history, you would not have to acknowledge the source. This information should be available in encyclopedias, almanacs, and other general sources.

But if you cite a more obscure fact that wouldn't be as readily verifiable, you should let your readers know where you found it. Likewise, you should acknowledge the sources of any arguable statements, claims, or judgments. The sources of statistics, research findings, examples, graphs, charts, and illustrations also should be acknowledged. This is not just a matter of plagiarism. People are especially skeptical about statistics and research findings if the source is not mentioned. For example, if you argue that the Internet has led to even greater marginalization of the rural poor in the United States, you might include statistics that in 1995, the households of rural poor (incomes less than $10,000) had the lowest levels of computer penetration—only 4.5 percent—of any population group. By contrast, 7.6 percent of households of the poor in central cities had computers. Failing to give the source of these statistics could undercut your argument, but since these statistics are from the U.S. Department of Commerce ("Falling through the Net: A Survey of the 'Have Nots' in Rural and Urban America," Washington, DC: U.S. Department of Commerce, July 1995), the source adds credibility.

Where most people get into plagiarism trouble is when they take words directly and use them without quotation marks or else change a few words and pass them off as their own words. It is easiest to illustrate where the line is drawn with an example. Suppose you are writing an argument about attempts to censor the Internet, and you want to examine how successful other nations have been. You find the following paragraph about China:

> China is encouraging Net use for business, but not what it considers seditious or pornographic traffic and "spiritual pollution." So the state is building its communications infrastructure like a mammoth corporate system—robust within the country, but with three gateways to the world, in Beijing, Shanghai, and Shenzhen. International exchanges can then be monitored and foreign content "filtered" at each information choke-point, courtesy of the Public Security Bureau.
> —Jim Erickson. "WWW.POLITICS.COM." *Asiaweek* 2 Oct. 1998: 42.

You want to mention the point about the gateways in your paper. You have two basic options: to paraphrase the source and to quote it directly.

If you quote directly, you must include all words you take from the original inside quotation marks:

> According to one observer, "China is encouraging Net use for business, but not what it considers seditious or pornographic traffic and 'spiritual pollution' " (Erickson 42).

This example is typical of MLA style. The citation goes outside the quotation marks but before the period. The reference is to the author's last name, which refers you to the full citation in the Works Cited list at the end. Following the author's name is the page number where the quote can be located. Since this particular article appeared only on one page, you do not have to include the page number. Notice also that if you quote material in quotation marks, then the double quote marks change to single quote mark. If you include the author's name, then you need to cite only the page number:

> According to Jim Erickson, "China is encouraging Net use for business, but not what it considers seditious or pornographic traffic and 'spiritual pollution' " (42).

Again, since the article appears on one page only, the correct form would be as follows:

> According to Jim Erickson, "China is encouraging Net use for business, but not what it considers seditious or pornographic traffic and 'spiritual pollution.' "

If the newspaper article did not include the author's name, you would include the first word or two of the title. The logic of this system is to enable you to find the reference in the list of Works Cited.

The alternative to quoting directly is to paraphrase. When you paraphrase, you change the words without changing the meaning. Here are two examples:

Plagiarized

> China wants its citizens to use the Internet for business, but not for circulating views it doesn't like, pornography, and "spiritual pollution." So China is building its communications infrastructure like a mammoth corporate system--well linked internally but with only three ports to the outside world. The Public Security Bureau will monitor the foreign traffic at each information choke-point (Erickson).

This version is unacceptable. Too many of the words in the original are used directly here, including much of one sentence: "is building its communications infrastructure like a mammoth corporate system." If an entire string of words is lifted from a source and inserted without using quotation marks, then the passage is plagiarized. The first sentence is also too close in structure and wording to the original. Changing a few words in a sentence is not a paraphrase. Compare the following example:

Acceptable paraphrase

> The Chinese government wants its citizens to take advantage of the Internet for commerce while not allowing foreign political ideas and foreign values to challenge its authority. Consequently, the Chinese Internet will have only three ports to the outside world. Traffic through

these ports will be monitored and censored by the Public Security Bureau (Erickson).

There are a few words from the original in this paraphrase, such as *foreign* and *monitored,* but these sentences are original in structure and wording while accurately conveying the meaning of the original.

Using Sources Effectively

The purpose of using sources is to *support* your argument, not to make your argument for you. Next to plagiarism, the worst mistake you can make with sources is stringing them together without building an argument of your own. Your sources help to show that you've done your homework and that you've thought in depth about the issue.

One choice you have to make when using sources is when to quote and when to paraphrase. Consider the following example about expressways:

Urban planners of the 1960s saw superhighways as the means to prevent inner cities from continuing to decay. Inner-city blight was recognized as early as the 1930s, and the problem was understood for four decades as one of circulation (hence expressways were called "arterials"). The planners argued that those who had moved to the suburbs would return to the city on expressways. By the end of the 1960s, the engineers were tearing down thousands of units of urban housing and small businesses to build expressways with a logic that was similar to the logic of mass bombing in Vietnam--to destroy the city was to save it (Patton 102). Shortly the effects were all too evident. Old neighborhoods were ripped apart, the flight to the suburbs continued, and the decline of inner cities accelerated rather than abated.

Not everyone in the 1950s and 1960s saw expressways as the answer to urban dilapidation. Lewis Mumford in 1958 challenged the circulation metaphor. He wrote: "Highway planners have yet to realize that these arteries must not be thrust into the delicate tissue of our cities; the blood they circulate must rather enter through an elaborate network of minor blood vessels and capillaries" (236). Mumford saw that new expressways produced more congestion and aggravated the problem they were designed to overcome, thus creating demand for still more expressways. If road building through cities were allowed to continue, he predicted the result would be "a tomb of concrete roads and ramps covering the dead corpse of a city" (238).

Notice that two sources are cited: Patton (Phil Patton, *Open Road: A Celebration of the American Highway* [New York: Simon & Schuster, 1986]) and Mumford (Lewis Mumford, "The Highway and the City" [1958]. Rpt. *The Highway and the City* [New York: Harcourt, Brace, 1963] 234–46).

The writer decided that the point from Patton about tearing down thousands of units of urban housing and small businesses to build expressways in the 1960s should be paraphrased but Mumford's remarks should be quoted directly. In both direct quotes from Mumford, the original wording is important. Mumford rejects the metaphor of arteries for expressways and foresees the future of cities as paved-over tombs in vivid language. As a general rule, you should use direct quotes only when the original language is important. Otherwise, you should paraphrase.

If a direct quote runs more than four lines, then it should be indented ten spaces and double-spaced. But you still should integrate long quotes into the text of your paper. Long quotations should be attributed; that is, you should say where the quote comes from in your text as well as in the reference. And it is a good idea to include at least a sentence or two after the quote to describe its significance for your argument. The original wording in the long quote in the following paragraph is important because it gives a sense of the language of the Port Huron Statement. The sentences following the quotation explain why many faculty members in the 1960s looked on the Port Huron Statement as a positive sign (of course, college administrators were horrified). You might think of this strategy as putting an extended quotation in an envelope with your words before and after:

> Critiques of the staleness and conformity of American education made the first expressions of student radicalism in the 1960s such as the "Port Huron Statement" from the Students for a Democratic Society (SDS) in 1962 appear as a breath of fresh air. The SDS wrote:
>
>> Almost no students value activity as a citizen. Passive in public, they are hardly more idealistic in arranging their private lives; Gallup concludes they will settle for "low success, and won't risk high failure." There is not much willingness to take risks (not even in business), no setting of dangerous goals, no real conception of personal identity except one manufactured in the image of others, no real urge for personal fulfillment except to be almost as successful as the very successful people. Attention is being paid to social status (the quality of shirt collars, meeting people, getting wives or husbands, making solid contacts for later on); much, too, is paid to academic status (grades, honors, the med-school rat race). But neglected generally is real intellectual status, the personal cultivation of mind. (238)

Many professors shared the SDS disdain for the political quietism on college campuses. When large-scale ferment erupted among students during the years of the Vietnam War, some faculty welcomed it as a sign of finally emerging from the intellectual stagnation of the Eisenhower years. For some it was a sign that the promise of John F. Kennedy's administration could be fulfilled, that young people could create a new national identity.

Note three points about form in the long quotation. First, there are no quotation marks around the extended quotation. Readers know that the material is quoted because it is blocked off. Second, words quoted in the original retain the double quotation marks. Third, the page number appears after the period at the end of the quotation.

Whether long or short, make all quotations part of the fabric of your paper while being careful to indicate which words belong to the original. A reader should be able to move through the body of your paper without having to stop and ask: Why did the writer include this quotation? or Which words are the writer's and which are being quoted?

MLA Documentation

Different disciplines use different styles for documentation. The two styles that are used most frequently are the APA style and the MLA style. *APA* stands for American Psychological Association, which publishes a style manual that is used widely in the social sciences (see Appendix B). *MLA* stands for the Modern Language Association, and its style is the norm for humanities disciplines, including English and rhetoric and composition.

Both MLA and APA styles use a Works Cited list placed at the end of a paper. Here's an example of an MLA Works Cited list:

Works Cited

Bingham, Janet. "Kids Become Masters of Electronic
    Universe: School Internet Activity Abounds."
    Denver Post 3 Sept. 1996, sec A: 13.
Dyrli, Odvard Egil, and Daniel E. Kinnaman. "Tele-
    communications: Gaining Access to the World."
    Technology and Learning 16.3 (Nov. 1995):
    79-84.

Center "Works Cited."

Double-space all entries. Indent all but first line five spaces.

Alphabetize entries by last name of authors or by title if no author is listed.

(continued)

Underline the titles of books and periodicals.

Ellsworth, Jill H. Education on the Internet: A Hands-On Book of Ideas, Resources, Projects, and Advice. Indianapolis: Sams, 1994.

Engardio, Pete. "Microsoft's Long March." Business Week 24 June 1996: 52-54.

National Center for Education Statistics. "Internet Access in Public Education." February 1998. NCES. 4 Jan. 1999 <http://nces.ed.gov/pubs98/98021.html>.

"UK: A Battle for Young Hearts and Minds." Computer Weekly 4 Apr. 1996: 20.

The Works Cited list eliminates the need for footnotes. If you have your sources listed on notecards, then all you have to do when you finish your paper is to find the cards for all the sources that you cite, alphabetize the cards, and then type your Works Cited list. For works with no author listed, alphabetize by the first content word in the title (ignore *a, an,* and *the*).

Some of the more common citation formats in MLA style are listed below. If you have questions that these examples do not address, you should consult the *MLA Handbook for Writers of Research Papers* (fifth edition, 1999) and the *MLA Style Manual and Guide to Scholarly Publishing* (second edition, 1998).

Books

The basic format for listing books in the Works Cited list includes the author's name (last name first), title (underlined), place of publication, short name of publisher, and date of publication. You find the exact title on the title page (not on the cover), the publisher, and the city (use the first city if several are listed). The date of publication is included in the copyright notice on the back of the title page.

Book by One Author

Ellsworth, Jill H. Education on the Internet: A Hands-On Book of Ideas, Resources, Projects, and Advice. Indianapolis: Sams, 1994.

Book by Two or More Authors

Scribner, Sylvia, and Michael Cole. The Psychology of Literacy. Cambridge, MA: Harvard UP, 1981.

Two or More Books by the Same Author

Berger, John. About Looking. New York: Pantheon, 1980.

- - -. Ways of Seeing. New York: Viking, 1973.

Translation

Martin, Henri-Jean. The History and Power of Writing. Trans. Lydia G.
    Cochrane. Chicago: U of Chicago P, 1994.

Edited Book

Bizzell, Patricia, and Bruce Herzberg, eds. The Rhetorical Tradition:
    Readings from Classical Times to the Present. Boston: Bedford,
    1990.

One Volume of a Multivolume Work

Habermas, Jürgen. Lifeworld and System, A Critique of Functionalist
    Reason. Trans. Thomas McCarthy. Boston: Beacon, 1987. Vol. 2 of
    The Theory of Communicative Action. 2 vols. 1984-1987.

Selection in an Anthology or Chapter in an Edited Collection

Merritt, Russell. "Nickelodeon Theaters, 1905-1914: Building an
    Audience for the Movies." The American Film Industry. Ed.
    Tino Balio. Rev. ed. Madison: U of Wisconsin P, 1985. 83-102.

Government Document

Malveaux, Julianne. "Changes in the Labor Market Status of Black
    Women." A Report of the Study Group on Affirmative Action to
    the Committee on Education and Labor. U.S. 100th Cong., 1st
    sess. H. Rept. 100-L. Washington: GPO, 1987. 213-55.

Bible

Holy Bible. King James Version.

[Note that the Bible is not underlined. No other publication information
besides the version is necessary.]

Periodicals

The necessary items to include are the author's name (last name first), title of
the article inside quotation marks, title of the journal or magazine (underlined), volume number (for scholarly journals), date, and page numbers. Many
scholarly journals are printed to be bound as one volume, usually by year, and
the pagination is continuous for that year. If, say, a scholarly journal is printed

in four issues and the first issue ends on page 278, then the second issue will begin with page 279. For journals that are continuously paginated, you do not need to include the issue number. Some scholarly journals, however, are paginated like magazines, each issue beginning with page 1. For journals that are paginated by issue, you should list the issue number along with the volume (e.g., for the first issue of volume 11, you would put 11.1 in the entry after the title of the journal).

Article in a Scholarly Journal—Continuous Pagination

Berlin, James A. "Rhetoric and Ideology in the Writing Class." College
English 50 (1988): 477-94.

Article in a Scholarly Journal—Pagination by Issue

Kolby, Jerry. "The Top-Heavy Economy: Managerial Greed and
Unproductive Labor." Critical Sociology 15.3 (Fall 1988): 53-69.

Review

Chomsky, Noam. Rev. of Verbal Behavior, by B. F. Skinner. Language 35
(1959): 26-58.

Magazine Article

Engardio, Pete. "Microsoft's Long March." Business Week 24 June
1996: 52-54.

Newspaper Article

Bingham, Janet. "Kids Become Masters of Electronic Universe: School
Internet Activity Abounds." Denver Post 3 Sept. 1996, sec A: 13.

Letter to the Editor

Luker, Ralph E. Letter. Chronicle of Higher Education 18 Dec. 1998,
sec B: 9.

Editorial

"An Open Process." Editorial. Wall Street Journal 30 Dec. 1998,
sec. A: 10.

Online Sources

Online sources pose special difficulties for systems of citing sources. Many online sources change frequently. Sometimes, you discover to your frustration that what you found on a Web site the previous day has been altered or in some cases no longer exists. Furthermore, basic information such as who put up a Web site and when it was last changed is often absent. Many print sources have also been put on the Web, which raises another set of difficulties. The basic format for citing a generic Web site includes the author's name (last name first), title of document in quotation marks, title of complete work or name of journal (underlined), date of Web publication or last update, the sponsoring organization, the date you visited, and the URL <enclosed in angle brackets>.

Web Site

"Composite Image of the 1995 Antarctic Ozone Hole." United States
    Environmental Protection Agency's Home Page 10 June 1998.
    USEPA. 4 Jan. 1999 <http://www.epa.gov/docs/ozone/science/
    hole/holecomp.html>.

Book on the Web

Rheingold, Howard. Tools for Thought: The People and Ideas
    of the Next Computer Revolution. New York, 1985.
    Brainstorms. 4 Jan. 1999 <http://www.well.com/user/hlr/
    texts/tftindex.html>.

Article in a Scholarly Journal on the Web

Browning, Tonya. "Embedded Visuals: Student Design in Web Spaces."
    Kairos 2.1 (1997): 4 Jan. 1999 <http://www.as.ttu.edu/kairos/2.1/
    features/browning/index.html>.

Article in a Magazine on the Web

"Happy New Euro." Time Daily 30 Dec. 1998. 4 Jan. 1999
    <http://cgi.pathfinder.com/time/daily/
    0,2960,17455-101990101,00.html>.

Personal Web Site

Vitanza, Victor. Victor's uncanny Web site. 4 Jan. 1999
    <http://www.uta.edu/english/V/Victor_.html>.

CD-ROM

Boyer, Paul, et al. The Enduring Vision, Interactive Edition. 1993 ed.
    CD-ROM. Lexington, MA: Heath, 1993.

Other Sources

Television programs, radio broadcasts, and movies are most often listed by title unless the focus is on the writer or director.

Interview

Williams, Errick Lynn. Telephone interview. 4 Jan. 1999.

Unpublished Dissertation

Rouzie, Albert. "At Play in the Fields of Writing: Play and Digital Literacy in a College-Level Computers and Writing Course." Diss. U of Texas at Austin, 1997.

Film

Stephen Speilberg, dir. Saving Private Ryan. DreamWorks and Paramount, 1998.

Television Program

"The Attitude." Ally McBeal. Fox. Dir. Allan Arkush, Daniel Attias, et al. Writ. David E. Kelley. Perf. Calista Flockhart, Courtney Thorne-Smith. 3 Nov. 1997.

Sound Recording

Glass, Phillip. "Low" Symphony. Point Music, 1973.

Speech (no printed text)

Gore, Albert. Remarks at the National Press Club. Washington. 21 Dec. 1993.

Speech (printed text)

Eberly, Rosa. "Inside and Outside Classrooms as Proto-Public Spaces." Conf. on Coll. Composition and Communication. Atlanta. 27 Mar. 1999.

Sample Argument Paper Using Sources

The paper that follows, by Chris Thomas, is an example of a student argument that uses sources well and that documents those sources appropriately.

Chris Thomas
10/24/98
Eng. 15 Sect. 20
Selzer

Should Race Be a Qualification to Attend College?
A Examination of Affirmative Action

Note: MLA style doesn't require a title page for student research papers, but many college instructors do. You should check with your instructor regarding his or her preference for this and other formats.

Imagine that you are an African American student like me and that it is your first day of classes at a prestigious university. As you make your rounds on campus, you become increasingly aware of the swift glances that you are receiving from some of your predominately white classmates. You assume that the looks are generated because you are among the few African American students around, but you soon learn that your assumptions were too shallow. A student that you begin to have a conversation with asks what you received on your SATs. You initially believe that this inquiry is just a piece of general freshman curiosity, but your classmate's line of questioning ends with the question, "Do you think that you got into school because of your race and affirmative action?" That leads you to feel resented by the classmate because of your presence in this university.

Believe it our not, thousands of African American students experience similar scenarios every year. These predicaments force African Americans to question their merit and sense of belonging and draws attention to the controversial issue of affirmative action and its relevance to college admissions. Let me explore both sides of the issue by clearly defining the policy, looking at its causes, assessing the facts, evaluating the policy, and examining conflicting ideas on what should be done in the future about affirmative action.

With reference to college admission, the definition of affirmative action is relatively simple. In his book Preferential Policies: An International Perspective, Thomas Sowell states, "What is called 'affirmative action' in the United States is . . . [a] government-mandated preferential policy toward government-designated groups" (13). There is general understanding that affirmative action is a program that aims to overcome the effects of past discrimination by giving preferential treatment to ethnic minorities and women. Barbara R. Bergmann's In Defense of

Affirmative Action confirms that "Affirmative Action planning and acting [are designed] to end the absence of certain kinds of people--those of who belong to groups that have been subordinated or left out from certain jobs and schools. The term is usually applied to those plans that set forth goals, required since the early 1970s, for government contractors and universities receiving public funds" (7). The Equal Opportunities Act of 1972 set up a right to act on such plans. Bergmann goes on to state, "[affirmative action] is an insurance company taking steps to break its tradition of promoting only white men to executive positions." The program is also seen as a means to producing a diverse learning and working environment.

In the case of African Americans, affirmative action was created as to compensate for a history of slavery and systemic racial discrimination. The program was initiated because American society had produced an atmosphere that was strictly conducive to white men's success and dominance. Affirmative action programs arose out of governmental and judicial decisions requiring efforts to remedy and continuing discrimination based on sex and race (Ponterotto 6). This program is an effort to "level the playing field" and to try to make it possible for African Americans to have an equal, fair, and just opportunity to succeed. One aim of the program is to help curb the negative stereotypes and stigmas that American society has bestowed upon African Americans. The ultimate goal of such programs is to enable these individuals, through educational and vocational achievement, to have greater access to socioeconomic opportunity and stability (Ponterotto 6). (For a full account of the history and intent of affirmative action, I recommend Affirmative Action on Campus by Joseph G. Ponterott et al.)

How does affirmative action work with reference to college admission? It is understood that preferential treatment in some respects is given to African American applicants. On college campuses, affirmative action's ideals are translated into combating sexism and racism and social acceptance of minority-group members (Ponterotto 6). In Ending Affirmative Action, Terry Eastland notes, "[Supreme Court] Justice Powell said in his Bakke opinion [referring to the University of California v. Bakke affirmative action case], that a university has the First Amendment freedom to make judgments about its educational mission. This freedom includes the latitude to select a student body [which] can help promote the educational environment most conducive to 'speculation, experiment, and creation' in which all students, minorities and non-minorities alike, benefit" (77).

If it is understood that affirmative action is implemented to justify for past discriminations of African Americans, then what's the problem? The debate lies not in the definition, causes, or goals of affirmative action in the college admission process, but in the contradictory evaluation policies that develop out of the process. Is affirmative action a good, bad, or fair program that should be used to assist African Americans in the college admission process? There are opposing arguments on this issue; there are those who believe that it is a just and necessary program and those who strongly oppose the issue. The components of the issue that have caused the greatest controversy are the qualifications of the African American applicants, the aims of the program, and the progression of the program.

Shouldn't the most qualified applicants to a university receive top priority in admissions? "The answers to such a question require a critical examination of just what is meant by 'best qualified'," states Norman Matloff in "Toward Sensible Affirmative Action Policies." Consider the question of admissions policy for any famous university, with many more applicants than open slots. Let us ask whether, say, applicants with higher SAT scores should get automatic priority in admissions over those with lower scores (Matloff 1). It goes without saying that "test scores alone [are] not the way to determine admission," according to John Furedy, professor of psychology at the University of Toronto (cited in Saha 1); standardized test scores are not perfect measurement tools, and thus they should not be over-applied in admissions decisions. Yet for most students, test scores will at least reliably predict whether the student's academic skills are "in the league with" those of typical students at the given school. In the January 24, 1995 issue of the Los Angeles Times, Norman Matloff affirms that "first one must keep in mind that neither SAT scores nor any other numeric measure will be a very accurate predictor of future grades. It thus makes no sense to admit one applicant over another simply because the first applicant had higher test scores." Even the staunchest supporters of standardized tests seem to agree "that the scores reflect only a small part of the factors that predict freshman grades, and far less of what it takes to graduate from college" (Lederman A36).

Supporters of affirmative action believe that an overemphasis shouldn't be placed solely on SAT scores. They believe that "you need to understand the degree to which race, gender, and religion affect that person. You need to look at that person as a whole," notes Earl Lewis, interim dean of the graduate school at the University of Michigan (cited in Saha 2), and family and collegiate background of the applicant should be taken into consideration. Supporters agree that academic strength should be the most important component of college admissions, but they also believe that an applicant's family background also influences the probability that a person will succeed in college. It is widely understood that students with parents or family members that attended college have a better chance at college success than those without such a history. Supporters of affirmative action also argue that past societal limitations have restricted African American students from colleges, thus producing a situation in which relatively few African Americans have a history of attending college to pass on to their children. Moreover, past discrimination has created a college environment for African Americans that isn't as conducive to college pursuits as white applicants. Supporters argue that affirmative action will help to gradually increase the number of African American family members that attend college. Supporters also believe that admissions should look at the well-roundedness of the applicant. They should look at situations such as the applicant's involvement in school, his or her living environment, and possible required work experiences which would account for not so stellar grades.

On the other hand, opponents of affirmative action say that the preferential aspects of the program overlook academically qualified white students. Opponents believe that preferential treatment should be given to those of strong academic caliber, not to those of a particular race, and they see admissions decisions as central to maintaining high institutional standards. "The students who are denied at Berkeley will move down one notch," says David Murray; "we must not throw out the thermometer [of test scores] because we don't like the temperature it's taking" (quoted in Lederman A37). As this quotation indicates, critics of affirmative action have a high regard for test scores: "Much of the discussion presumes that the tests are a very profound measure of academic preparation, and can really predict how well people do in college," notes Claude Steele, a psychology professor at Stanford University (quoted in Lederman A37).

Another element of debate is the actual goals of affirmative action in college admissions. Supporters contend that the main goal of the program is to "level the playing field" in all aspects of society by giving qualified African American applicants the opportunity to attend college. The supporters argue that giving this preferential treatment to African Americans will provide minorities the opportunity "to defy the pernicious stereotypes and stigmas cast upon them by others"--for example, that African Americans are lazy, unsuccessful, and are strictly drug and sex driven (Lewis 2). Upholders of affirmative action argue that "the whole point of employing racial preferences in admissions is to change the composition of the student body--to bring more members of 'favored' groups into the institution," thus diversifying the college atmosphere (Thernstrom 36).

While opponents of affirmative action in college admission often concede that the program has been needed as an aid to stop past discrimination, they strongly believe that now "a dual system of criteria, based solely on race, strikes most Americans of all races as offensive" (Maguire 52). They vehemently argue that affirmative action is "reverse discrimination." They believe that affirmative action is "the 'ignorant' way of fighting discrimination. There is one simple rule to fight discrimination: do not discriminate," notes Furedy (cited in Saha 2). They affirm that one cannot fight discrimination with reverse discrimination targeted towards white Americans.

Opponents also claim that the supposed beneficiaries of the program, African Americans, in fact get hurt the most by negative effects of affirmative action. Clint Bolick, for instance, in The Affirmative Action Fraud, states that "preference policies may do their beneficiaries more harm than good. Race-based diminution of admissions standards inevitably causes a mismatch between students' abilities and the demands of the school" (79). Eastland too concedes that "being treated differently in order to be treated equally--a 'benign' act, according to advocates of affirmative action--has had its costs" (72), which can be described as a general idea that African Americans' degrees will have a low value.

This degree-devaluing of African Americans is possible because "people who are accepted [to college with the help of affirmative action] have a smear attached to them; it will be assumed that they were accepted not for their merit, but for their race" (Furedy, cited in Saha 1), that they were able to obtain it because of their race, not because of their academic abilities. It will also lead African American students to question their sense of belonging. Opponents state that if standards for admission are lowered when considering the admission of African American students, then these programs will "distort what is now a level playing field and bestow preferential treatment on undeserving minorities because of their skin" (Lewis 1).

There is, then, much debate over the evaluation of affirmative action and its link to college admission of African Americans. Both supporters and opponents have strong arguments on the issue. Both sides state why the program is good or bad and have an arguable and justifiable argument for their beliefs. Where, then, should we go from here?

Supporters believe that affirmative action in college admission of African Americans should continue to be practiced. Syndicated columnist William Raspberry states that he has thoroughly interviewed "two eminent American educators [who] have taken a good hard look at affirmative action in college admissions, and their conclusion is that by virtually any reasonable measure, affirmative action works." Advocates believe that affirmative action is still needed because "without the deconstruction of white power and privilege, how can we legitimately claim that the playing field is level" (Lewis 22), even if African Americans are no longer discriminated and suppressed to quite the extent that they once were. In the words of Kerry Colligan, "you need to talk about the debt this country has to pay. You cannot negate 300 years of slavery and 100 years of oppression" (2).

Thomas   8

On the other hand, opponents believe that the affirmative action policies college admissions follow should be curbed because it is an unfair act of "reverse discrimination" that causes racial tension from resentful white Americans. Opponents believe that "[g]roups seen as newly favored because of their race or ethnicity may become targets of the majority's animosity, or they may be seen as needing special treatment because of their supposed inferiority" (Ponterotto 6). They suggest that the program be made unconstitutional because it violates both the 14th Amendment, which guarantees equal protection under the law, and Title VI of the 1964 Civil Rights Act, which forbids discrimination in programs receiving federal financial aid (Colligan 1). Realizing that discrimination is still a problem, some opponents suggest that "the focus should be on education in the K-12 sector in order to prepare everyone equally well . . . for entrance exams [for college]" (Doyle 1).

Exactly where does this leave us? The critics that attack affirmative action are correct when they say that affirmative action corrupts the purity of the process. Extreme care must be taken in determining if affirmative action in the admission of African Americans to college should be practiced, for how long, and to what degree. While the policies of affirmative action are not perfect and they do raise some legitimate concerns, they take us away from a system that is inherently unfair to some groups. "The active deconstruction of the white privilege that grew out of virulent American racism affords African Americans a greater chance at equal opportunity and will have the side effect of forcing us to re-evaluate a society that unfairly disadvantages minorities" (Lewis 4). The issue is more confusing if you consider that "affirmative action prefers individuals on the basis of their group membership, [not considering that] those minorities with academic credentials competitive with regularly admitted students may nonetheless be regarded with skepticism as affirmative action admittees" (Eastland 90). Therefore, further research on and evaluation of the issue is definitely needed to see if the progression or regression of the program's aims will uphold the aims of the respective arguing sides of the issue.

Thomas 10

Works Cited and Consulted

Barr, Margaret J., et al. Affirmative Action on Campus. San Francisco: Jossey-Bass, 1990.

Bergmann, Barbara R. In Defense of Affirmative Action. New York: Basic, 1996.

Bolick, Clint. The Affirmative Action Fraud. Washington: Cato Institute, 1996.

Colligan, Kerry. "Panelists Discuss History of Affirmative Action, Lawsuit." The University Record 53 (26 Nov. 1997). 14 Dec. 1998 <http://www.umich.edu/~newinfo/U_Record/Issues97/Nov/ afhist.htm>.

Doyle, Rebecca A. "Students Express Views on Racism, Discrimination." The University Record 53 (26 Nov. 1997). 14 Dec. 1998 <http://www.umich.edu/~newinfo/U_Record/Issues97/Nov/ afhist.htm>.

Eastland, Terry. Ending Affirmative Action: The Case for Colorblind Justice. New York: Basic, 1996.

Kahlenberg, Richard D. The Remedy. New York: Basic, 1996.

Lederman, Douglas. "Persistent Racial Gap in SAT Scores Fuels Affirmative Action Debate." The Chronicle of Higher Education 30 Oct. 1998: A36-38.

Lewis, Brian C. "An Ethical and Practical Defense of Affirmative Action." 1996. 18 Dec. 1998 <http://www.princeton.edu/ ~bclewis/action>.

Maguire, Timothy. "My Bout with Affirmative Action." Commentary 93 (April 1992): 50-52.

Matloff, Norman. "Why Not a Lottery to Get Into UC?" 24 Jan. 1995. 18 Dec. 1998 <http://www.heather.cs.ucdavis.edu/pub/ AffirmativeAction/LAT.NM>.

Matloff, Norman. "Toward Sensible Affirmative Action Policies." King Hall (UC Davis) Law School Advocate Nov. 1994. 18 Dec. 1998.

Thomas   11

<http://www.heather.cs.ucdavis.edu/pub/AffirmativeAction/
Advocate>.

McWhirter, Darien A. The End of Affirmative Action. New York: Birch
Lane P, 1996.

Ponterotto, Joseph G., et al. Affirmative Action on Campus. San
Francisco: Jossey-Bass, 1990.

Raspberry, William. "Despite the Myths, Affirmative Action Works."
Centre Daily Times 4 Oct. 1998: 9A.

Saha, Paula. "Panel Presents Perspectives on Diversity in Higher
Education." The University Record 53 (26 Nov. 1997).
18 Dec. 1998 <http://www.umich.edu/~newinfo/U_Record/
Issues97/Nov/affac.htm>.

Sowell, Thomas. Preferential Policies: An International Perspective.
New York: William Morrow, 1990.

Thernstrom, Stephan. "Farewell to Preferences." Public Interest 130
(Winter 1998): 34-49.

Zelnick, Bob. Backfire: A Reporter's Look at Affirmative Action.
Washington, DC: Regner, 1996.

Chapter 15

Effective Revision

Skilled writers know that the secret to writing well is rewriting. Even the best writers often have to revise several times to get the result they want. If you want to become a better writer, the best advice consists of three words: *Revise, revise, revise.* To be able to revise effectively, you have to plan your time. You cannot revise a paper effectively if you finish it at the last minute. You have to allow what you write to sit for a while before you go back through it. Allow at least a day to let what you write cool off. With a little time, you gain enough distance to "resee" it, which, after all, is what revision means.

You also have to have effective strategies for revising if you're going to be successful. The biggest trap you can fall into is starting off with the little stuff first. *Don't sweat the small stuff at the beginning.* If you see a word that's wrong or a misplaced comma, the great temptation is to fix the errors first. But if you start searching for the errors, then it's hard to get back to the larger concerns that ultimately make your argument successful or unsuccessful. A better strategy is to divide revising into three separate stages:

1. Switch from writer to reader.
2. Focus on your argument.
3. Focus on your style and proofread carefully.

Switch from Writer to Reader

First, pretend that you are someone who either is uninformed about the issue you are writing about or is informed but holds an opposing viewpoint. If possible, think of an actual person and pretend to be that person. Read your argument aloud all the way through. When you read aloud, you often hear clunky phrases and catch errors; but do no more in this stage than put checks in the margins that you can return to later. Once again, you don't want to get bogged down with the little stuff. What you are after in this stage is getting an overall sense of how well you accomplished what you set out to do.

1. *Your claim.* When you finish reading, can you summarize in one sentence what you are arguing? If you cannot, then you need to focus your claim. Then you need to ask yourself what's at stake in your claim? Who benefits by what you are arguing? Who doesn't? If what you're arguing is obvious to everyone and all or nearly all would agree with you, then you need to identify an aspect on which people would disagree and restate your claim.

2. *Your good reasons.* What are the good reasons for your claim? Would a reader have any trouble identifying them? What evidence is offered to support these good reasons and how is the evidence linked to the claim (the "so what?" question in chapter 2)? Note any places where you might add evidence and any places where you need to explain why the evidence is relevant.

3. *Your representation of yourself.* To the extent that you can, forget for a moment that you wrote what you are reading. What impression do you have of you, the writer? Is the writer believable? Has the writer done his or her homework on the issue? Does the writer take an appropriate tone? Note any places where you can strengthen your credibility as a writer.

4. *Your consideration of your readers.* Do you give enough background if your readers are unfamiliar with the issue? Do you acknowledge opposing views that they might have? Do you appeal to common values that you share with them? Note any places where you might do more to address the concerns of your readers.

Use this stage to make a list of your goals in the revision. You might have to write another draft before you move to the next stage.

Focus on Your Argument

Now it's time to go through your argument in detail. Your analysis will help you to figure out how to accomplish the goals on your list.

1. *Find your main claim and circle it. What kind of claim is it?*
   - A claim of definition (see chapter 5)? *X is (or is not) a Y because it has (or does not have) features A, B, and C.*
   - A claim of causation (see chapter 6)? *X causes (or does not cause) Y or X causes Y, which in turn causes Z.*
   - A claim of evaluation (see chapter 7)? *X is a good (bad, the best, the worst) Y if measured by certain criteria (aesthetic, practical, or moral).*

■ A claim from a narrative (see chapter 8)? *My experience shows something needs to be changed.*

■ A rebuttal argument (see chapter 9)? *It is wrong (or misguided or irresponsible) to claim X.*

■ A proposal (see chapter 10)? *We should (or should not) do X.*

2. *Check whether key terms are adequately defined.* What are your key terms? Are they defined precisely enough that your argument holds up? Consider this example:

> *If a person is just in his initial actions (i.e., going to war), he will tend to act justly throughout the situation. If a person is unjustified in his initial actions, however, he will have no reason to act justly throughout the rest of the situation. In the Six Day War, the Israelis were justified in going to war and fought a just war throughout. In Vietnam, the American had no justification for going to war, and thus fought unjustly throughout.*

What do "just" and "unjust" mean in this paragraph? Evidently, whatever the writer wants them to mean. This paragraph is a true hall of mirrors. If your argument depends on a critical distinction such as that between "just" and "unjust," you are obligated to be as specific as possible in defining these terms.

3. *Analyze your organization.* Turn to the Steps in Writing exercise at the end of chapters 5–10 that best fits your argument (or chapter 4 if you are doing an analysis). The exercises will help you to determine what kind of good reasons you need. For example, if you have a definition argument, go to the Steps in Writing exercise at the end of chapter 5. You should be able to identify the criteria for your definition. How many criteria do you offer? Where are they located? Are they clearly connected to your claim?

4. *Examine your evidence.* If you noted places where you could use more evidence when you read through the first time, now is the time to determine what kinds of additional evidence you need. Evidence can be examples, personal experiences, comparisons, statistics, calculations, quotations, and other kinds of data that a reader will find relevant and compelling. Decide what you need and put it in.

5. *Consider your title and introduction.* Many students don't think much about titles, but they are very important. A good title makes the reader want to see what you have to say. Be as specific as you can in your title, and if possible, suggest your stance. Then, in the introduction, you want to get off to a fast start and convince your reader to keep reading. You might need to establish right away that a problem exists. You might have to give some background. You might need to discuss an argument by someone else that you are addressing. But above all, you want to convince your reader to keep reading.

6. *Consider your conclusion.* Restating your claim usually isn't the best way to finish. The worst endings say something like "In my paper, I've said this."

Think about whether there is a summarizing point you can make, an implication you can draw, or another example you can include that sums up your position. If you are writing a proposal, your ending might be a call for action.

7. *Analyze the visual aspects of your text.* Does the font you selected look attractive using your printer? Do you use the same font throughout? Are you consistent if you use more than one font? Would headings and subheadings help to identify key sections of your argument? If you include statistical data, would charts be effective? Would illustrations help to establish key points? For example, a map could be very useful if you are arguing about the location of a proposed new highway.

Focus on Your Style and Proofread Carefully

In your final pass through your text, you should concentrate on the style of your argument and eliminate as many errors as you can.

1. *Check the connections between sentences.* Notice how your sentences are connected. If you need to signal the relationship of one sentence to the next, use a transition word or phrase. For example, when you find two sentences that are closely connected, you should ask what the relationship is. If you need to signal the relationship, use a transitional word or phrase, as in the following example:

   > Silent Spring *was widely translated and inspired legislation on the environment in nearly all industrialized nations.* Silent Spring *changed the way we think about the environment.* ———➤
   >
   > Silent Spring *was widely translated and inspired legislation on the environment in nearly all industrialized nations.* **Moreover,** *the book changed the way we think about the environment.*

2. *Check your sentences.* If you notice that a sentence was hard to read when you read your paper aloud or it doesn't sound right, think about how you might rephrase it. If a sentence seems too long, you might break it into two or more sentences. If you notice a string of short sentences that sound choppy, you might combine them. If you notice any run-on sentences or sentence fragments, fix them.

3. *Eliminate wordiness.* When writing a draft, people tend to be wordy. Sometimes, they use long expressions that can easily be shortened ("at this point in time" ———➤ "now"). Sometimes, they become repetitive, saying,

a sentence or two later, about the same thing they said before. See how many words you can take out without losing the meaning.

4. *Use active verbs.* Any time you can use a verb besides a form of *be* (is, are, was, were) or a verb ending in *-ing,* take advantage of the opportunity to make your style more lively. Sentences that begin with "There is (are)" and "It is" often have better alternatives ("It is true that exercising a high degree of quality control in the manufacture of our products will be an incentive for increasing our market share." ⟶ "If we pay attention to quality when we make our products, more people will buy them"). Notice too that active verbs often cut down on wordiness.

5. *Include people when possible.* Compare the following:

   > *Mayoral approval of the recommended zoning change for a strip mall on Walnut Street will negatively impact the traffic and noise levels of the Walnut Street residential environment.* ⟶

   > *If the mayor approves the zoning change recommended by the Planning Commission to allow a strip mall on Walnut Street, people who live on the street will have to endure much more noise and traffic.*

   Including people makes your writing more emphatic. People relate better to people than to abstractions. Putting people in also introduces active verbs because people do things.

6. *Know what your spelling checker can and can't do.* Spelling checkers might be the greatest invention since peanut butter. They turn up many typos and misspellings that are hard to catch. But spelling checkers do not catch wrong words (e.g., "to much" should be "too much"), omitted endings (e.g., "three dog" should be "three dogs"), and similar errors. You still have to proofread carefully to eliminate misspellings.

7. *Use your handbook to check items of mechanics and usage.* Nothing hurts your credibility more than leaving many errors in what you write. A handbook will help you to identify the most common errors (e.g., it's = it is) and answer questions of usage. Readers probably shouldn't make such harsh judgments when they find errors, but in real life they do. We've seen job application letters tossed in the reject pile because an applicant made a single glaring error. The conventions of punctuation, mechanics, and usage aren't that difficult to master, and you'll become a lot more confident when you know the rules or at least know how to look up the rules.

Appendix A

Working Effectively in Groups

Until recently, one of the biggest differences between writing on the job and writing in college courses was that writing in the workplace is often done by teams of people—especially important writing tasks such as reports, analyses, and proposals. Almost without exception, people in occupations that require a college education write frequently on the job. Much of that writing is done in collaboration rather than alone. Even people who don't have experience writing collaboratively find that when they move into managerial positions, they often are responsible for employees who must work and write in teams. Furthermore, they are responsible for all that comes out of their units, so if a particular document is poorly written, they suffer the consequences.

Collaborative writing isn't confined to the workplace. Word-processing programs make it easy to compose newsletters for organizations, and the World Wide Web makes it even easier for several people to work on a project from different locations. You likely will be writing a great deal with other people in the future, and the better you understand this process, the more enjoyable and more productive it will be for you. If you have played on competitive sports teams, you know that it takes time for a team to come together. Successful athletic teams recognize that different team members have different styles and abilities and that the key is to find ways to blend these styles and abilities so that each team member can contribute to the team's goals. Athletic teams, however, have the advantages of playing together over several months under the direction of a coach who assigns roles, conveys expectations, and assesses progress.

In many cases, writing teams collaborate on only one project. Often, no one is in a supervisory role, and the team members are expected to determine what needs to be done, decide the necessary roles, and monitor the progress of the project. Members have to be player and coach at the same time, and they are often under serious time pressure. Successful writing team members have skills that enable them to determine overall goals, the work required, and who will be responsible for what tasks; to monitor progress along the way; to improve constantly; and to ensure quality in the finished product. People who are members of effective writing teams understand what a team needs to do.

1. *Determine the goals and identify tasks.*
   - First determine the goals of the project. Write down the goals as specifically as you can.
   - Next determine what tasks are required to meet those goals. Again, be as specific as you can. Write down the tasks on notecards, and then arrange them in the order in which they need to be completed.
   - Then assess whether the team has the skills and resources to perform those tasks. If you do not have the necessary skills and resources, then you have to adjust the goals to what you can realistically expect to accomplish.

2. *Make a work plan.*
   - Use the notecards to make a time line that lists the dates when specific tasks need to be completed. Charts are useful tools for keeping track of progress.
   - Assign tasks to team members. Find out whether anyone possesses additional skills that could be helpful to the team.
   - Determine a process of monitoring progress. Set up specific dates for review, and assign team members to be responsible for reviewing work that has been done.

3. *Understand the dynamics of a successful team.*
   - Teamwork requires some flexibility. Different people have different styles and contribute in different ways. Keep talking to each other along the way.
   - It may be desirable to rotate roles during the project.

4. *Deal with problems when they come up.*
   - If a team member is not participating, find out why.
   - If team members have different ideas about what needs to be done, then find time to meet so that the team can get on the same page.
   - Get the team together if you are not meeting the deadlines you established in the work plan and devise a new plan if necessary.

5. *Have realistic expectations about the pluses and minuses of working as a group.*

   - The big benefit of working in a group is that you can potentially accomplish a great deal more than you could working alone. Participating as a team member can be personally rewarding.
   - Working in groups can have disadvantages. They can require more time because different people bring different perspectives that need to be discussed. The perennial problem with groups is what do you do when a team member isn't doing his or her share or if a team members puts in a lot of work but doesn't produce a satisfactory result.

Appendix B

APA Documentation

Disciplines in the social sciences (anthropology, government, linguistics, psychology, sociology) and in education most frequently use the APA (American Psychological Association) documentation style. This appendix gives you a brief overview of the APA style. For a detailed treatment you should consult the *Publication Manual of the American Psychological Association,* fourth edition (1994).

The APA style has many similarities to the MLA style described in chapter 14. Both styles use parenthetical references in the body of the text with complete bibliographical citations in a list at the end. The biggest difference is the emphasis on the date of publication in the APA style. When you cite an author's name in the body of your paper with APA style, you always include the date of publication. Also, you include the page number:

> By the end of the 1960s, the engineers were tearing down thousands of units of urban housing and small businesses to build expressways with a logic that was similar to the logic of mass bombing in Vietnam--to destroy the city was to save it (Patton, 1986, p. 102). Shortly the effects were all too evident. Old neighborhoods were ripped apart, the flight to the suburbs continued, and the decline of inner cities accelerated rather than abated.
>
> Not everyone in the 1950s and 1960s saw expressways as the answer to urban dilapidation. Lewis Mumford (1958) challenged the circulation metaphor. He wrote: "Highway planners have yet to realize that these arteries must not be thrust into the delicate tissue of our cites; the blood they circulate must rather enter through an elaborate network of minor blood vessels and capillaries" (p. 236).

Notice that unlike MLA, a comma is placed after the author's name and the abbreviation for page is included—for example, (Patton, 1986, p. 102).

The APA list of works cited is entitled "References":

Center "References."

Double-space all entries. Indent all but first line five spaces.

Alphabetize entries by last name of authors or by title if no author listed.

Authors' initials listed rather than first names.

Only first words and proper nouns capitalized in titles.

Underline titles of books and periodicals; no quote marks for articles.

APA specifies a different format for work submitted for publication, so consult *Publication Manual of the American Psychological Association* for the proper format.

References

Bingham, J. (1996, September 3). Kids become masters of electronic universe: School Internet activity abounds. Denver Post, p. A13.

Dyrli, O. E., & Kinnaman, D. E. (1995, November). Telecommunications: Gaining access to the world. Technology and Learning, 16(3), 79-84.

Ellsworth, J. H. (1994). Education on the Internet: A hands-on book of ideas, resources, projects, and advice. Indianapolis, IN: Sams.

Engardio, P. (1996, June 24). Microsoft's long march. Business Week, 52-54.

National Center for Education Statistics. (1998, February). Internet Access in Public Education. Retrieved May 21, 1998 from the World Wide Web: http://nces.ed.gov/pubs98/98021.html

UK: A battle for young hearts and minds. (1996, April 4). Computer Weekly, 20.

The References list eliminates the need for footnotes. If you have your sources listed on notecards, then all you have to do when you finish your paper is to find the cards for all the sources that you cite, alphabetize the cards, and then type your References list. For works with no author listed, alphabetize by the first significant word in the title (ignore *a, an,* and *the*).

Books

The basic format for listing books in the Works Cited list includes the author's name (last name first, initials), date of publication, title (underlined), place of publication, and short name of publisher. You find the exact title on the title page (not on the cover), the publisher, and the city (use the first city if several are listed). The date of publication is included in the copyright notice on the back of the title page. Use the abbreviation for pages (pp.) for chapters in a book.

Book by One Author

Ellsworth, J. H. (1994). Education on the Internet: A hands-on book of
ideas, resources, projects, and advice. Indianapolis, IN: Sams.

Book by Two or More Authors

Scribner, S., & Cole, M. (1981). The psychology of literacy. Cambridge,
MA: Harvard University Press.

Translation

Martin, H.-J. (1994). The history and power of writing (L. G. Cochrane,
Trans.). Chicago: University of Chicago Press.

Edited Book

Bizzell, P., & Herzberg, B. (Eds.). (1990). The rhetorical tradition:
Readings from classical times to the present. Boston: Bedford.

One Volume of a Multivolume Work

de Selincourt, E., & Darbishire, H. (Eds.). (1958). The poetical works
of William Wordsworth (Vol. 5). Oxford, England: Oxford
University Press.

Selection in an Anthology or Chapter in an Edited Collection

Merritt, R. (1985). Nickelodeon theaters, 1905-1914: Building
an audience for the movies. In T. Balio (Ed.), The American
film industry (Rev. ed., pp. 83-102). Madison: University of
Wisconsin Press.

Unpublished Dissertation

Rouzie, A. (1997). At play in the fields of writing: Play and digital
literacy in a college-level computers and writing course. Unpub-
lished doctoral dissertation, University of Texas, Austin.

Periodicals

The necessary items to include are the author's name (last name first, initials), title of the article, title of the journal or magazine (underlined), volume number (for scholarly journals), date, and page numbers. For articles in
newspapers, use the abbreviation for pages (p. or pp.). Many scholarly journals are printed to be bound as one volume, usually by year, and the pagination is continuous for that year. If, say, a scholarly journal is printed in four

issues and the first issue ends on page 278, then the second issue will begin with page 279. For journals that are continuously paginated, you do not need to include the issue number. However, some scholarly journals are paginated like magazines, each issue beginning with page 1. For journals that are paginated by issue, you should list the issue number along with the volume (e.g., for the first issue of volume 11, you would put *11*(1) in the entry after the title of the journal).

Article in a Scholarly Journal— Continuous Pagination

Berlin, J. A. (1988). Rhetoric and ideology in the writing class. College
    English, 50, 477-494.

Article in a Scholarly Journal—Pagination by Issue

Kolby, J. (1988, Fall). The top-heavy economy: Managerial greed and
    unproductive labor. Critical Sociology, 15(3), 53-69.

Review

Chomsky, N. (1959). [Review of the book Verbal behavior]. Language,
    35, 26-58.

Magazine Article

Engardio, P. (1996, June 24). Microsoft's long march. Business Week,
    52-54.

Magazine Article—No Author Listed

UK: A battle for young hearts and minds. (1996, April 4). Computer
    Weekly, 20.

Newspaper Article

Bingham, J. (1996, September 3). Kids become masters of electronic
    universe: School Internet activity abounds. Denver Post, p. A13.

Electronic Sources

The World Wide Web has become an important scholarly resource since the last edition of the *Publication Manual of the American Psychological Association.* APA likely will revise its guidelines in the next edition.

Web Site

Environmental Protection Agency. (1998, June 10). Composite image of
the 1995 Antarctic ozone hole [Posted on the World Wide Web].
Washington, DC: Author. Retrieved January 4, 1999 from the
World Wide Web: http://www.epa.gov/docs/ozone/science/hole/
holecomp.html

Article in a Scholarly Journal on the Web

Browning, T. (1997). Embedded visuals: Student design in Web spaces.
Kairos, 2(1). Retrieved January 4, 1999 from the World Wide Web:
http://www.as.ttu.edu/kairos/2.1/features/browning/index.html

Article in a Magazine on the Web

Happy new Euro. (1998, December 30). Time Daily. Retrieved January 4,
1999 from the World Wide Web: http://cgi.pathfinder.com/time/
daily/0,2960,17455-10 1990101,00.html

Film

Speilberg, S. (Director). (1998). Saving Private Ryan [Film]. Hollywood,
CA: DreamWorks and Paramount.

Recording

Glass, P. (1973). "Low" Symphony [CD]. New York: Point Music.

Index

Credits